TAKING THE FEAR
OUT OF ECONOMICS

TAKING THE FEAR
OUT OF ECONOMICS

John Curran

Business Press
Thomson Learning™

Australia • Canada • Denmark • Japan • Mexico • New Zealand • Philippines
Puerto Rico • Singapore • South Africa • Spain • United Kingdom • United States

Taking the Fear out of Economics

Copyright © 2000 John Curran

Business Press is a division of Thomson Learning. The Thomson Learning logo is a registered trademark used herein under license.

For more information, contact Business Press, Berkshire House, 168–173 High Holborn, London, WC1V 7AA or visit us on the world wide web at: http://www.itbp.com

British Library Cataloguing-in-Publication Data
A catalogue record for this book is available from the British Library

First edition published 2000 Thomson Learning

ISBN 1–86152–474–9

Typeset by LaserScript, Mitcham, Surrey
Printed in the UK by TJ International, Padstow, Cornwall

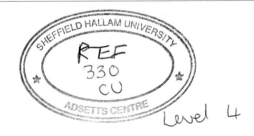

THOUGHT

On 30 June 1998, England played Argentina in the quarter final of the World Cup. The game saw the dismissal of David Beckham. Remember? The score was two all at the end of extra time and the match was decided by penalties. England lost. David Batty missed one of the penalties and admitted that it was the first penalty he had ever taken. He had not even practised taking penalties during his entire professional career. Indeed, penalty practice was not included in England training sessions.

Practice, practice, practice . . .

CONTENTS

Chapter 3   Indifference analysis — behind the demand curve   31

Chapter 4   The supply curve — movement along and shift of   68

FIGURES AND TABLES

Figures

Tables

PREFACE

'Always introduce your paper!'

This book has been written for people who have a fear of microeconomics, but who have to learn about microeconomics. The usual reason for having to learn anything is to pass an assessment. The book will be of use to people who believe that they will never understand microeconomics. It is possible that many of you have had bad experiences with economics textbooks. Economics textbooks can be boring, overlong and full of theory with no supporting real world examples. The typical reaction to fear is to hate the thing causing the fear. Many people hate microeconomics. It causes them fear.

What I have tried to do in this book is quite straightforward: to make microeconomics as simple as possible. I want people to be able to say 'That's simple' after reading a topic. I have written a simple book. The word simple is used either as a term of abuse or praise. I think it should always be used in praise. To make things simple to understand is some achievement. Interestingly, the Microsoft Word thesaurus suggests the following replacements for simple: clear, lucid, intelligible, unmistakable and understandable. The word simple is in good company.

The aims of the book are:

✓ To provide a comprehensive but simple introduction to microeconomics, assuming no prior knowledge.

✓ To emphasise the importance of microeconomics as a tool for gaining insights into the behaviour of customers and firms. Theory is nothing if it does not provide insights.

✓ To stress the importance of practice. Learning is an activity. It is a doing thing. You cannot learn without practising. Gary Player, the world class golfer said 'The more I practice the luckier I get!' Start getting lucky with microeconomics by practising. Unfortunately, teachers can only teach you. They cannot learn you. Only you can learn. Learning can be fun.

✓ To overcome the fear factor. The first three aims will help you to move from a state of fear to a position of confidence.

The underlying learning philosophy is that understanding is preferable to memory. Memory fades, whereas understanding remains. Microeconomics can be an enjoyable subject. When you have read a section of the book, ask yourself the simple question 'What understanding have I gained from working through that section?' The objective should always be understanding and insights but not a desperate attempt at remembering. If you understand then you will remember. Memory does not guarantee understanding. There is no guarantee that memorising one answer will lead you to the next answer.

The key to understanding is practice. By the end of this book, you will become fed up with my emphasis on practice. Unfortunately, learning is an activity and the activity is practice. The more you practice the more you will understand. Practice makes perfect. You cannot overcome the fear factor without practising your microeconomics. Practice, then practice some more and finish off with some final practice.

ACKNOWLEDGEMENTS

The writing of this book has been the result of me sitting in front of the computer and learning to type. All that practice. The ideas are not mine. They are the result of the people I have met over the 25 years I have been learning and teaching economics. I was fortunate to have the support of Bob Greenhill and Barry Ricketts at the then City of London Polytechnic. I was struggling with economics but Bob and Barry give me encouragement and help. They emphasised the importance of practice. Colleagues at the University of North London and the Polytechnic of North London have listened to my ideas on teaching economics to the many and not the few. I would like to thank John Sedgwick, Stuart Archbold, Mike Pokorny, Neil Dorward and Bob Morgan. I have purposely avoided using economists as reviewers for the book. This could be a major criticism of the style and content but I did not want the book to be for teachers, or its content controlled by teachers. I wanted the book to be for students. They are the learners. Arijana Tandara took on the task of being the student reviewer. She has played an important part in the development of the book and acted as the first proofreader. I asked Arijana to take on the role of students who struggle with microeconomics and tell me what she thought the book told them. She did this job superbly and instigated many changes and refinements. Arijana was not the only student to be part of the student review team. Every student I have taught since August 1978 at Simon Fraser University in Canada has in some way or another helped to shape this book. Jill Garlick contributed to the graphics and the general layout of the book. She also acted as a reader and greatly improved the clarity of the final product. Maggie Smith of International Thomson Business Press was the commissioning editor. She was supportive of the original idea and continued her support during the writing of the book.

To them all, I owe a debt of gratitude. Unfortunately, I alone am responsible for the outcome. Finally, I would like to thank my mother for persuading me to go to college and Sheree, my partner, and our daughter Alice for their unstinting support during the writing of this book.

KEY TO SYMBOLS

   Practice/exercise/do this

   What's in this chapter/section? In a nutshell

   What does this mean? Definition of term

   How does that work? Explanation of process/difficult bit of theory tackled in stages/connected to or explanation of figure or table.

   Encouragement symbol

   Fear/difficulty symbol

   Case study/longer example

   Write this down/learn this

   Summary/the story so far in easy-to-swallow chunks

Important fact/ write it in bigger letters/highlight it and don't forget it.

 Here's a tip to help you remember how to understand this bit

 Example – short and snappy

MICROECONOMICS AND THE FEAR FACTOR

We have nothing to fear but fear itself.
FRANKLIN D. ROOSEVELT

Introduction

Microeconomics looks at economic issues that affect consumers and firms in their daily activities. These activities include

✓ buying and selling goods and services
✓ deciding on the price to sell the goods and services at
✓ controlling costs and producing profits
✓ maximising consumer utility and business profits.

Microeconomics can be a difficult subject to master but mastery of microeconomics can provide real insights into the decision-making process of businesses and consumers. Microeconomics should be viewed as a means to an end. The end is passing assessment in microeconomics and understanding that the microeconomic problem is scarcity. We all want to pass the assessment but there is only a limited amount of time. Unfortunately, the work involved in gaining the mastery can be challenging and intimidating. The fear factor relates to a number of issues. The scarcity aspect permeates the coverage of microeconomics.

The fear factors

Students are fearful of microeconomics for many reasons. For many students it is a completely new topic. The subject includes mathematics – and many people do not like numbers. Diagrams are an essential part of the economist's toolbox and they play a big role in the way concepts are explained. Finally, for many students economics is a compulsory core module despite the fact that their programmes have very little to do with economics.

Confidence and change

Studying and attempting to conquer a new skill throws up challenges. People are naturally fearful of failure. In education, the test of skills acquisition is the ability to pass assessments. Students need to pass to progress. They need to face the acquisition of the new skill with confidence but they usually approach the challenge with fear and a lack of confidence. This is as true of microeconomics as it is of learning to pass the driving test.

The key to the challenges of confidence and change is the correct support environment and practice. Gary Player, the world-class South African golfer, maintained that 'The more I practice the luckier I get!' Practice breeds confidence. Unfortunately, students without the correct support framework lack confidence in their ability to conquer the skill and tend not to practice. A vicious circle of self-fulfilling failure occurs.

Microeconomics is a new challenge. With the correct help, it can be mastered and significant benefits can be realised. But remember: learning is a doing activity. It is necessary to practice, to be active. Very little learning takes place in any area of activity without practice. Practice makes perfect.

I find microeconomics difficult

Many students find economics difficult. I found microeconomics difficult. If I fail to practice I can still find microeconomics challenging. There seems to be a feeling among members of the public that economics is a difficult subject to understand and master. This is probably because economics is not introduced to students in the early years of their education. But remember that the most difficult thing you ever conquered was learning to read and write. Think back to the initial difficulty you experienced with reading and writing but you do both activities without a second thought now.

If the majority of the public find economics difficult then imagine the advantageous position you will put yourself in by being able to master the subject. Most business decisions in one way or another concern the application of microeconomics. Should British Rail run fewer trains outside peak periods? What are the benefits of opening supermarkets on Sunday? The answers to both questions are to be found in microeconomics. You will be able to answer these questions by the end of this book. It is a question of confidence, support and practice.

I am not going to become an economist

The vast majority of students studying economics will not become economists. There are very few economists in the United Kingdom. Very few students studying history go on to become historians. Economics is a vocation for very few people. Sadly, I am one of them.

The purpose of studying microeconomics is to gain insights into the behaviour of consumers and businesses. These insights can be applied in any number of careers. A leisure and tourism student may take only one module in economics but that module could provide the student with a number of insights and applications into the workings of the economics of a leisure centre. Should the price of swimming pool tickets be increased during weekday lunchtimes? What are the benefits of introducing a leisurecard? Again, these business dilemmas can be addressed by mastering microeconomics. The insights can be gained from only a relatively general coverage of microeconomic topics.

The analytical tools

Microeconomics uses various analytical tools. These are part of the challenge and the fear. For many students the analytical tools are new and difficult. Economics has its own language and method. The language and method can create fear.

The analytical tools are not there to frighten you but to help. Once you become familiar with them you will quickly realise how helpful they can be.

Numbers

Microeconomics uses numbers. Some people are afraid of numbers. 'I cannot even do simple sums without a calculator.' I hear you say. Go into a shop and look at the numbers confronting you. There is the price of the product you are thinking about buying. There is the number of rival products that you could buy as an alternative. Look at the supermarket bill and the amount of numerical information contained. You are responsible for all the information on the bill. You selected the items, paid the bill and received the change. There is no need to be fearful of numbers in microeconomics.

Diagrams

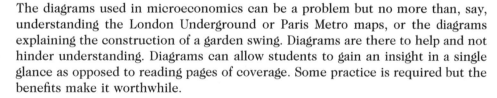

The diagrams used in microeconomics can be a problem but no more than, say, understanding the London Underground or Paris Metro maps, or the diagrams explaining the construction of a garden swing. Diagrams are there to help and not hinder understanding. Diagrams can allow students to gain an insight in a single glance as opposed to reading pages of coverage. Some practice is required but the benefits make it worthwhile.

The amount of theory involved

Economics is seen as being overly dependent on theory. The core issue is not to allow the theory to control us but rather to use the theory for our purposes. Theory is no good if it does not provide us with insights. If theoretical devices fail to provide insights and understanding then they are not worthy of consideration. Only theory producing insights will be used.

There is a theory behind the successful and safe overtaking of the car in front. It requires that the driver know the approximate speed of the car to be overtaken, the speed of the cars approaching, the conditions of the road, the width of the road and so on. If these factors were constructed as a theoretical model then people would argue that overtaking was an impossible event. The theory of overtaking may be complex but drivers overtake other cars every second of the day. The practice of overtaking shows that the theory of overtaking can be conquered. We may make mistakes but it does not stop us practising our overtaking. We should use the same approach with microeconomics.

The language used

Economics introduces new words into your vocabulary. Every discipline does this. I run, slowly. I suffer from tendinitis in my ankles. I was told that this was due to overpronation. I had never heard of overpronation. It simply means that I have a tendency to run on the outside of my feet. A cure for this problem is to see a podiatrist (a foot doctor) and have orthoses made (inserts making your feet land on the sole and not the edge). I now know these strange words. My tendinitis is under control and my understanding of running injuries has increased. I have gained insights and a bigger vocabulary!

    The new words introduced to you in microeconomics are there to help you gain insights, not create barriers.

Getting rid of the fear element

The strategy to be adopted in removing the fear factor is to enjoy microeconomics. I enjoy running but I also have a fear factor. Will I finish the race?

    Microeconomics can be enjoyed if the objective is understanding and insights, and not a desperate need to remember. If you understand then you will remember. Memory, unfortunately, does not guarantee understanding. The key to understanding is practice. The more you practice, the greater the skills and insights gained. I am always amazed by the skills exhibited by skateboarders. They fall over but they get up and carry on. Making mistakes teaches them the correct methods. You cannot make omelettes without breaking eggs.

Learning microeconomics is sequential

Microeconomics is like using a series of building blocks. If you get to a point where the understanding is not happening then stop stacking bricks and return to the point where the difficulty started. You will gain nothing from continuing. You will become disillusioned and frustrated. Your confidence will suffer and the fear factor will return. Return to the level or building block where you were happy. If you can swim or cycle then you will have experienced times when it was difficult to breathe correctly or ride without the stabilisers. Practice and help allowed you to overcome these difficulties.

My shopping trip and microeconomic insights

I have been studying economics for 28 years. I started with an O level, then an A level followed by a degree and finally a masters. I have been teaching economics since 1978. Each day my understanding of microeconomics allows me to gain insights into the decision-making processes of firms and consumers.

Consider a typical shopping trip and the microeconomic issues I come across. I decide to have my hair cut. The hairdresser, Andy's, charges a **price** of £5.50 on weekdays and £6.50 on Saturdays for the same haircut. It **costs** Andy the same amount to cut my hair on a Thursday or a Saturday. The difference in **price** means that Andy makes a bigger **profit** on Saturdays. Why does Andy charge a higher **price** on Saturday?

After my haircut, I go to the local supermarket. I see that the supermarket is open on Sunday. What is the purpose of opening the supermarket on Sunday? Will the supermarket charge higher **prices** on Sunday than on Saturday? I get to the checkout and see that the supermarket has changed the **technology** used. This must increase their **costs** but what will it do to their **profits**? Why have they introduced this new **technology**? What will it mean for the **labour efficiency** of the checkout workers?

I am thinking of going into central London to buy a pair of running shoes. I need to know the **price** of a return ticket and discover that it is more expensive to travel into central London if I start my journey before 9.30am. Why is the **price** higher in the morning rush hour when **demand** is very high, the trains are packed and I have to stand?

The words in bold type are in everyday use but they are also microeconomic terms. Microeconomics uses the same words as we use every day. Remember that microeconomics is simply a subject that tries to explain what consumers and businesses do each day.

How to use the book

The purpose of this book is to remove your fear of microeconomics. Removing the fear factor requires work. I have done my bit. Now it is time for you to do your bit. You need to practise and to generate insights.

Learn from insights

The book attempts to tell the story of microeconomics by intertwining theory and evidence. The examples are the evidence and help to explain the theory. Try to generate your own examples. These will help you to gain insights into microeconomics. The more insights you can generate the better will be your understanding of microeconomics. Your fear of microeconomics will disappear.

Practice, practice, practice!

The key to understanding anything is practice. Each chapter of the book covers a topic in microeconomics. The chapters are broken into sections and each section has at least one practice question at the end of the section. I have avoided placing the practice questions at the end of the chapter as I think the time to practice is immediately after you have read the section. I suggest that you read the section then try the practice questions. You will always find the answer in the section but to help you with your understanding you can find my solutions to the practice questions at the end of the chapter. I have attempted to keep the answers as simple and as direct as possible. If you have problems with the practice question then return to the section containing the practice question and review it. It would be easy simply to read the sections and avoid the practice questions but that would be wrong. You are reading this book because you are frightened by microeconomics. You need to confront that fear. The way to build confidence is through successful practice. Remember that learning is activity. It is not passive. The learning activity is practice.

Practice 1.1

During the next hour, complete a diary of any microeconomic events you experience. List any questions the events pose. By the end of the book, you will be able to answer these questions. This is the purpose of economics.

The layout of the book

The book is divided into 14 chapters. Each chapter:

✓ summarises the topics to be covered
✓ explains the theory with appropriate examples, case studies, figures, etc.
✓ gives practice questions
✓ reviews the key points learned
✓ provides answers to the practice questions (hooray!).

Chapter 14 (Taking the fear out of assessments in microeconomics), concentrates on producing a strategy for making assessments easier to pass. The key to passing assessments is to practice and each of the 13 chapters covering microeconomics provides opportunities for you to test your understanding.

    Chapters 2 and 4 introduce you to demand and supply and the factors that influence demand and supply decisions. They are important building blocks and it is essential that you read and understand them. Again, practice is the key. Chapter 3 on indifference analysis is a difficult chapter. This chapter tries to explain the theory behind the demand curve and is optional. If you have indifference analysis covered in your microeconomics module then this chapter is important. If you do not have coverage of indifference analysis in your programme then you can survive without reading Chapter 3. Chapter 5 on production is required reading. This chapter takes you behind the supply curve.

The coverage of production leads naturally to costs (Chapter 6). Production requires factors such as labour and capital and these factors receive payments that are business costs. With knowledge of the cost side of the firm (Chapter 6) and the revenue side (Chapter 2) we are in a position to examine profits in Chapter 7. Chapters 8 and 9 are devoted to price elasticity. Students find elasticity difficult. Chapter 8 looks at elasticity and movement along the demand curve, while Chapter 9 examines elasticity and shift of the demand curve. The issue of price determination is covered in Chapter 10. The question posed is whether price is market determined or administered. Chapters 11 and 12 look at how markets are structured. Perfect competition and monopoly are covered in Chapter 11, while Chapter 12 examines monopolistic competition and oligopoly. The final micro-economics coverage is on the market for factors of production (Chapter 13). This is a demanding chapter. You can find brief definitions and descriptions of the important concepts in the Glossary.

Summary

Microeconomics can appear to be difficult but understanding microeconomics can generate many insights. The key to understanding is tuition and practice. Learning is an activity. You must practice. Reading alone is not sufficient. I hope that this book will help you to understand microeconomics and remove the fear factor. Let us see if the opening chapter on demand reduces your demand for Valium!

Answers for Chapter 1

Answer 1.1

There is no definitive answer. Microeconomics surrounds all of us in our daily activities. Simply list the questions and return to answer them as you progress through the book.

THE DEMAND CURVE – MOVEMENT ALONG AND SHIFT OF

Don't panic

DOUGLAS ADAMS, *A HITCH HIKER'S GUIDE TO THE GALAXY*

This will help

This chapter covers the factors explaining demand, movement along and shifts of the demand curve and the information to be obtained from the demand curve. The chapter is the first subject of the book. No prior knowledge is expected or required.

This chapter is an essential building block for the chapters on indifference curve analysis (Chapter 3), elasticities (Chapters 8 and 9), market structures (Chapters 11 and 12) and price determination (Chapter 10). Every student should read this chapter. Try the practice questions. They will increase your understanding.

Introduction

Demand analysis is an excellent opportunity to conquer any fears you have concerning microeconomics. This is because you, as a consumer, spend a lot of time, effort and money on demanding goods and services. Just think about the number of things that you purchased yesterday and today. Again, think about the goods and services you would like to purchase, but are prevented from purchasing by lack of income. The goods and services you purchased or demanded yesterday were caused by a number of factors. Did you purchase a newspaper? Does that newspaper have rivals? Was yesterday hot? Did you buy any soft drinks or alcohol to quench your thirst?

By the end of this chapter you will understand:

✓ what demand is
✓ what a demand curve is
✓ why changes in the price of the good or service will lead to movement along the demand curve

✓ why changes in the other factors explaining demand will lead to a shift of the demand curve

✓ how total revenue reacts to the above changes.

What is demand?

We as individuals have wants. I would like a top of the range BMW, a yacht, a holiday home in Italy and many other things. Unfortunately, I do not have enough income to make these wants effective. I would have an effective demand for these items if I had the necessary income. My demand for the BMW is not effective. It would only be effective if I was willing and able to buy a BMW. I am not part of the market demand for BMWs. The market demand is made up by the people who are willing and able to purchase BMWs. I have insatiable wants but my effective demand is controlled by my income. If only . . .

The demand curve

The demand curve shows the diagrammatic relationship between the price of the good and the quantity demanded of the good (see Figure 2.1). Price is found on the vertical axis and quantity demanded is placed on the horizontal. If we were examining the demand curve for oranges then we would see the price of oranges on the vertical and the quantity demanded of oranges on the vertical. The demand

FIGURE 2.1   The demand curve

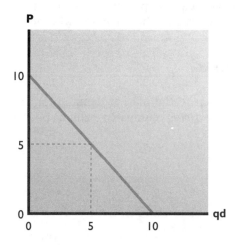

curve shows what happens to the demand for oranges at different prices. The demand curve is part of the economist's toolbox. It is a figure or picture of the demand relationship. A picture can sometimes paint a thousand words. The demand curve simply aids analysis.

The factors explaining demand

There are a number of factors explaining the demand for a good or service. These factors are called the explanatory, determining or causal factors. Demand is explained, determined or caused by these factors. Changes in demand are explained, determined or caused by changes in these factors. This can be represented as:

$$qd = f(\overset{-}{p}, \overset{-}{p_c}, \overset{+}{p_s}, \overset{+}{Y}, \overset{+}{T}, \overset{-}{r}, \overset{?}{E}, \ldots)$$

where

qd = the total quantity demanded in a particular market

p = the price of the good or service in a particular market

p_c = the price of complements

p_s = the price of substitutes

Y = income

T = tastes

r = the rate of interest

E = expectations.

The sign above each of the explanatory variables shows what will happen to demand if the explanatory variable increases. For example, if the price of the good or service (p) increases then demand will decrease. This is the meaning of the negative sign above price (p). Above income (Y) there is a positive sign. This shows that if income increases then demand will increase.

Practice 2.1

What will happen to the market demand for Playstation if the firm engages in a successful advertising campaign which positively affects people's tastes for Playstation?

Movement along the demand curve – price and quantity demanded

The first relationship examined is that between price (p) and quantity demanded (qd). All the other factors explaining demand will be ignored or held constant. They will not change. This is the *ceteris paribus* (Latin: 'all other things being equal') assumption. The *ceteris paribus* assumption allows us to analyse one thing or factor at a time. This makes the analysis easier.

An increase in price will generally cause the total quantity demanded to decrease. This relationship generates the demand curve for this particular market and is shown in Table 2.1.

Table 2.1 The demand and price schedule

P	QD
10	0
9	1
8	2
7	3
6	4
5	5
4	6
3	7
2	8
1	9
0	10

What makes quantity demanded equal zero?

Prices of 10 and above lead to quantity demand being zero. There will always be a price at which demand in the market will be zero. The price of a pint of lager is about £2 at present. Is it realistic to think of people paying £10 for a pint of lager? If £10 were the price per pint that caused market demand for lager to be zero, then £10 would be the intercept on the price axis. At prices equal to and above £10 market demand would be zero. There would be positive market demand at prices less than £10.

The price and quantity demanded information is reproduced in Figure 2.1. The data produce a downward sloping demand curve, showing that price decreases lead to increases in demand. In general, the relationship between price changes and demand is negative and the demand curve is downward sloping.

Practice 2.2

What price would make you not demand and not drink your favourite soft drink? What would you drink as an alternative or substitute?

Decreasing price increases demand

The demand curve starts at the minimum price producing zero demand. In the earlier example, the minimum price producing no demand is 10. As the price decreases, the quantity demanded increases. The firm can use a decrease in price to increase demand. A price decrease from 6 to 5 leads the quantity demanded to increase from 4 to 5:

p	qd
6	4
5	5

There has been movement along the demand curve.

Changes in the price of the good or service under consideration lead to a change in quantity demanded and movement along the demand curve.

It is very important to understand that the 'movement along' factor is the change in the price of the good or service.

Practice 2.3

What happens to demand in Table 2.1 if price increases from 2 to 3?
Place a finger on p = 2 and qd = 8. Does your finger move along the demand curve as price increases to 3? What happens to quantity demanded?

The demand curve in the real world? The Fresh Fry Restaurant

Can you spot the mistake? The Fresh Fry Restaurant offers a deal on pieces of chicken. The deal is shown in Table 2.2.

Table 2.2 The Fresh Fry Restaurant offer

Pieces of chicken	Price per piece	Total price
1	90p	90p
2	90p	£1.80
3	88.33p	£2.65
4	86.25p	£3.45
6	90.83p	£5.45
8	81.25p	£6.50

If you purchase one piece of chicken it is priced at 90p, whereas three pieces have a total price of £2.65 and a price per piece of chicken of 88.33p. The price has fallen and should act as an incentive to purchase more pieces of chicken. At this stage there appears to be a downward sloping demand curve for pieces of chicken. Strangely, the price per piece rises to 90.83p if you purchase six pieces of chicken. It would be cheaper to purchase two lots of three pieces at a total price of £5.30 (2 × £2.65) rather than purchase six pieces at a total price of £5.45. The restaurant has not understood the downward sloping demand curve and movement along it.

The Fresh Fry offer can be converted into a demand curve. This is shown in Figure 2.2. The demand curve is not continuously downward sloping. Fry Fresh hope to entice customers to purchase more pieces of chicken by offering lower prices for increased quantities but this only works up to a purchase of four pieces. If customers want to purchase six pieces then they can get a better deal by purchasing four pieces and two pieces separately. This was not the intention of the restaurant. Understanding a very basic piece of microeconomics allows us to gain an insight into why this business has made an embarrassing mistake. It would be surprising if customers did not spot the upward sloping part of the Fresh Fry demand curve. They may not understand microeconomics but they know when they are being diddled!

Practice 2.4

Suggest a pricing structure for Fresh Fry whereby the price of each piece of chicken falls as more pieces of chicken are purchased. You could use a spreadsheet.

FIGURE 2.2 The Fresh Fry offer demand curve

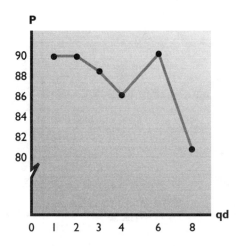

Shift of the demand curve
– a change in demand

The Fresh Fry example argues that the movement along factor is a change in price. The other factors explaining demand are:

L R R R L ?
$(p_c, p_s, Y, T, r, E, ...)$

Changes in each of these determinants of demand will cause the demand curve to shift. The direction of the shift of the demand curve for an **increase** in each of the causal or explanatory variables is indicated by the letter above the variable. Hence R for rightward shift and L for leftward. If income (Y) increases then the demand curve will shift to the right (R). We will examine each of the shift factors.

The price of complements and quantity demanded

A complement is any good or service that is consumed with another good or service. A classic example of two complements is a rowing boat and the oars. **If the two goods are complements then the relationship between the quantity demanded of good B and the price of good A is negative.** Two more complements are Walkmans and batteries. If the price of Walkmans increases then fewer Walkmans will be demanded (movement along the demand curve). In addition, there will be a fall in the demand for batteries (shift of the demand curve). The increase in the price of Walkmans leads

FIGURE 2.3 The demand curve for batteries –
an increase in the price of a complement

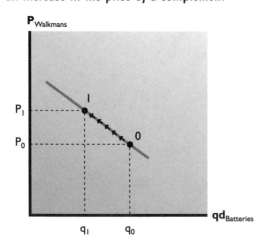

FIGURE 2.4 The price of Walkmans and the
demand for batteries

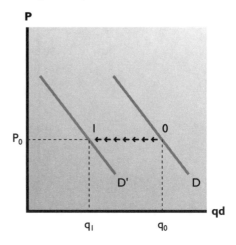

to a decrease in the demand for batteries. The relationship is negative. In Figure 2.3, the price of Walkmans (on the vertical axis) increases and the demand for batteries (on the horizontal axis) decreases. The relationship is negative.

In Figure 2.3 the price of Walkmans increased. This is shown as the price increase, p_0 to p_1. The demand for batteries falls from q_0 to q_1. The relationship is negative and indicates that the two products are complements.

We can now examine what happens to the demand curve for batteries following the increase in the price of Walkmans. The only factor to have changed is the price of Walkmans. All the other explanatory factors have stayed constant. This is the *ceteris paribus* assumption. The price of batteries remains constant (p_0) but the demand curve for batteries shifts to the left. Demand falls from q_0 to q_1. The leftward shift of the demand curve for batteries has been caused by the higher price of Walkmans and the reduced demand for Walkmans. This leftward shift is shown in Figure 2.4.

The higher price of Walkmans led to a movement along the demand curve for Walkmans. There was movement up the demand curve. Fewer Walkmans are demanded. The complement good, batteries also experience a fall in demand, as shown in Figure 2.3. There is a shift of the demand curve for batteries. The price of batteries remains unchanged at p_0. The demand curve for batteries shifts to D'. The shift is to the left.

Another example of complements is the Gameboy machine and the associated game disks. They are perfect complements. They cannot be used separately. If the Gameboy machine increases in price, then there will be movement up the demand curve for Gameboy machines as fewer Gameboy machines will be demanded. In addition, the number of game disks will experience a decrease in demand. The demand curve for the game disks will shift to the left. These changes are shown in Figure 2.5.

FIGURE 2.5 The demand curves for Gameboys and associated games following an increase in the price of Gameboys

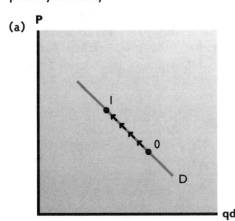

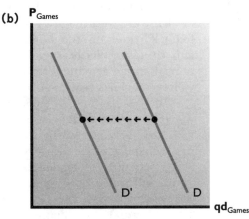

Figure 2.5a shows that an increase in the price of Gameboys leads to a movement along the Gameboys demand curve and fewer Gameboys are demanded. Figure 2.5b shows that the increase in the price of Gameboys leads to a fall in the demand for disks. The price of disks is unchanged but fewer batteries are demanded. There is a shift of the demand curve for disks to the left.

Practice 2.5

Cars and car insurance are good complements. Car insurance is a legal requirement for car use. If the price of cars increase then what would you expect to see happen to:

✓ the demand for cars
✓ the demand for car insurance?

Graph the figures for:

✓ the price of cars and the demand for cars
✓ the price of car insurance and the demand for car insurance.

What has happened to the price of car insurance? Think about *ceteris paribus*.

The price of substitutes and a change in demand

Substitutes are goods or services the public sees as rivals. Substitutes compete with each other. One example of substitutes is Nike and Reebok running shoes. If the two goods are substitutes then the relationship between an increase in the price of Nike shoes and the demand for Reebok shoes is **positive**. If Nike increases the price of its shoes then the demand for Nike shoes will decrease (movement along). In addition, the demand for Reebok shoes will increase (shift to the right). The relationship between the increase in the price of Nike shoes and the demand for Reebok shoes is **positive**. This positive relationship is shown in Figure 2.6 with the price of Nike shoes on the vertical axis and the demand for Reebok shoes on the horizontal axis. *Therefore, **the relationship between substitutes or rivals is positive**. Nike increased the price of their shoes. This led to a fall in the demand for Nike shoes (movement along) and a switch in demand to Reebok shoes (shift of).

Another example of substitutes or rivals is that of the daily UK newspapers the *Telegraph* and *The Times*. If the price of the *Telegraph* is increased then the quantity demanded will decrease. If the two papers are substitutes then the demand for *The Times* will increase. The demand curve for the *Telegraph* will experience a movement up the demand curve, while the demand curve for *The Times* will shift to the right. Figure 2.7 shows what happens to the demand for the *Telegraph* and *The Times* following an increase in the price of the former. The *Telegraph* loses market share by increasing price (movement along). The benefactor is *The Times*, which gains market share (shift of).

Practice 2.6

List three goods or services you will purchase today. List the alternative or substitute goods or services you would consider buying. Are the substitutes good or poor substitutes?

Are Safeway baked beans the same as Heinz baked beans?

FIGURE 2.6   The price of Nike and the demand for Reebok

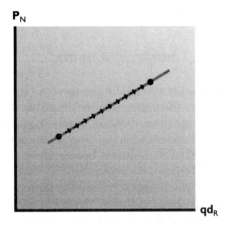

FIGURE 2.7   The demand curves for the *Telegraph* and *The Times* following an increase in the price of the *Telegraph*

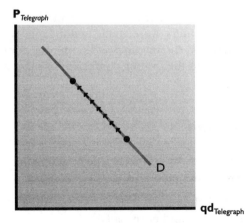

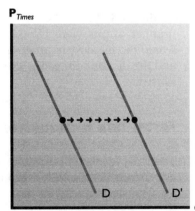

Practice 2.7

The gas market in the United Kingdom has been made competitive in that domestic users of gas can buy their gas from a number of suppliers. You use British Gas as your supplier. You receive literature from a rival company, Altancit Gas, which promises to undercut the British Gas price by 10 per cent. British Gas has announced that it will not be lowering prices.

What will the promised price cut mean for the demand curves of:

 British Gas

✓ Altancit Gas?

Show, using figures, what the price change will mean for the demand curves of British Gas and Altancit Gas.

Income and a change in demand

An increase in income will lead to an increase in quantity demanded. The demand curve will shift to the right. The relationship between demand and income is positive. An example of an increase in income was the windfall shares given to the holders of building society saving accounts and mortgages in 1997 when the building societies converted to the status of banks. Many recipients of the windfall cashed in their shares and increased their income. The increase in income created an increase in the demand for goods and services. The main recipient of the increase in income was the holiday package industry which experienced a significant increase in the demand for package holidays in Spain as shown in Figure 2.8. The only thing that has changed is the level of income, all the other factors influencing demand are held constant, the *ceteris paribus* assumption. The increase in income led to the demand for holidays increasing. The demand curve for holidays shifts to the right.

Practice 2.8

In the mid-1980s, the UK government restructured the coalmining industry. A number of pits were closed and the miners were made redundant. What effect would the pit closure programme have on the incomes of the mining communities and the demand for goods and services in the mining communities? Use a figure to illustrate this.

Tastes and a change in demand

Taste is a personal thing, influenced by hobbies, peer group pressure or advertising. **The relationship between demand and tastes is positive.**

 I am a keen, if slow, runner and thus have a 'taste' for running magazines, running shoes, shorts, t-shirts, socks and corn pads!

✓ I play football on a Monday evening. The teams are made up of friends from college days. After football, we retreat to the pub to watch the Monday night football on Sky. I drink lager. This demand or taste for lager is mainly explained by peer group pressure or the presence of my friends.

✓ Advertising has a large impact on many of my consumption decisions. My summer holiday destination is primarily explained by the advertising information contained in the holiday brochures.

Television advertising seeks to shift the demand curve for the advertised products to the right. If the latest advertising campaign for Gap Jeans were successful we would expect the demand curve for Gap Jeans to shift to the right. This is shown in Figure 2.9.

If advertising is effective, then tastes are positively influenced and the demand curve for the advertised product shifts to the right.

In the 1999 cricket World Cup two matches were played at Chelmsford:

Date	Teams	Ticket price
17 May 1999	New Zealand v. Bangladesh	£16
29 May 1999	Zimbabwe v. South Africa	£20

The higher price for the Zimbabwe v. South Africa match is a reflection of the belief that this fixture has a higher taste factor than the New Zealand v. Bangladesh game. The ground capacity is the same and the weather is not known at the time of the ticket sales. The organisers of the cricket World Cup and their marketing advisers believe that they can take advantage of this increase in tastes by increasing price.

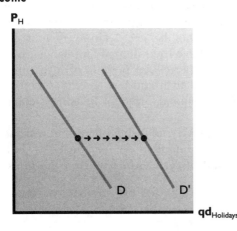

FIGURE 2.8 The demand curve for Spanish package holidays following an increase in income

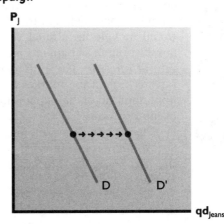

FIGURE 2.9 The demand curve for Gap Jeans following a successful television advertising campaign

The relatively high price of Levi 501 jeans is a reflection of the power of advertising in shifting people's tastes towards those jeans.

BT provide their customers with the free 1471 service that gives you the telephone number of the last call to your number. For unanswered calls this acts as a free answerphone. This service increases the tastes for telephone calls and is a very clever marketing weapon.

Practice 2.9

In April 1998 trading standards officers in Liverpool alleged that a large number of the baby walkers on sale in the UK were unsafe. What effect will this allegation have on the demand for baby walkers? Show the effect in a figure.

Practice 2.10

List the goods or services you demand that are influenced by:

✓ personal tastes
✓ peer group pressure
✓ advertising.

Practice 2.11

What does E-mail mean for people's tastes for letter and telephone communication?

The rate of interest and a change in demand

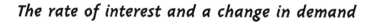

The rate of interest only affects the demand for durable goods and services. The relationship between demand and interest rates is negative. Durables are consumed over a period of time; their purchase may involve credit agreements and include goods such as fitted kitchens, double glazing and cars. Durables services would include an annual two-week package holiday for a family of four. Non-durables, such as bananas and beer, will not have their demand influenced by the rate of interest. The United Kingdom has experienced periods of high interest rates. The housing market has seen periods of high and low activity. One of the important factors in explaining shifts of the demand curve for housing is changes in interest rates.

Figure 2.10 shows the reduced level of activity following higher interest rates.

An increase in interest rates causes the demand curve for houses to shift to the left. Mortgages are more expensive and buyers withdraw from the housing market.

Practice 2.12

Interest rates fall from 7 per cent to 5 per cent. List five goods or services you would expect to experience an increase in demand.

Expectations and a change in demand

Expectations depend on our view of the future. The future is uncertain but expectations can aid our economic knowledge. What do you think will happen to the demand for package holidays this summer? If you think demand will be high then you should book your holiday early to guarantee you get the holiday you want. If you believe that demand will be low then you can wait and get the holiday you want, probably, at a discount price.

Expecting holiday demand to be high will cause the demand curve to shift to the right. There will be a rush of early bookings. Book now and avoid any possible disappointment.

With unemployment low, and falling, during early 1998, we tried to book our family holiday early. On trying to book the holiday our local travel agent informed me that there was very little availability. This was especially true for people wanting to fly from Luton, Gatwick and Stanstead. These airports serve the relatively prosperous south-east of England. The expectation that popular destinations would be fully booked caused the demand curve for holidays to shift to the right. This is shown in Figure 2.11.

When people are optimistic or confident about the future, they have a tendency to increase their demand for goods and services. The expectation of job security shifts the demand curve to the right.

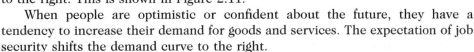

FIGURE 2.10   The demand curve for houses and an increase in interest rates

FIGURE 2.11   The demand curve for Spanish package holidays and the expectation that holiday availability is low

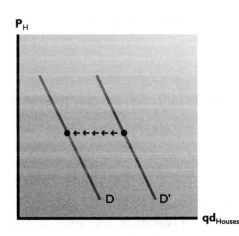

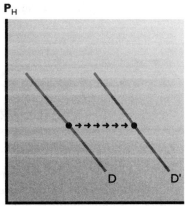

Practice 2.13

The housing market appears to have peaked. You expect the price of houses to fall. As a first time buyer do you buy now or in six months' time?

Review

We have covered the important factors explaining market demand. It is time to consolidate the coverage with a brief summary before moving on to total revenue.

Movement along

If the price (**p**) changes, then there is movement along the demand curve. Thus:

> price change leads to movement along the demand curve

Shift of

If any of the explanatory variables p_s, **Y, T increase**, then the demand curve shifts to the **right**. Thus:

> increase in any of p_s, Y, or T causes the demand curve to shift
> to the right

If any of the explanatory variables p_c, **r increase**, then the demand curve shifts to the **left**. Thus:

> increase in p_c or r causes the demand curve to shift to the left

The information given by the demand curve — total revenue

The demand curve produces a lot of information and insights. In this section, we will only look at total revenue.

Total revenue is the result of multiplying price and quantity demanded. If price is £4 and quantity demanded is 6, then total revenue is £24. Total revenue is another expression for sales revenue. Total revenue is the outcome of selling the good or service. We can use the demand schedule of Table 2.1 to calculate total revenue. This is shown in Table 2.3.

Table 2.3 **Price, quantity demanded and total revenue**

P	QD	TR
10	0	0
9	1	9
8	2	16
7	3	21
6	4	24
5	5	25
4	6	24
3	7	21
2	8	16
1	9	9
0	10	0

The demand schedule in Table 2.3 shows that price falls lead to increases in demand. The total revenue obtained by the firm from selling the good or service can be read from the total revenue profile. Figure 2.12 shows how total revenue changes as price changes.

The total revenue profile starts at total revenue of zero when price is 10. It rises to a high of 25 units of total revenue when price is 5 and then falls back to zero when price is zero. The total revenue profile is dome shaped. Remember the Millennium Dome.

Practice 2.14

If you wanted to increase the firm's total revenue then would you lower price from 4 to 3?

A shift of the demand curve and the resulting total revenue profile

If the demand curve shifts to the right due to an increase in, say, tastes then a new demand schedule results. The new demand schedule produces a new total revenue profile. The new information is presented in Table 2.4.

Table 2.4 **The demand schedule and total revenue profile after the demand curve shifts to the right**

P	QD	TR
12	0	0
11	1	11
10	2	20
9	3	27
8	4	32
7	5	35
6	6	36
5	7	35
4	8	32
3	9	27
2	10	20
1	11	11
0	12	0

FIGURE 2.12 The total revenue profile and the demand curve

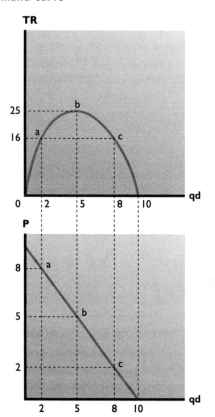

FIGURE 2.13 The demand curves and the resulting total revenue profiles

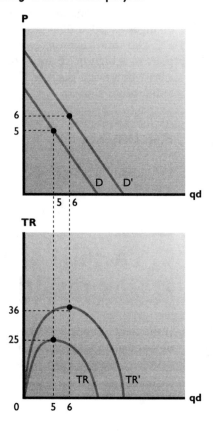

Some points to note

✓ The price at which demand is zero is now 12 and not 10. The demand curve has shifted up by two from 10 to 12. This is an indication of the increase in tastes. The intercept on the price axis has increased from 10 to 12.

✓ 1998 was a World Cup year, remember! The taste for various World Cup merchandising shifted the demand curve for World Cup products to the right. The price of World Cup replica shirts was higher than the price of Premiership shirts. This reflected the change in tastes.

✓ Consumers are willing to pay higher prices at each level of demand. Before the demand shift a price of £5 led to a demand of five. After the demand shift consumers demand five at a price of £7. Figure 2.13 shows the old and new demand curves and the old and new total revenue profiles.

The new demand curve (D') is to the right of the old demand curve. The new total revenue profile (TR') is above the old total revenue profile, and the highest total revenue is now 36 at a price of £6 and a quantity of six.

Practice 2.15

Draw a demand curve. Now subject the demand curve to a fall in income. Immediately below your demand curve figure, draw the two total revenue profiles.

Summary

This chapter has attempted to introduce you to the concept of demand. You should now understand that:

✓ The demand curve is generally downward sloping. Just think of the reaction to happy hour.

✓ If price changes then there is movement along the demand curve. A lower price leads to an increase in demand.

✓ Shift of the demand curve is the result of changes in the other factors influencing demand.

✓ Total revenue can be calculated by multiplying quantity demanded by price. This is the sales revenue. Again, changes in any of the factors influencing demand will produce changes in total revenue.

The chapter has attempted to show that knowledge of demand can generate many insights. These include transport pricing, family holidays and economic activity and happy hour. Maybe it is time to take advantage of a local happy hour deal before looking at the rest of the book.

The next chapter looks at indifference analysis. This is a relatively difficult topic. If you do not need to know about indifference analysis then you can skip it. You will not lose anything if you do. If you do need to understand indifference analysis, however, then read Chapter 3.

Answers for Chapter 2

Answer 2.1

The demand curve will shift to the right. A successful advertising campaign by Playstation will increase brand loyalty and demand. Remember the *ceteris paribus* assumption. Only one factor changes, the others remain constant, including price.

Answer 2.2

Obviously, the answer is personal to the respondent. I would not buy Coca-Cola if the price increased by 5 pence per 500ml can. I would switch to a cheaper alternative such as Pepsi.

Answer 2.3

There is movement along the demand curve. The price increase, from two to three, leads to a decrease in demand, from eight to seven. The important element to understand is that a change in the price of the product produces a movement along the demand curve.

Answer 2.4

My solution is:

Pieces of chicken	Price per piece	Total price
1	90p	90p
2	85p	£1.70
3	80p	£2.40
4	75p	£3.00
6	70p	£4.20
8	65p	£5.20

Hopefully, the incentive of lower prices will increase demand by moving the consumers down the demand curve.

Answer 2.5

✓ The demand for cars will experience a movement up the demand curve. There will be fewer cars demanded, *ceteris paribus*.

✓ The demand for car insurance will shift to the left. If fewer cars are being demanded (movement along), then there will be a fall in the demand for insurance services (shift of), *ceteris paribus*.

✓ The price of cars and the demand for cars figure shows that there has been a movement along the demand curve. In this case, fewer cars have been demanded so the movement is up the demand curve. The figure looks like:

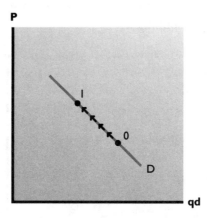

✓ The price of car insurance and the demand for car insurance figure shows that the increase in the price of cars has caused the demand curve for car insurance to shift to the left. Car insurance is a complement to car usage. As the demand for cars falls so does the demand for car insurance. The figure looks like:

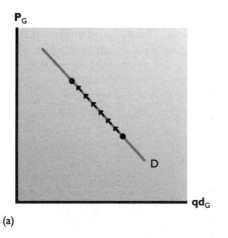

(a)

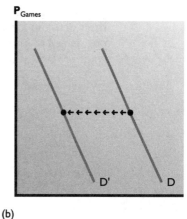

(b)

Answer 2.6

Again, this is a personal response. We went shopping yesterday. I bought the following: a pair of Adidas running shorts, lunch for three in BhS and a haircut at Andy's. The alternatives are: a pair of Nike running shorts, lunch at Fresh Fry and getting my hair cut at a different hairdresser.

Answer 2.7

✓ The demand curve for British Gas will shift to the left.
✓ Atlancit will experience movement down their demand curve.
✓ The figures look like:

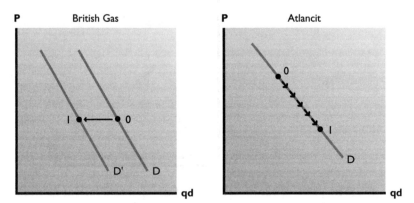

Answer 2.8

The mining communities would see their income decline and they would reduce their demand for goods and services. The demand curves of the goods and services purchased by the mining community would shift to the left. The figure for a typical good or service purchased, say eating out, would look like:

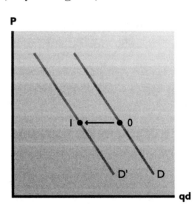

Answer 2.9

The allegation would reduce the taste for baby walkers and shift the demand curve for baby walkers to the left. The figure for baby walkers would look like:

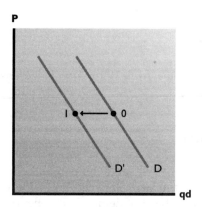

Answer 2.10

Again, a personal issue but my demand is influenced by:

✓ personal tastes for running equipment such as blister-free socks
✓ peer group pressure for beer when it is my turn to buy
✓ advertising for holidays via the brochures.

Answer 2.11

The introduction and increasing use of E-mail will lead to a decrease in the demand for letter and telephone communication. Do you use E-mail as an alternative to letters and telephone calls? Do businesses?

Answer 2.12

The five areas in which I would expect to see the demand curve shift to the right are:

✓ housing
✓ cars
✓ double glazing
✓ holidays
✓ computers.

Answer 2.13

I would advise the first time buyer to postpone buying a house now if house prices are expected to fall. Why buy something now when you expect it to be cheaper in six months' time?

Answer 2.14

No, lowering price from 4 to 3 will decrease total revenue. Look at the total revenue profile.

Answer 2.15

The fall in income will shift the demand curve to the left. The new total revenue profile will start at zero, but will lie inside the old total revenue profile and will finish at a lower level of demand. The figure will look like:

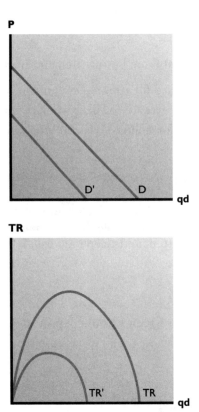

3

INDIFFERENCE ANALYSIS — BEHIND THE DEMAND CURVE

Keep it simple, stupid

This will help

This chapter attempts to provide a theoretical reason to explain why demand curves are normally downward sloping. Chapter 2 used casual empiricism or gut reaction to argue that price reductions lead to increases in demand and movement down the demand curve. The chapters on demand (Chapter 2) and price elasticity (Chapter 8) will help to prepare you for the material covered in this chapter. There is no escaping the fact that students find indifference analysis difficult. The coverage is usually presented in an abstract manner and it is difficult to understand what insights can be gained from studying indifference analysis. As a student I found the topic very confusing and only really came to terms with it when I had to teach it! Yet again, practice. The quote at the beginning of this chapter is typical of the attitude of a number of economists to this topic. Indeed, many colleagues, on hearing that I had undertaken to write this book, asked 'Are you covering indifference analysis?' Obviously, I am. The reasons are that the topic:

✓ is covered in the majority of microeconomics modules; indifference analysis can be part of the assessment strategy
✓ does provide useful insights into demand analysis
✓ is covered in other modules such as labour economics to examine the work-leisure trade-off.

Introduction

Shops attempt to move consumers down the demand curve by offering sales discounts. A classic example of this is the January sales. The expectation is that the demand curve is downwards sloping. It is an empirical factor but lacks theoretical underpinning. Indifference analysis seeks to provide the theoretical underpinning.

By the end of this chapter you will understand:

✓ the theory of utility maximisation
✓ the implications of budget constraints
✓ what happens when price changes – movement along the demand curve
✓ what happens when income changes – shift of the demand curve
✓ the different outcomes of price changes:
  – income and substitution effects
  – total revenue and price elasticity
  – normal, inferior and Giffen goods.

Utility maximisation

One of the most important assumptions in microeconomics is that consumers are utility maximisers. This simply means that consumers try to get the most satisfaction they can from the goods and services purchased, given their income. This is reasonable. For example, I do not smoke. I get no utility or satisfaction from smoking. I do not spend any of my income on the consumption of cigarettes for my own use. It would be irrational.

In microeconomics, it is assumed that consumers purchase a combination of goods and services to maximise their total utility. Utility or satisfaction is derived from the consumption of the goods and services purchased. I like drinking lager. I get utility or satisfaction from drinking lager. Thankfully, I can buy lager as I have the necessary income. I like the idea of owning an ocean-going yacht. It would give me lots of utility but unfortunately I do not have enough income! Life is so unfair. So I try to get the most from the purchases I make given my income. If only I were rich.

Practice 3.1

Write down a good, or a service, which gives you no utility or satisfaction.

Total and marginal utility

As usual, last Monday was a football night. As usual, it was up to the pub after the exercise. The pints went down a treat after all that exercise! The first pint was wonderful. The second pint was good. But, eventually, I had had enough pints and it was time to go. I got more satisfaction or utility from my first pint than I did from my last pint. I was experiencing the microeconomic concept of diminishing marginal utility. Table 3.1 shows my Monday night experience of total and marginal utility from drinking pints of lager.

Pint	Total utility	Marginal utility
None	Zero	
First	50 utils at	50 utils between
Second	80 utils at	30 utils between
Third	100 utils at	20 utils between
Fourth	110 utils at	10 utils between

Table 3.1 **Monday night drinking – total and marginal utility**

As Table 3.1 shows, my total utility increased the more pints of lager I consumed. The first pint gave me 50 utils (utils are simply a way of measuring satisfaction), while the second pint added 30 utils to my total utility. The change in my total utility from 50 utils to 80 utils was 30 utils. This was the marginal utility of the second pint. The marginal utility column shows that I enjoyed the first pint more than I enjoyed the second. The marginal utility of the first pint was 50 utils and the marginal utility from the second pint was only 30. My marginal utility continued to diminish as more lager was consumed, but my total utility increased. After four pints it was time to go home. I did not feel like drinking any more lager. The marginal utility from the fourth pint was only 10 utils. This was much less than the first pint.

My drinking experience is consistent with microeconomic theory:

✓ *my **total utility** increased as long as the marginal utility was positive*

✓ my **marginal utility diminished as I drank more lager.**

If I had continued to drink beyond the fourth pint then my marginal utility would have eventually become zero and then negative. Is this when people are sick, literally, of drinking lager? *Note that my **total utility is at its peak when marginal utility is zero**.* Total utility decreases thereafter. Figure 3.1 shows my total utility and marginal utility experience from drinking pints of lager.

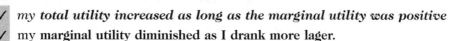

Please note that total utility happens **at** the pints, whereas marginal utility happens **between** the pints. My total utility from the first pint is 50 utils and two pints give me a total utility of 80 utils. These happen at the pints. My marginal utility from drinking the second pint is 30 utils. This is the change in my total utility. It happens **between** the end of first pint and the end of the second pint. It is plotted at 1.5 pints, which is halfway between the end of the first pint and the end of the second pint. This is an important concept. Give it some thought. Remember, total *at* and marginal in *between*.

The essential factors to take from this section are that:

✓ consumers are assumed to be utility maximisers

✓ marginal utility is usually diminishing.

Practice 3.2

From the following information calculate the marginal utility of eating chocolates and plot the figure for total utility and marginal utility against chocolates. When does the consumption of a good turn into a bad?

Chocolates	Total utility
1	10
2	18
3	24
4	28
5	30
6	30
7	28

Utility maximisation, again

In microeconomics the consumer maximises utility by purchasing the combination of two goods, x and y, which generate the highest total utility given the consumer's income. The analysis is carried out in two dimensional space. This is similar to the demand curve. Economists love working in two dimensions and thus using graphs and figures.

I am a drinker who does not smoke. More pints of lager increase my total utility up to the point where my marginal utility from an extra pint equals zero. As I do not smoke, I get no utility from cigarettes. My total utility from lager and cigarettes is explained only by my consumption of lager. Extra cigarettes do nothing to increase my total utility. I would never give up pints of lager in exchange for cigarettes. Giving up lager for cigarettes would clearly reduce my total utility.

FIGURE 3.1 Monday night drinking – total utility (TU) and marginal utility (MU)

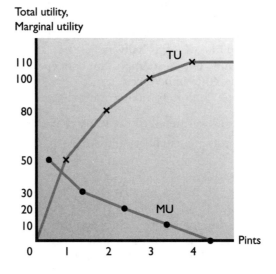

Table 3.2 My total utility and different combinations of pints and cigarettes

	Outcome 1	Outcome 2	Outcome 3	Outcome 4
Pints	5	5	4	6
Cigarettes	50	100	130	0
Total utility	100	100	80	110

Table 3.2 shows that I am:

✓ Indifferent between outcomes 1 and 2. Both outcomes produce the same total utility of 100. I am given an extra 50 cigarettes but my total utility stays the same. What is the marginal utility of the extra cigarettes?

✓ Not indifferent between outcomes 2 and 3. I prefer outcome 2. Taking away a pint of lager and giving me 30 extra cigarettes reduces my total utility by 20. As far as I am concerned, the two outcomes are different. Given the choice I would choose outcome 2. Again, I am not indifferent between outcomes 2 and 3.

✓ Obviously, I prefer outcome 4 to all the other outcomes. Why?

The four outcomes are plotted in Figure 3.2 with pints of lager on the vertical and cigarettes on the horizontal.

The line between 5 pints and 50 cigarettes and 5 pints and 100 cigarettes is one of my indifference curves. Both combinations produce the same total utility of 100. I am totally indifferent between the two combinations. The combination 4 pints and 130 cigarettes produce a lower total utility of 80 and lies below the above combinations. My favourite combination is 6 pints and no cigarettes. I am a drinker who does not smoke, therefore my indifference curves are horizontal if lager is on the vertical axis.

FIGURE 3.2 My indifference curve mapping between pints and cigarettes

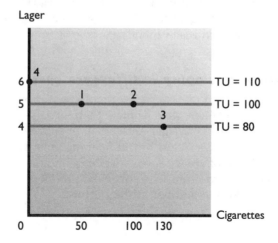

Practice 3.3

Using the framework of Figure 3.2, with lager on the vertical axis, what would an indifference curve look like for a non-drinking smoker? Which indifference curve would the teetotal smoker aim for?

The shape of the indifference curve

My indifference curve between lager and cigarettes is horizontal if lager is on the vertical axis. But if you are a smoker who drinks then your indifference curve between lager and cigarettes will not be a vertical line. Taking lager away reduces your total utility. To keep you indifferent you must receive more cigarettes to compensate for the loss of the pints of lager, as shown in Table 3.3.

Table 3.3 Keeping total utility the same

	Option 1	Option 2	Option 3
Cigarettes	30	30	35
Lager	5	4	4
Total utility	100	90	100

You are indifferent between options 1 and 3. Both options give the same total utility. Option 2 would shift you to a lower indifference curve. To compensate for the loss of one pint of lager you need to be compensated by 5 extra cigarettes.

Practice 3.4

What is the marginal utility of the fifth pint of lager? What is the marginal utility of each of the extra 5 cigarettes? (It is important to make sure you understand these answers and how to reach them.)

A downward sloping indifference curve

If you are a smoker who drinks, therefore, your indifference curve will be downward sloping. Less lager must be compensated for by more cigarettes to keep you indifferent. When you are indifferent your total utility is unchanged. The shape of the indifference curve depends on the psychology of each individual consumer and their attitude to particular products. **In general, indifference curves are steep at the top and flat at the bottom.**

Practice 3.5

Two of your friends like takeaway meals. Friend 1 prefers Indian takeaways to Chinese while friend 2 is the opposite. Both friends will eat either sort of food. Sketch indifference curves for both friends.

The general view of the indifference curve

The reason why the indifference curve is steep at the top of the curve is because the consumption of lager is high and the consumption of cigarettes is low. **When consumption is relatively high, the resulting marginal utility is relatively low and when consumption is relatively low, marginal utility is relatively high.**

Consumption and marginal utility	
High consumption	*Low marginal utility*
Low consumption	High marginal utility

When consumption is high, marginal utility is low. This is an important concept to understand. Can you remember the stomach ache you had after eating all those Easter eggs? Did you want to eat more chocolate?

Figure 3.3 shows the shape of an indifference curve that has the property of high consumption, low marginal utility and low consumption, high marginal utility.

FIGURE 3.3 **The general view of the indifference curve**

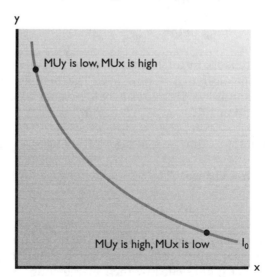

Think of the general view figure as the ski jumper coming down the ski jump at the Winter Olympics. At the top of the jump, the slope is steep and at the take-off point, the slope has flattened out.

Practice 3.6

Put cigarettes on the horizontal axis and lager on the vertical axis. What happens to the marginal utility of cigarettes as we move up the indifference curve? What happens to the marginal utility of lager?

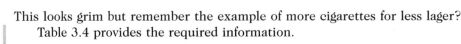

The slope of the indifference curve

Let us keep this simple! The slope of the indifference curve is:

$$\frac{\text{Marginal utility of cigarettes}}{\text{Marginal utility of lager}}$$

This looks grim but remember the example of more cigarettes for less lager? Table 3.4 provides the required information.

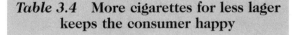

Table 3.4 More cigarettes for less lager keeps the consumer happy

	Option 1	Option 3
Cigarettes	30	35
Lager	5	4
Total utility	100	100

The change in total utility is zero. The change in lager is minus one and the change in cigarettes is plus five. The marginal utility of lager is ten and the marginal utility of cigarettes is two. Now for equations:

Equation 1:

Δ in total utility = Δ in lager*MU of lager + Δ in cigarettes*MU of cigarettes

(where Δ = change)

Zero = $-1 * 10 + 5 * 2$

Thankfully, equation 1 works. The loss of the pint of lager (-1) multiplied by its marginal utility (10) is completely offset or compensated by the gain in cigarettes (5) multiplied by their marginal utility (2).

Equation 1 can be re-arranged to produce equation 2.

$$-\Delta \text{ in lager * MU of lager} = \Delta \text{ in cigarettes * MU of cigarettes}$$
$$\left(\begin{array}{c} -1 \quad * \quad 10 \\ 10 \end{array}\right) = \begin{array}{c} 5 \quad * \quad 2 \\ = \quad 10 \end{array}$$

It works again! Remember when you change sides you change signs. The slope of the indifference curve is Δ in lager/Δ in cigarettes. Repeating equation 2 and rearranging this equation produces:

$-\Delta$ in lager * MU of lager = Δ in cigarettes* MU of cigarettes
$-\Delta$ in lager/Δ in cigarettes = MU of cigarettes/MU of lager

We can multiply both sides by minus one to produce:

Δ in lager/Δ in cigarettes = $-$MU of cigarettes/MU of lager

The slope of the indifference curve is $-$MU of cigarettes/MU of lager. I do not smoke so my MU of cigarettes is zero. My indifference curves are horizontal if lager is on the vertical axis. This is because the slope of my indifference curves equal zero. The slope equals:

Δ in lager/Δ in cigarettes = $-$zero/MU of lager = zero

Table 3.5 summarises the slope of the indifference curve.

Table 3.5 The slope of the indifference curve

Cigarettes consumption is low Lager consumption is high	MU cigarettes is high MU lager is low	Slope is steep
Cigarettes consumption is high Lager consumption is low	MU cigarettes is low MU lager is high	Slope is flat

Practice 3.7

Your consumption of x is high, while your consumption of y is low. You consume both x and y and have no great preference for either. With y on the vertical axis, what is the slope of your indifference curve? Is it steep or flat?

Enter money

Unfortunately, our income sets limits on our consumption of goods and services. That £6 million yacht would make me very happy. Each Saturday night I wait in anticipation for the lottery numbers. Our budget constraint controls our consumption.

The budget constraint (BC) for the consumption of lager and cigarettes is given by:

BC = price of lager*lager consumed + price of cigarettes*cigarettes consumed

Say that the price of lager is £2 per pint, the price of cigarettes is 15p each and your income or budget is £30 per week. Table 3.6 shows how the budget can be spent.

Table 3.6 Spending the budget

Amount spent	Lager	Cigarettes
All spent on lager	15 pints	0
All spent on cigarettes	0	200
£15 on lager/£15 on cigarettes	7.5 pints	100

If you spend all your income on lager, then you can buy a maximum of 15 pints (£30 ÷ £2). You can buy 200 cigarettes (£30 ÷ 15p) if you spend all your income on cigarettes. Spending half your budget on lager and cigarettes allows for 7.5 pints and 100 cigarettes. Figure 3.4 shows the information from Table 3.6.

Practice 3.8

Given:

income = £100
price of takeaway curry = £12.50
price of bottle of wine = £5

FIGURE 3.4 The budget constraint

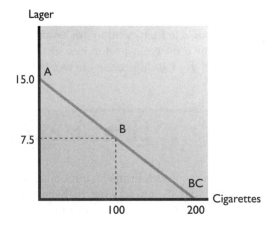

construct a budget constraint with curries on the vertical axis. Is it possible to consume seven curries and four bottles of wine given your income of £100? If you spend £50 on wine, what is the maximum number of curries you can purchase without going to the bank manager?

The slope of the budget constraint

The budget constraint (BC) for lager and cigarettes is given by:

BC = price of lager*lager consumed + price of cigarettes*cigarettes consumed

or

$$BC = p_l *l + p_c *c$$
where
p_l = the price of lager
p_c = the price of cigarettes
l = lager
c = cigarettes.

The positions A and B of Figure 3.4 are:

Position	BC	p_l	l	p_c	C
A	£30	£2	15	15p	0
B	£30	£2	7.5	15p	100

The entire budget is spent on combinations A and B. The change in the budget constraint (ΔB) is:

$$\Delta B = p_l *\Delta l + p_c *\Delta c$$

The change in ΔB, from A to B, is zero. So:

$$p_l *\Delta l = -(p_c *\Delta c)$$

and

$$\Delta l/\Delta c = -p_c/p_l$$

is the slope of the budget constraint.
Using our real numbers:

$$\Delta B = p_l *\Delta l + p_c *\Delta c$$
$$0 = £2* -7.5 + 15p*100$$
$$-(15p*100) = £2* -7.5$$
$$-15p/£2 = -7.5/100$$

The first expression is $-p_c/p_l$ and the second is $\Delta l/\Delta c$.

Now it is time for a cup of tea, or maybe something stronger, then it will be on to bringing the indifference curve and the budget constraint together to see where the consumer maximises utility.

Practice 3.9

A consumer has total income of £100 and purchases bread and water. The price of bread is £1 per loaf and the water is 50p per bottle. If water is on the vertical axis, what is the slope of the consumer's budget constraint?

Utility maximisation, at last

The consumer attempts to get to the highest indifference curve given the budget constraint. The budget constraint is the crucial factor. Utility maximisation is shown in Figure 3.5.

The consumer would like to live on indifference curve I_1 but, unfortunately, the consumer's budget constraint (BC) prevents this. Utility is maximised at the bliss point on indifference curve I_{max}. At the bliss point, the slopes of the indifference curve and the budget constraint are the same. Thus:

$$-p_c/p_l = -MU_c/MU_l$$

This can be rearranged to show the utility maximising condition:

$$MU_l/p_l = MU_c/p_c$$

The condition says that utility maximisation occurs when the marginal utility of lager relative to the price of lager equals the marginal utility of cigarettes relative to the price of cigarettes. This condition can be generalised and extended to all the products the consumer purchases, such that:

$$MU_l/p_l = MU_c/p_c = MU_x/p_x$$

where x represents all the other purchases made. This condition looks frightening but Figure 3.5 shows that indifference curve I_{max} is the highest given the consumer's budget constraint. Look at indifference curve I_0. The consumer could live on this indifference curve between points C and D but, clearly, this indifference curve is below I_{max}. At point D, the slope of indifference curve is flatter than the slope of the budget constraint. So:

$$-p_c/p_l > -MU_c/MU_l$$

and

$$MU_l/p_l > MU_c/p_c$$

This indicates that lager gives more marginal utility relative to its price than cigarettes. Lager yields more satisfaction than cigarettes at the margin allowing for their prices. The consumer should move away from cigarettes and purchase more lager. This would move the consumer away from point D and onto a higher indifference curve. The prices of lager and cigarettes remain the same but the marginal utility of lager falls while the marginal utility of cigarettes increases. The consumer would continue to move up the budget constraint until the condition:

$$MU_l/p_l = MU_c/p_c$$

was re-established. This condition is the utility maximising condition.

Practice 3.10

Prove that at point C in Figure 3.5 the consumer finds cigarettes yield more marginal utility relative to their price than lager. What advice would you give to this utility maximising consumer?

Price changes

If the price of cigarettes falls then the budget constraint will rotate towards the north-east in Figure 3.4. The budget constraint will have the same intercept on the lager axis (the price of lager stays the same) but the slope of the budget constraint will be flatter than before the price fall. This is shown in Figure 3.6.

FIGURE 3.5 Maximising utility

FIGURE 3.6 The budget constraint and a fall in the price of cigarettes

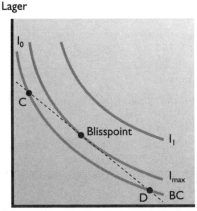

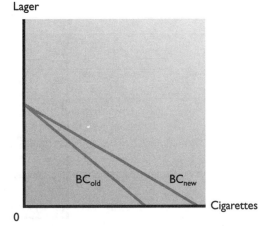

The consumer can now move to a new indifference curve. Normally, we would expect the consumer to purchase more cigarettes. This is shown in Figure 3.7 along with the resulting demand curve for cigarettes.

The consumer shifts from indifference curve I_{old} to I_{new} and purchases more cigarettes (c_1 as opposed to c_0). We have the demand curve relationship for a fall in price leading to a rise in demand. This relationship now has a theoretical underpinning. Indifference analysis provides theoretical support for the existence of a downward-sloping demand curve.

Practice 3.11

Show the effect of a rise in the price of cigarettes on the demand for them. Use indifference analysis and produce a demand curve.

FIGURE 3.7 Maximising utility after a fall in the price of cigarettes

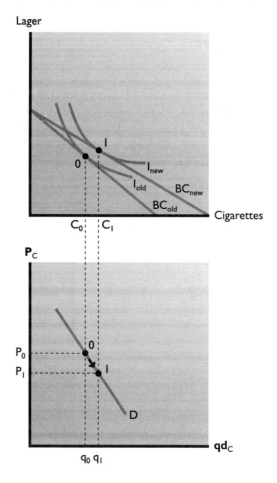

Income changes

When income increases the budget constraint shifts to the right. The shift is a parallel one and is shown in Figure 3.8.

The shift of the budget constraint allows the consumer to purchase more cigarettes and lager. This shows that both goods are normal. The new utility maximising bliss point and the resulting demand curves for cigarettes are shown in the Figure 3.9. The bliss point is the point where the consumer maximises utility. It is where the indifference curve touches the budget constraint.

Again, **indifference analysis has provided theoretical support for the assertion that an increase in income leads to an increase in demand through a shift of the demand curve.**

FIGURE 3.8 The budget constraint and an increase in income

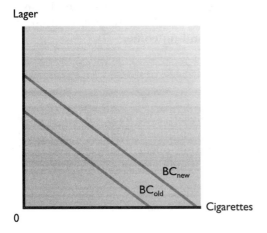

FIGURE 3.9 Utility maximisation and an increase in income

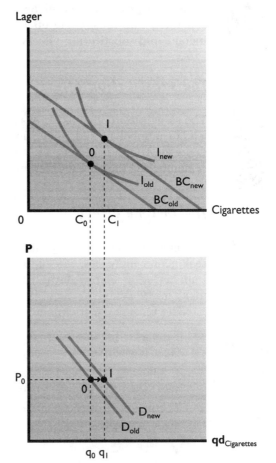

Practice 3.12

What is the difference between a fall in price and an increase in income as far as the budget constraint is concerned?

Practice 3.13

Using indifference analysis, show the effect of a fall in income on a normal good. Produce the resulting demand figure.

Income and substitution effects of a price change

When the price of a good or service changes, the effect on demand can be separated into an income effect and a substitution effect. In combination, the income and substitution effects show the demand outcome.

The substitution effect

The substitution effect is always negative. It is negative because a fall in price will lead to an increase in demand, and because a rise in price will lead to a decrease in demand. You can remember that the substitution effect is always negative by remembering that the indifference curve is negatively sloped.

The income effect

The income effect can be positive, negative or zero. If the price of lager falls, my real income increases. One of the products I buy is now cheaper and, in real terms, I am better off. Happy days! This is the opposite of inflation or rising prices that make me worse off.

The income effect concerns what I do with the change in real income:

✓ If my real income increases (and I purchase more lager) then the income effect is positive.

✓ If, following the real income increase, I do not change my consumption (of lager) then the income effect is zero.

✓ If I consume less (lager) following the increase in real income then the income effect is negative.

The substitution and income effects together

Income and substitution effects are typically examined by looking at three types of goods: normal, inferior and Giffen. This approach is followed but, first, Table 3.7 shows a summary of the income and substitution effects of each type of good.

Table 3.7 Income and substitution effects: normal, inferior and Giffen goods following a price decrease

Good	Income effect	Substitution effect	Overall effect
Normal	Positive. Buy more of the good	Negative. Buy more of the good	Buy more of the good
Inferior	Negative. Buy less of the good The substitution effect dominates the income effect	Negative. Buy more of the good	Buy more of the good
Giffen	Negative. Buy less of the good The income effect dominates the substitution effect	Negative. Buy more of the good	Buy less of the good An upward sloping demand curve

In the Table 3.7 the substitution effect is negative. To repeat, the substitution effect is always negative. For a price reduction, a negative substitution effect leads to more of the good being purchased. For a price increase, a negative substitution effect produces a fall in demand.

Practice 3.14

As a student, you need to purchase textbooks. They are vitally important and sometimes quite enjoyable. The price of textbooks increases due to the imposition of VAT. What will this mean for your real income? What will this price increase mean for your purchases of textbooks!?

The normal good

The normal good situation is when a price decrease (in the price of lager) prompts the consumer to have a negative substitution effect (buy more lager) and a positive income effect (buy more lager). The overall outcome is to purchase more lager, which is normal. It is certainly normal for me!

Two types of indifference curve figures can be constructed for a decrease in the price of lager. Figure 3.10 shows a situation where a fall in the price of lager leads to:

✓ a decrease in the amount spent on lager and thus an increase in the total expenditure on curries. The example is lager and curries with lager on the horizontal axis. Lager is price inelastic (see Chapter 8), and

✓ both goods experience positive income effects and are thus normal goods.

Some calculations

✓ The substitution effect. Use the old indifference curve I_0 and the new budget constraint BC_1. What? It can be done. Slide the new budget constraint BC_1 down so that it is parallel and touches the old indifference curve I_0. This happens at point S and coincidences at l_S and c_S. The movement along the old indifference curve I_0 from point 0 to point S shows the substitution effect. The consumer buys fewer curries (c_0 to c_S) and more lager (l_0 to l_S). The relatively cheaper lager (the price drop has made lager relatively cheaper) is substituted for the relatively more expensive curries (the price drop in lager makes curry relatively more expensive). The consumer buys more lager and fewer curries.

✓ The income effect. The income effect is measured from point S on the old indifference curve I_0 to point 1 on the new indifference curve I_1. Curry and lager are normal goods as the income effect leads to increases in both. The income effect for lager is l_S to l_1 and for curries it is c_S to c_1.

✓ The price elasticity of lager. The price of lager decreased and the amount spent on lager fell. Lager is price inelastic. How do I know this? There are two ways.

FIGURE 3.10   Income and substitution effects: Lager is price inelastic

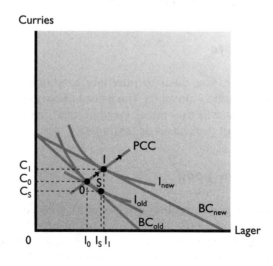

First, you can look at what has happened to expenditure on curries. The price of curries stayed the same but the number of curries purchased increased. Money income stayed the same so more of the money income is spent on curries and less on lager. Second, you can construct a price consumption curve (pcc) between points 0 and 1. The price consumption curve shows what happens to the products following a price change. If the price consumption curve is upward sloping then the product experiencing the price change is inelastic.

✓ The resulting demand curves for lager and curries. Figure 3.11 shows the demand curve for lager with (D_{S+Y}) and without (D_S) the income effect. Note that the demand curve for lager is steeper in the absence of the income effect. The inclusion of the income effect makes the demand curve flatter. The demand curve without the income effect will always be downward sloping.

Figure 3.12 shows the demand shift with (D_{S+Y}) and without (D_S) the income effects. The income effect dominates the substitution effect and leads to an increase in the demand for curries. This suggests that lager and curries are complements (see Chapter 2).

Practice 3.15

The price of lager increases. Sketch the demand curve for this normal good with and without the income effect. The demand curve without the income effect should be the steeper. Is it?

FIGURE 3.11 **The demand for lager: with and without the income effect**

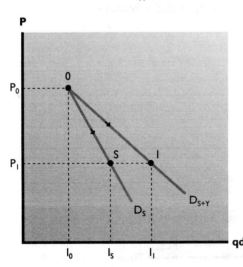

FIGURE 3.12 **The demand for curries: with and without the income effect**

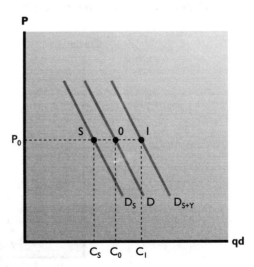

Practice 3.16

Try to construct an indifference curve figure in which a price increase in lager produces less lager and fewer curries being purchased. Show the income and substitution effects of the price increase for the demand for lager. You will need lager on the horizontal axis. Remember that the substitution effect uses the old or original indifference and the new budget constraint. Go on, try it!

The two goods are substitutes

It is possible to construct an indifference curve figure where the two goods are substitutes. This is shown in Figure 3.13. Two substitutes would be curries and pizzas. Thankfully, I do not know anybody who eats both at the same time!

Figure 3.13 possesses a number of features:

✓ The price of pizzas has fallen and this leads to the bliss point moving from point 0 to point 1.

✓ The substitution effect (always measure this first) uses I_0 and the new budget constraint BC_1. To do this, we shift the BC_1 line down to the old indifference curve I_0. Remember that the shift of BC_1 is a parallel shift. This produces point S. The substitution effect is more pizzas (p_0 to p_S) and fewer curries (c_0 to c_S).

✓ The income effect is more pizzas (p_S to p_1) and more curries (c_S to c_1). Both goods are normal. Interestingly, the curry income effect is positive (c_S to c_1) but is dominated by the negative curry substitution effect (c_0 to c_S). Thus, overall less curries are consumed at point 1 than at point 0. This suggests that the two products are substitutes.

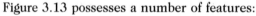

FIGURE 3.13 Curries and pizzas: indifference analysis and substitutes

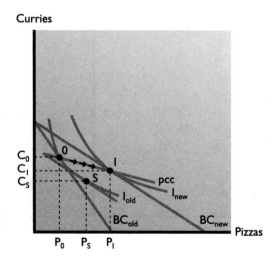

✓ Pizzas are price elastic. The price consumption curve (pcc) is downward sloping. Less money is spent on curries. The price of curries stayed the same but the overall quantity fell. If less money is spent on curries, more money must be spent on pizzas. The price of pizzas falls and more money is spent on pizzas. Pizzas must be price elastic.

Again, the demand curves for pizzas and curries can be constructed with and without the income effect. The demand curve (Figures 3.14 and 3.15) shows that:

✓ The demand for pizzas is steeper in the absence of the income effect.

✓ The demand for curries experiences a shift from point 0 to point 1. This shows that the two products are substitutes. The income effect is positive (point S to point 1) but not sufficiently so to overcome the negative substitution effect (point 0 to point S).

Practice 3.17

Now the price of pizzas increases. Produce an indifference curve figure showing that the demand for pizzas is price elastic.

The case of the inferior good

An inferior good is one which experiences a **negative income effect** following a price reduction for the good. The overall demand for the good increases following the price reduction as the negative income effect does not overwhelm the substitution

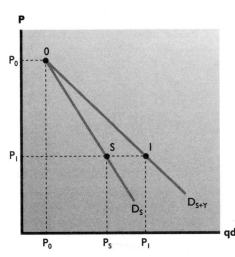

FIGURE 3.14 The demand for pizzas: with and without the income effect

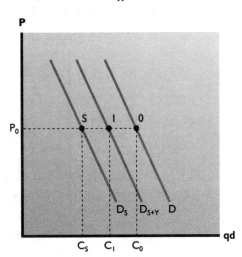

FIGURE 3.15 The demand for curries: with and without the income effect

effect. An example of an inferior good is bus and coach travel. Students and pensioners are typical users of coaches. They are, typically, on relatively low incomes and are prepared to sacrifice time and comfort in exchange for low fares. As students move into the world of work, they travel by private car, train or plane. **Inferior goods have a negative income elasticity** (Chapter 9). Figure 3.16 shows the implications of a fall in the price of coach journeys. In the analysis, a student needs to travel to and from college each day by bus. This takes up a lot of the student's precious income and there is very little income left to indulge in her favourite pastime of watching the great Glasgow Celtic. The fall in the price of coach travel creates a substitution effect of more coach travel and fewer Celtic games (point 0 to point S) but when the income effect (point S to point 1) enters the figure the overall result is fewer coach journeys and more Celtic games.

We can summarise the outcomes of Figure 3.16 in Table 3.8.

Table 3.8 **Substitution and income effects: coach journeys as an inferior good**

Product	Substitution effect	Income effect	Overall
Celtic games	(f_0 to f_S). Fewer games	Positive (f_S to f_1). More games	Increase in demand: income effect overwhelms substitution effect
Coach journeys	Negative (c_0 to c_S). More journeys	Negative (c_S to c_1). Fewer journeys	Increase in demand: substitution effect dominates negative income effect

FIGURE 3.16   Indifference analysis: coach journeys as an inferior good

Celtic games

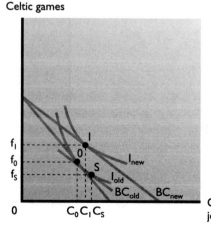

Figure 3.16 shows that the demand for coach journeys is price inelastic (see Chapter 8). The price of Celtic games is unchanged but more games are attended. More money is spent on football matches and less on coach journeys.

Figure 3.17 shows the effects of the fall in the price of coach travel on the demand for Celtic games (shift of) and coach journeys (movement along). The two products are complements as the demand for Celtic games shifts to the right following the fall in the price of coach travel.

Presumably, our Celtic fan uses the coach system to travel to Celtic games.

Practice 3.18

Allow the price of coach journeys to increase. Using an indifference figure, show the impact of this price increase on the demand for Celtic games and coach journeys. Show the income and substitution effects of the price change on the demand for coach journeys. Remember that the substitution effect uses the old indifference curve and the parallel shift of the new budget constraint.

The Giffen good

A Giffen good is a good with an upward sloping demand curve. An increase in price leads to an increase in demand. The Giffen good is one of the tricks of the economist's act. As with all tricks it is an illusion. All textbooks cover the Giffen good and a number comment on its somewhat controversial nature. The story behind the Giffen good is that communities living a subsistence existence eat a

FIGURE 3.17 The resulting demand curves for Celtic games and coach journeys

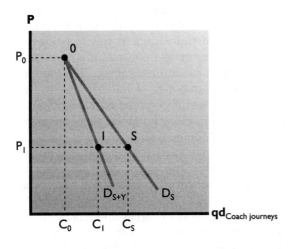

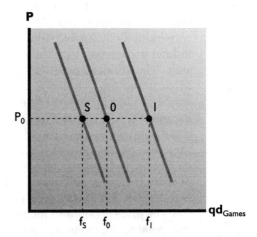

diet consisting mainly of a staple product. The Giffen good, which is a particular type of inferior good, accounts for a very large proportion of a consumer's expenditure. In Ireland, during the first half of the nineteenth-century, it was potatoes, while in Asia it is rice. Robert Giffen, a nineteenth century social scientist inquired into the strange statistical finding that agricultural communities purchased more of a staple (bread and potatoes) at higher prices. This produced an upward-sloping demand curve! Potatoes in Ireland in the 1840s are the classic example of Giffen goods. Unfortunately, there has not been another occurrence of a Giffen good since then despite the considerable amount of research carried out by economists. With all this in mind, it is time to cover the indifference analysis of the Giffen good. Table 3.9 summarises the income and substitution effects of a rise in the price of a Giffen good.

Table 3.9   Substitution and income effects: potatoes as a Giffen good

Increase in the price of potatoes

Product	Substitution effect	Income effect	Overall
Meat (normal good)	(m_0 to m_S). More meat demanded	Negative (m_S to m_1). Less meat demanded	Decrease in demand: income effect overwhelms substitution effect
Potatoes (Giffen good)	Negative (p_0 to p_S). Fewer potatoes demanded	Positive (p_S to p_1). More potatoes demanded	Increase in demand: income effect dominates negative substitution effect

Remember that the price of potatoes has increased so the budget constraint rotates towards the south-west and becomes BC1. The substitution effect is measured by using the old or original indifference curve I_0 and the new budget constraint BC_1. Again, shift the new budget constraint until it touches the old indifference curve. Remember that the shift of the budget constraint is a parallel shift. The result is point S. We have the normal substitution effect. *The income effect is the key.* The consumer is spending the majority of her income on the staple product, potatoes. The increase in the price of potatoes reduces her real income and she reacts by consuming less meat but more potatoes. She consumes more potatoes because the reduction in her real income is so dramatic (remember that she spends most of her meagre income on potatoes) that she must sacrifice meat and purchase potatoes in order to survive. The potato income effect is **positive** (p_S to p_1) and overwhelms the negative substitution effect (p_0 to p_S). That is the story. The outcome is shown in Figure 3.18.

The price of potatoes increases. The resulting demand curves for meat (shift of) and potatoes (movement along) show that the demand for meat shifts to the left when the income effect is included. The demand for potatoes is downward-sloping only if the substitution effect is included, but **upward-sloping** when the income effect is added. An upward-sloping demand curve? Yes, but look at the requirements. It is a strange story. Figure 3.19 shows the resulting demand curves for meat and potatoes.

The demand curve for meat shifts to the left overall, while the demand curve for potatoes is upward sloping when the income effect is added up to substitution effect.

FIGURE 3.18 Indifference analysis: potatoes as a Giffen good

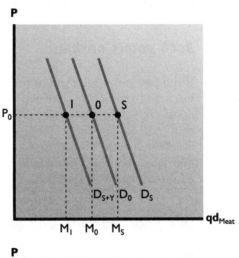

FIGURE 3.19 The demand curves for meat and potatoes

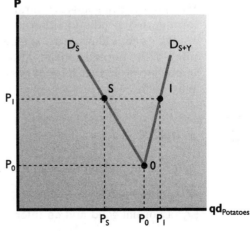

Practice 3.19

It is 1849 in the west of Ireland and the price of potatoes falls. What do you expect this will do to the demand for potatoes? Show the outcome in an indifference curve map. Has the demand for meat increased? It should have!

Changes in income

The purpose of this section is to introduce the income consumption curve (ycc) into the analysis. The income consumption curve shows what happens to the demand for the two products when income changes. A change in income produces a parallel shift in the budget constraint. We will look at two situations. The first is when both the goods are normal. The second case considers a normal good and either an inferior or Giffen good.

Both goods normal

If the two goods are normal then the ycc is upwards sloping. We have argued that lager and curries are normal goods. They are usually consumed by 'abnormal' people but they are normal goods. Figure 3.20 shows the upward-sloping nature of this ycc.

The upward-sloping income consumption curve argues that a consumer will purchase more of both goods following an increase in income. This is why the goods are known as normal.

One good normal, one good Giffen or inferior

If one of the two goods is inferior or Giffen then the ycc slopes downward. The ycc for a normal good and either an inferior or Giffen good is shown in Figure 3.21.

The ycc is downward sloping. This suggests that a consumer will purchase more of the normal good and less of the inferior/Giffen good following an increase in income. Note that it is not possible to have inferior or Giffen goods on both axes. Why not?

Practice 3.20

Demonstrate, using the ycc, the result of a fall in income for:

✓ normal goods
✓ a normal good and an inferior good.

Summary

'At last!' I hear you say. This has not been an easy chapter. Indifference analysis is only required by students who have it included in their economics module or those who are very curious people.

The key to understanding indifference analysis is to conquer the substitution effect:

✓ Remember to use the old indifference curve and shift the new budget constraint parallel to meet the old indifference curve.

✓ Once you have successfully carried out the substitution effect, the rest of the analysis, including the income effect, follows without too many problems.

✓ The chapter contains numbers and algebra but with practice (that word again) what looks complicated can be overcome.

The next chapter looks at the supply curve but for now try to sketch the indifference curve map for a decrease in the price of tea with coffee on the vertical axis. Practice, practice, practice ...

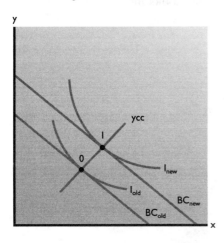

FIGURE 3.20 The income consumption curve: both goods are normal

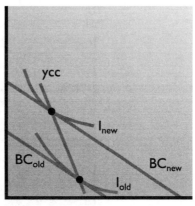

FIGURE 3.21 The income consumption curve: inferior good or Giffen good

Answers for Chapter 3

Answer 3.1

As you know I get no utility from the consumption of cigarettes or cigars. In addition, I do not watch 'Catchphrase', the TV quiz show. You can assume that I get no utility from 'Catchphrase'.

Answer 3.2

Marginal utility is the change in total utility.

Chocolates	Total utility	Marginal utility
1	10	10
2	18	8
3	24	6
4	28	4
5	30	2
6	30	0
7	28	−2

Chocolates become a bad with the consumption of the seventh chocolate. The seventh chocolate yields a negative marginal utility. The negative marginal utility indicates that chocolate has become a bad.

The figure for total utility and marginal utility looks like:

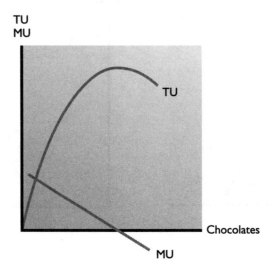

Answer 3.3

The non-drinking smoker has vertical indifference curves if lager is on the vertical axis. More pints of lager do not increase total utility. They are not substituted for fewer cigarettes. The non-drinking smoker will aim for the vertical indifference giving the maximum number of cigarettes. The figure looks like:

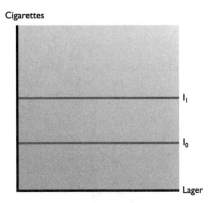

Answer 3.4

Ten and two, respectively. An extra pint increases total utility from 90 to 100, so the marginal utility is ten. Five extra cigarettes increase total utility by ten. The marginal utility of each of the cigarettes is two.

Answer 3.5

Indian takeaways are on the vertical and Chinese food on the horizontal. Friend 1 will have a downward sloping indifference curve that is flatter than that of friend 2. Friend 1 prefers Indian food and will require more Chinese food to compensate for the loss of each Indian meal. Friend 2 is the opposite. The loss of each Chinese meal must be compensated for by ever more Indian meals. The figure looks like:

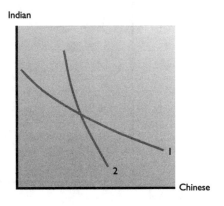

Answer 3.6

The marginal utility of cigarettes increases as we move up the indifference curve, the marginal utility of lager falls and fewer cigarettes are consumed and more lager is purchased. Fewer cigarettes increase the marginal utility of cigarettes, while more lager reduces the marginal utility of lager.

Answer 3.7

The slope of the indifference curve is relatively flat. The slope is given by $(-MU_x/MU_y)$. The marginal utility of x is low and the marginal utility of y is high. This makes the slope relatively flat. The indifference curve looks like:

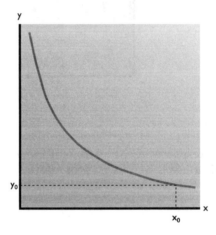

Answer 3.8

The budget constraint, with curries on the vertical axis, looks like:

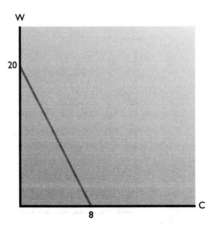

It is not possible to consume seven curries and four bottles of wine given your income (£100) as it would require an income of £107.50.

If you spend £50 on wine then the maximum number of curries you can have is four.

Answer 3.9

The slope of the budget constraint is -2. There are two ways of reaching this result.

1. The maximum number of bottles of water is 200 and the maximum number of loaves is 100. If we give up all the bottles of water (-200), we can have all the loaves ($+100$). The ratio is $-200/+100$ or -2.
2. The slope of the budget constraint is ($-p_b/p_w$) with water on the vertical. Therefore, the slope is $-£1/50p$ or -2.

Answer 3.10

The consumer should discover that:

$$-p_c/p_l < -MU_c/MU_l$$

or, in words, that the slope of the indifference curve is greater than the slope of the budget constraint. This shows that cigarettes yield more marginal utility relative to their price than does lager. This follows from:

$$MU_l/p_l < MU_c/p_c$$

and should lead the consumer to purchase more cigarettes and less lager. This moves the individual to a higher indifference curve along the budget constraint in the direction of the bliss point.

Answer 3.11

The effect of an increase in the price of cigarettes should normally be to:

1. lead to a movement up the demand curve for cigarettes
2. shift the consumer to a lower indifference curve. Whether the consumer buys more or less of the other good depends on the relationship between the two goods. If they are substitutes then more of the other good is purchased. If they are complements then less of the other good is purchased.

The demand and indifference curve figures look like:

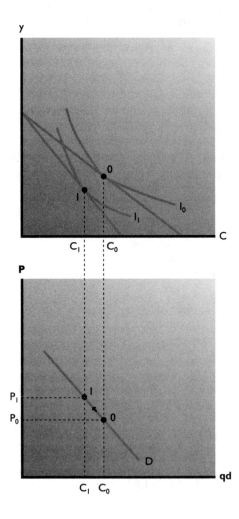

Answer 3.12

A price decrease rotates the budget constraint, while an increase in income shifts the budget constraint.

Answer 3.13

A fall in income will lead to the demand for a normal good decreasing. There will be a shift of the demand curve to the left. The indifference curve outcome and the resulting demand figures look like:

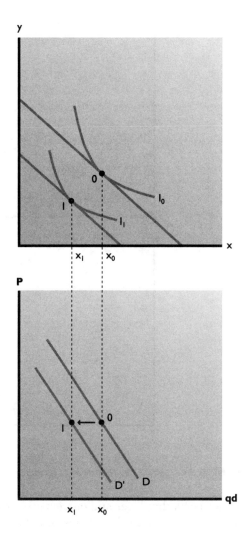

Answer 3.14

1. The price increase will reduce your real income. The reduction will vary with the amount of your income spent on textbooks. If you spend a large percentage of your income on textbooks then the reduction will be large.
2. If textbooks are a normal good, you will buy fewer textbooks following the price increase.

Answer 3.15

If the price of lager increases, we would expect the demand for this normal good to fall. There would be movement up the demand curve. We can analyse the price increase with and without the income effect. The two effects look like:

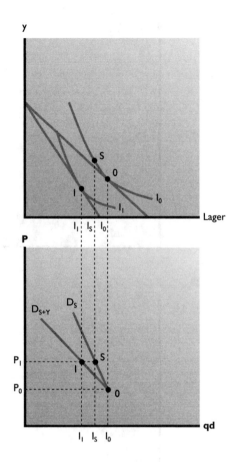

Answer 3.16

This question suggests that lager and curries are complements. An increase in the price of lager leads to less lager being demanded (movement along) and also fewer curries being purchased (shift of). The indifference outcome looks like:

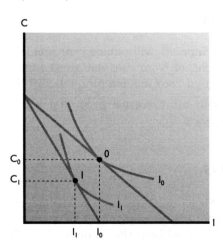

Answer 3.17

If pizzas are price elastic following a price increase then the amount spent on pizzas will fall. The amount spent on curries will rise. The price of curries stays the same so more curries have to be purchased in order to increase the amount spent on them. The price consumption curve will be upward sloping. The indifference figure will look like:

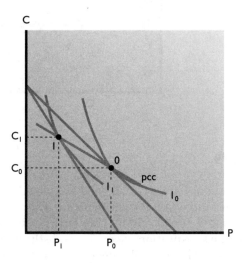

Answer 3.18

Remember that:

1. coach journeys are an inferior good and possess a negative income effect
2. coach journeys and Celtic games are complements.

An increase in the price of coach journeys will possess an income effect and a substitution effect. The substitution effect will be fewer coach journeys and more Celtic games. This is measured along the original indifference curve (point 0 to point S). The income effect uses the new indifference curve. With the negative income effect for coach journeys, the consumer will increase the demand for coach journeys following the price increase (point S to point 1). This, however, will be dominated by the substitution effect and the overall outcome will be fewer coach journeys (point 0 to point 1). In addition, fewer Celtic games will be attended, which is a shame. The indifference figure looks like:

Games

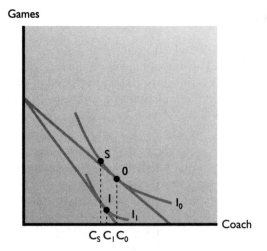

Answer 3.19

Given that potatoes are a Giffen good, we would expect a decrease in the price of potatoes to lead to a fall in their demand. There would be a movement down the upward sloping demand curve. This is the result of the negative income effect dominating the substitution effect. The substitution effect is to buy more potatoes and less meat. The overall effects are fewer potatoes and more meat. The indifference figure looks like:

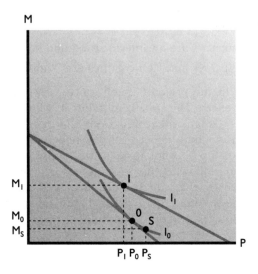

Answer 3.20

1. A fall in income will shift the demand curve for a normal good to the left. The indifference outcome will be to reduce the purchase of each of the normal goods.

2. A fall in income will shift the demand curve for an inferior good to the right. If the two goods are normal and inferior, the income consumption curve will be downward sloping with the normal good on the vertical axis.

3. The figures look like:

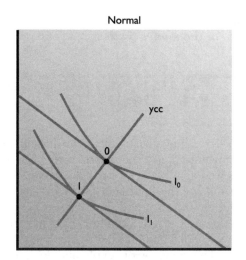

Normal

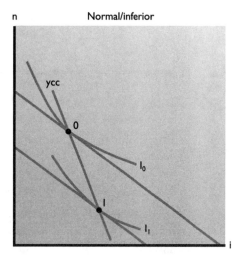

Normal/inferior

THE SUPPLY CURVE – MOVEMENT ALONG AND SHIFT OF

Where is the nearest bookshop?
I must buy an economics textbook!

This will help

You should read Chapter 2 before reading this chapter, as this chapter is the counterpart to demand. We, as consumers, are the demanders, while businesses are the suppliers. Each can be viewed as a blade of a pair of scissors. The blades work best together. This chapter follows the approach taken in Chapter 2. This chapter is brief because lots of the groundwork and practice was covered in that chapter. Economics is fairly sequential. Understanding one aspect, such as demand, makes the following topic, say elasticity, easier to comprehend. Demand will help you to understand supply. The coverage of supply and demand will make understanding price determination (Chapter 10) a lot easier.

Introduction

Supply analysis is, like the coverage on demand, an excellent opportunity to conquer any fears you have concerning microeconomics. Like the chapter on demand, this chapter is one of the essential building blocks for understanding microeconomics. If you get the basics right then the more difficult parts are more easily managed.

The goods and services you purchased yesterday were supplied by somebody. The act of demand is matched by supply. When you purchase a newspaper, it is an act of demand. For the newsagent it is an act of supply.

By the end of this chapter you will understand:

✓ what a supply curve is
✓ what changes in the price of the good or service will mean for the level of supply (the movement along aspect)

✓ why changes in the other factors explaining supply will lead to a shift of the supply curve

✓ the factors explaining the slope of the supply curve.

The supply curve

The supply curve shows the diagrammatic relationship between the price of the good and the quantity supplied of the good. It is the opposite of the demand curve. As with the demand curve, however, price is found on the vertical axis and quantity supplied is placed on the horizontal. If we were examining the supply curve for oranges, for example, we would see the price of oranges on the vertical and the quantity of oranges supplied on the horizontal. The supply curve shows what happens to the supply for oranges at different prices. The supply curve is, like the demand curve, part of the economist's toolbox.

The factors explaining supply

There are a number of factors explaining the supply of a product. Changes in the explanatory factors lead to changes in supply. The explanatory factors include:

$$qs = f(\overset{+}{p}, \overset{-}{p_{fop}}, \overset{+}{Tech}, \overset{?}{Aims}, \overset{?}{E}, \ldots)$$

where

qs = the total quantity supplied in a particular market

p = the price of the product

p_{fop} = the price of factors of production

Tech = technology

Aims = the aims or objectives of businesses

E = expectations.

The sign above each of the explanatory variables shows what will happen to supply if the explanatory variable increases. The sign above p is positive. This indicates that an increase in price should lead to an increase in supply. Above the p_{fop} factor there is a negative sign. This indicates that an increase in the price of factors of production will lead to a decrease in supply.

Practice 4.1

What will happen to supply if there is an increase in technology? Can you think of an example of an increase in technology?

Movement along the supply curve

The first relationship examined is that between price and quantity supplied. All the other factors explaining supply will be held constant. This is the *ceteris paribus* assumption. ***An increase in price will normally cause the total quantity supplied to increase***. Table 4.1 shows the relationship between price and quantity supplied.

Table 4.1   **The relationship between price and quantity supplied**

P	QS
0	0
1	2
2	4
3	6
4	8
5	10
6	12
7	14
8	16
9	18
10	20

The schedule shows that price and quantity supplied move together. The relationship is positive.

The schedule can be seen in Figure 4.1.

FIGURE 4.1   **The supply curve**

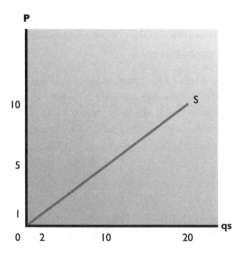

The reason why the supply curve is argued to be upwards sloping concerns the notion of profits (Chapter 7). Businesses can aim to maximise profits. A higher price will, *ceteris paribus*, lead to higher profits. The firm has an incentive to increase production and supply. There is movement up the firm's supply curve.

A classic example of an increase in price leading to an increase in supply is the housing market in the United Kingdom. During the late 1990s the housing market recovered and boomed. The price of houses increased. Our house was purchased in September 1996 for £200 000. By the summer of 1998 the market price had increased to over £300 000. This is a big increase and the number of homeowners putting their houses on the market has increased. They can obtain a price in excess of the price they originally paid. There are profitable opportunities available for sellers and positive equity.

Ask your local estate agent to comment on the state of the housing market, then look at the number of properties on sale. There should be a positive relationship.

Another example of higher prices leading to an increase in supply is the craze thing. In the summer of 1998 the craze thing was yo-yos. The fact that prices were high led everybody to stock and sell yo-yos. Again, there was a positive relationship between price and supply. The profits to be had from selling yo-yos explained the positive relationship between price and supply.

Practice 4.2

Draw a supply curve where a relatively small increase in price leads to a relatively large increase in output.

Increasing price leads to an increase in supply

As price increases, quantity supplied also increases. The increase in price acts as an incentive to increase supply. The price increase from 7 to 8 leads to supply increasing from 14 to 16:

p	qs
7	14
8	16

There has been movement along the supply curve. The movement along factor is the price of the product.

Practice 4.3

Using Table 4.1, what happens to supply if price falls from 5 to 4?

Place your finger on p=5 and qs = 10. Does your finger move along the supply curve as price decreases to 4?

Shift of the supply curve

We have covered the movement relationship between price and quantity supplied. The other factors explaining supply are:

L   R   ?   ?
(P$_{fop}$, Tech, Aims, E, . . .)

Changes in each of these determining factors will cause the supply curve to shift. The letter, R for rightward shift and L for leftward shift, above the explanatory factors show the direction of the shift of the supply curve caused by an increase in each of the causal variables. If, for example, technology (Tech) increases then the supply curve will shift to the right.

The price of factors of production and quantity supplied

The factors of production include workers, buildings, electricity, raw materials, management, capital equipment and technology. In combination, the factors of production create the product supplied. The factors of production have to be paid for. These are the costs of the business. I enjoy getting my monthly salary as a factor of production, but as far as my employer is concerned it is a cost.

Increases in the price of factors of production such as wages, salaries, interest rates lead to the supply curve shifting to the left. The most intuitively appealing explanation is that an increase in the price of a factor of production will be passed on to the consumer in the form of a higher price. The high wages paid to footballers such as David Beckham and Michael Owen have been passed on to football fans in the form of higher match tickets. This intuitive explanation is shown in Figure 4.2.

The typical explanation for the supply curve shifting to the left following an increase in the price of a factor of production is not intuitively appealing. The firm finds it unprofitable to maintain the existing level of supply after the cost increase. Their selling price remains unchanged and the firm reacts by reducing its supply. Again, the supply curve shifts to the left. This is an awkward story.

Practice 4.4

Workers seek and obtain a higher rate of pay. What will this mean for the supply curve of the product they produce?

Technology and quantity supplied

Technology is a vitally important aspect of the production process. Examples of technology include the laptop computer, the supermarket checkout point and the ticket machine in your local railway station. The supermarket checkout point has introduced technological improvements through the scanner, the conveyor and the information provided by the electronic cash register. Each of these technological improvements has improved the productivity of the checkout worker. The worker can deal with more shoppers in a given period. The increased efficiency of the checkout worker will increase the supply of shoppers through the checkout. This is shown in the Figure 4.3.

Practice 4.5

The government plans improvements to road technology such as smart traffic lights and bus-only lanes. If the improvements are successfully introduced then what would you expect this to mean for the supply of public transport from buses?

The aims of businesses and quantity supplied

Businesses have various aims. The principal aims are profit maximisation and market share. If profit maximisation is the aim, movement along and shifts of the supply curve can be explained by this analysis. Higher prices produce higher profits, *ceteris paribus*, and lead to a movement up the supply curve. Changes in the shift factors will also have consequences for the profit position of the firm. Lower wage rates may encourage the firm to hire more workers, produce more and make higher profits.

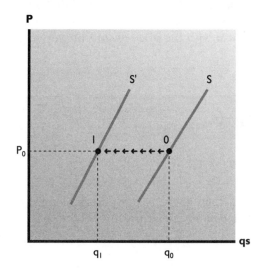

FIGURE 4.2 An increase in the price of a factor of production and the supply curve

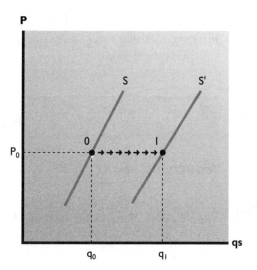

FIGURE 4.3 An increase in technology and the supply curve

If market share is the dominant aim, firms may be willing to sacrifice profits to protect their market position. Supermarkets appear to be very concerned with their market share and seek to maintain and indeed increase their share. If their workforce obtain a wage increase then conventional supply analysis would argue that the supply curve should shift to the left. The market share firm may decide to absorb the cost increase by reducing their profits, thus maintaining their level of output and market share. We can only predict supply changes when we know the aims of the particular business. This is the reason for the question mark over the 'Aims' variable.

Practice 4.6

Graph the supply reaction of the market share firm following an increase in wages. What has happened to price and quantity supplied?

Expectations and quantity supplied

Expectations, as with beauty, are in the eye of the beholder. If a firm expects the price of a factor of production to increase, say electricity, then it would be sensible to increase present production and stockpile the resulting production. In the United Kingdom the coalminers took strike action from March 1983 to March 1984. The National Coal Board increased production in anticipation of the strike action. The result was very high levels of coal stocks (shift of the supply to the right). This prevented the strike (shift of the supply curve to the left) from having a significant effect.

Practice 4.7

Spanish airport workers decide to hold a strike over the weekend of 31 July 1998. What would you expect this to mean for the supply of catering services at Spanish airports over that weekend? Graph your answer with the price of catering services on the vertical axis.

Review

Movement along

If the price of the good or service changes, then there is movement along the supply curve. Thus **price changes lead to movement along the supply curve.**

Shift of

If the following explanatory variables increase (wages and salaries (w), interest rates (r), price of raw materials ($p_{materials}$), strike activity) then the supply curve shifts to the left. **Thus increase in any of w, r, $p_{materials}$, or strikes leads to shift to the left.**

If the following explanatory variables increase (technology, productivity, efficiency) then the supply curve shifts to the right. Thus **increase in any of technology, productivity or efficiency lead to shift to the right**.

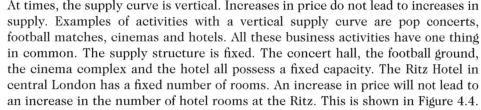

The supply curve in the real world

There is no doubt that increases in price will lead to increases in supply. The supply curve experiences movement along. It is also true that shifts of the supply curve are the result of changes in wages, technology and expectations. However, the shape of the supply curve is not always upwards sloping. This section looks at real-world situations where the supply curve is vertical and horizontal.

Supply is fixed

At times, the supply curve is vertical. Increases in price do not lead to increases in supply. Examples of activities with a vertical supply curve are pop concerts, football matches, cinemas and hotels. All these business activities have one thing in common. The supply structure is fixed. The concert hall, the football ground, the cinema complex and the hotel all possess a fixed capacity. The Ritz Hotel in central London has a fixed number of rooms. An increase in price will not lead to an increase in the number of hotel rooms at the Ritz. This is shown in Figure 4.4.

The supply curve in Figure 4.4 shows that supply is fixed. This is the same type of supply curve as for a Spice Girls concert. The concert hall has fixed seating capacity.

Practice 4.8

A holiday firm books a Spanish hotel for the summer season. The firm offers two-week holidays. They aim to fill the fixed capacity. Unfortunately, their bookings for the last two weeks in September are only 50 per cent of capacity. What price advice would you offer the firm to make sure capacity usage increases to 100 per cent? Graph the supply curve. Graph your demand curve advice.

Supply is flexible

Just as the supply curve can be vertical, there are also occasions when the supply curve is horizontal. An horizontal supply curve indicates that the supplier is prepared to sell unlimited amounts of the product at a fixed price. One example is car production. Ford decides on a price for the Mondeo and is happy to supply as much as is demanded at the price. Figure 4.5 shows the horizontal supply curve.

Knowing the shape of the supply curve allows us to engage in real-world analysis. During France 98, the demand for games involving England outstripped the fixed supply. The official ticket price for first-round games was £14.50, while the unofficial, black market price was as high as £400 for the England–Romania game. Clearly, the supply curve for this game was not horizontal. Neither was it upwards sloping.

Practice 4.9

Graph the demand and supply curve for the England–Romania game.

Summary

I am sure that you were happy that this chapter was brief. The brevity is a reflection of the previous demand coverage, not that supply analysis is unimportant. Supply analysis is very important. Businesses need to make very important decisions on output, price and reactions to changes in wages and technology. The key points to take from this chapter are:

FIGURE 4.4 The Ritz Hotel supply curve

FIGURE 4.5 The Ford Mondeo supply curve

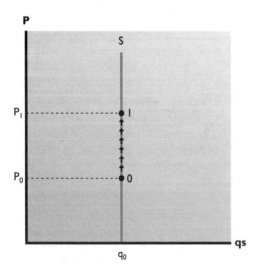

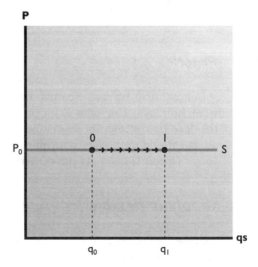

✓ price changes produce movement along the supply curve

✓ changes in the other factors influencing supply create a shift of the supply curve

✓ the slope of the supply curve is usually thought to be upward sloping but there are situations when the supply curve is vertical (fixed supply) and horizontal (perfectly flexible).

The next chapter leads on from this chapter. Reading and understanding this chapter on supply will help you to understand Chapter 5.

Answers for Chapter 4

Answer 4.1

The supply curve will shift to the right if there is an increase in technology. More products can be supplied at the existing price. An example of this is personal computers.

Answer 4.2

The supply curve will be relatively flat. A small increase in price has produced a large increase in supply. The figure looks like:

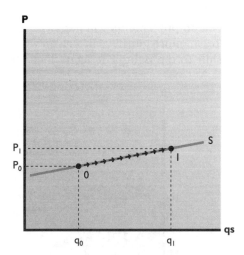

Answer 4.3

If price falls from 5 to 4, then supply decreases from 10 to 8.

Answer 4.4

The supply curve will shift to the left. The figure looks like:

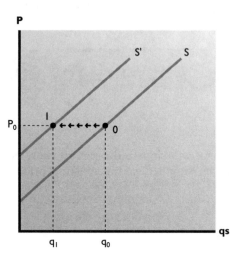

Answer 4.5

The technological improvements will increase the productivity of buses. Each bus will be able to travel more journeys in a given work period. The supply curve of bus journeys will shift to the right. The figure looks like:

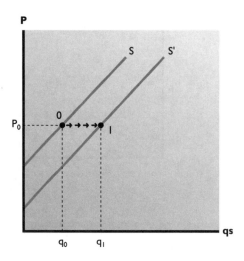

Answer 4.6

The market share firm will absorb the wage cost increase. Profits will be sacrificed at the expense of market share. The firm's supply curve will not be affected. Their profits will be affected. There will be no reaction! The figure looks like:

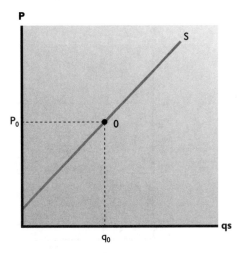

Answer 4.7

The supply of catering services should shift to the left. Thankfully, the strike did not happen. It was the day of our flight to Ibiza! If the strike had taken place then the figure would have looked like:

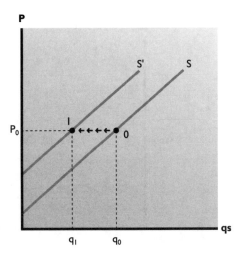

Answer 4.8

Obviously, the supply curve is vertical. This represents the fixed capacity. Price is too high to match demand of 50 per cent with the fixed capacity of 100 per cent. The firm should lower price along the demand curve until demand equals supply and all capacity is full. The figure looks like:

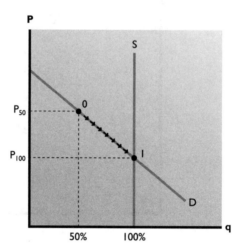

Answer 4.9

The supply curve was again vertical. The official FIFA price per ticket was too low and more tickets were demanded than were supplied. The result was the presence of ticket touts. The figure looks like:

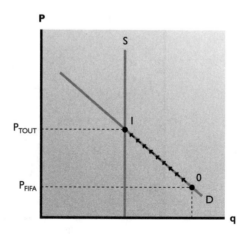

PRODUCTION – BEHIND THE SUPPLY CURVE

Production costs.

This will help

You are advised to read Chapter 4 before reading this chapter. Firms produce output and need to bring together factors of production to produce their output. Workers are paid wages as compensation for being a factor of production. Unfortunately for employers, these wages give rise to costs. To produce a product requires factors and the factors have to be paid. That is the story of this chapter.

Introduction

If you are reading this chapter then it is probably because you are studying economics at college or school. Your school or college is a production centre. The product they produce is educational services. You, the student, are the output. To produce the educational services the schools and colleges need to combine factors of production. Look around your school or college and you will see the factors of production used in producing the educational services. There is the building, the teachers, the technology, the management, energy, such as electricity and gas, the land and the raw materials.

By the end of this chapter you will understand:

- ✓ what factors of production are
- ✓ how factors of production are separated into fixed and variable factors
- ✓ the short- and long-runs
- ✓ the production function
- ✓ returns to factors and factor efficiency
- ✓ paying for the factors of production
- ✓ the production possibility curve.

The factors of production

The factors of production used in writing this book were the computer, the study and the writer, me. Any business needs to combine factors of production in order to produce the firm's output. The factors of production include the following:

✓ labour
✓ capital equipment
✓ land
✓ technology
✓ management
✓ energy
✓ raw materials.

This is a fairly abstract list. We can give it real-world reality by using the example of a McDonald's restaurant. The people who serve us are the labour. The capital equipment is the building, the table and chairs, the counter, the fryers and the cash machines. The land is literally the land on which the restaurant stands. Technology includes the computer system used to generate more French fries and Big Macs if stocks are running low and the use of smart lights in the toilets to control electricity usage. The man in the white shirt who smiles at us and frowns at the workers represents management. Energy is required to light the building and cook the food. The raw materials include the food and the packaging. In combination, the factors of production produce the output of the McDonald's restaurant. Have a look the next time you are in a McDonald's. There is microeconomics all around you.

The factors of production can be separated into fixed and variable factors. The separation into fixed and variable factors allows us to identify the factors that can be changed quickly and the factors that cannot be changed quickly. As far as the McDonald's restaurant is concerned, the factors of production can be separated into fixed and variable factors as shown in Table 5.1.

Table 5.1   McDonald's fixed and variable factors

Fixed factors	Variable factors
Capital equipment	Labour
Land	Energy
Technology	Raw materials
Management	

The key to separating the factors into fixed and variable factors is how quickly the factors can be changed. Factors that can be changed quickly, such as longer shifts for the existing workers, more part-time workers and keeping the lights on longer each day, are defined as variable factors. Alternatively, factors that take a long time to change, such as capital equipment and land, are described as fixed factors.

In the short-run only variable factors can be changed or varied. Fixed factors cannot be altered in the short-run. If the McDonald's restaurant wished to increase its output of food in the short-run then it would increase the factors that are capable of being changed quickly. These are the variable factors. McDonald's would:

✓ buy more raw materials such as hamburgers or chicken nuggets (my daughter's favourite)
✓ use their cooking equipment for longer and hence use more electricity
✓ maybe employ more part-time workers.

They could not change any of the fixed factors. It would be impossible to change the size of the building or the fryers. The fixed factors are, in the short-run, fixed.

Practice 5.1

List the fixed and variable factors at your local supermarket.

The short-run and the long-run

To make the analysis easy (that word again) all the variable factors are classified as labour (L), while the fixed factors are denoted by capital (K). Using this approach, we can examine how McDonald's will increase and decrease its output in the short-run. This introduces us to the production function, which shows the relationship between output (Q) and the factors of production (L, K). The McDonald's production function in the short-run, with capital fixed, shows that changes in output are the sole result of changes in variable factors. This is shown in Figure 5.1.

The short-run production function shows that capital is fixed ($\underline{K}$) and output (Q_0 to Q_1) can only increase if labour increases (L_0 to L_1). Changes in output can only come from changes in the variable factors. The main variable factor is usually labour. When output is planned to change the number of workers employed also changes. In July 1998 Rover, the car producer, decided that demand for its cars was falling and reacted to this fall in demand by reducing output. Rover laid off 1500 workers. The workers are a variable factor and are usually the first factor to be reduced when businesses face demand problems.

In the long-run, McDonald's can change all of its factors. It could move to a new building, introduce new technology or implement new management strategies. If it introduced new technology, the existing workforce would become more efficient. The long-run production function results from a change in at least one of the firm's fixed factors. For example, McDonald's may have increased the number of seats in the restaurant. This would allow McDonald's to increase output. Alternatively, McDonald's could introduce superior cookers. This would speed up cooking times. The production implication of introducing new cookers is shown in Figure 5.2.

McDonald's can increase output (Q_0 to Q_1) by shifting to the new production function (PF_1). The new production function is the result of introducing new cookers. More hamburgers can be cooked by the existing workers (L_0).

Practice 5.2

Use the example of your local supermarket to explain how it could increase output in both the short- and the long-run.

The short-run

I think I can hear you asking the question 'How long is the short-run?'. An excellent question. Well done. Now for the answer. The length of the short-run depends on the sophistication of the fixed factors. The more sophisticated the capital structure the longer the time it takes to change fixed factors. Two examples will help to show the length of the short-run. Fred runs a hamburger van outside Charlton's football ground. His capital structure is his rather small old van. Charlton has been promoted and Fred expects demand to increase for hamburgers. He decides to trade his small van in for a bigger one. The bigger van has better cooking technology and Fred expects to be able to make more hamburgers per hour than previously. Fred's short-run is a fast one. He can change his capital factors quickly.

FIGURE 5.1 McDonald's production function in the short-run

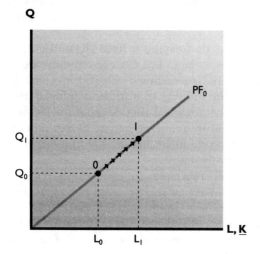

FIGURE 5.2 McDonald's production function in the long-run

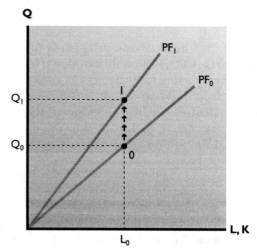

Charlton also expects demand to increase and has put in place plans to increase the seating capacity of the ground. It will not happen as quickly as Fred's buying his new van. It will take some time. It usually takes at least a year to build a new grandstand. The short-run for Charlton, therefore, is at least a year, if not longer. The length of the short-run depends on the characteristics of the capital structure of the organisation.

Practice 5.3

Your school/college plans to renovate the building where you have most of your lectures. How long will it take to renovate this part of the capital structure completely?

Returns to variable factors and factor efficiency

Firms can, and should, examine the efficiency of their variable factors of production. The principal variable factor to be analysed is labour. Returns to labour can be measured using a short-run production function. The short-run production function diagram showed the relationship between output (Q) and the factors of production, variable labour (L) and fixed capital (K). The exact nature of the production relationship, in the short-run, can be examined by looking at the numerical examples shown in Table 5.2.

Table 5.2   Returns to labour in the short-run – constant, increasing and decreasing

Constant returns		Increasing returns		Decreasing returns	
Output	Labour	Output	Labour	Output	Labour
0	0	0	0	0	0
5	1	5	1	5	1
10	2	11	2	9	2
15	3	18	3	12	3
20	4	26	4	14	4
25	5	35	5	15	5

Constant returns

The relationship between output and labour is constant. Each time labour is increased by one worker the resulting increase in output is five. The change is constant at five and the firm is experiencing constant returns to labour. *Each worker does the same amount of work.* Firms would be happy with constant returns as it gives them a measure against which they can gauge the performance of their staff. In this case, it is five units of output per work period.

Increasing returns

Each worker produces more than the last worker does. The first worker produces five, while the second worker takes output up to 11 in total and thus adds six units. The third worker adds seven to the total. Finally, the fifth worker adds nine. The additions to output are five, six, seven, eight and finally nine. The additions are increasing. This is increasing returns. Businesses would love to experience increasing returns. If you contrast increasing returns with constant returns then you can see that output is higher with increasing returns. It is difficult, if not impossible, to imagine real-world situations where workers are paid the same wage and each newly employed worker produces more than the previous worker.

Decreasing returns

Each worker produces less at the margin that the previous worker. The first worker produces five, while the second worker only adds four and takes the total to nine. The subsequent increases are three, two and one. Returns per extra worker are decreasing. Would managers tolerate a situation in which they employed extra workers at the same wage and saw each newly employed worker produce less extra than the previous worker did? I think not.

Labour efficiency

Firms would like to see their workers give them increasing returns, as this is the most efficient of the three returns examined here. If returns are increasing, worker efficiency is increasing. Worker efficiency is constant if returns to labour are constant. Each additional worker performs at the same pace as the previous and the next. Returns decreasing to labour indicate falling or decreasing efficiency as far as the workers are concerned.

The three examples can be graphed and appear in the Figure 5.3.

An easy way to understand Figure 5.3 is to remember that the constant returns line is straight, the increasing returns line looks like the letter 'J' and, finally, the decreasing returns line is the opposite of the increasing returns line.

Practice 5.4

A firm employs 30 workers. The first ten workers give the firm increasing returns, the next ten workers employed produce constant returns and the last ten workers employed contribute decreasing returns. Graph the continuous production function for the 30 workers.

Sainsbury's and constant returns to labour

If we take the example of checkouts in Sainsbury's supermarkets, we see that constant returns are achieved there. The checkout stations are part of the capital structure. Each checkout worker has a checkout station equipped with scanner, conveyor belt and electronic cash machine. On Monday when there are few shoppers in the store, the number of checkouts open is low. On a Saturday afternoon when the store is packed with shoppers, most of the checkouts are open. The length of the queue and the amount of work each checkout worker performs are controlled by us, the shoppers. Every shopper tries to go to the shortest queue which very quickly becomes the size of the queues either side. The performance of the checkout workers is monitored by the cash machine. Look at your receipt. It shows the amount of money you spent, the items purchased and the time. The cash machine information can be analysed to see if the worker is performing to an acceptable standard. Remember the time when you joined a short queue but spent a long time in that queue? There was a trainee on the checkout. So the workers receive training, have their performance supervised and the shoppers ensure that constant returns happen. Figure 5.4 shows that returns to labour are constant.

The workers perform the same as one another. When demand is low only two checkouts are open. Busy periods have all checkouts open but the queues are the same as when demand is low.

Practice 5.5

What returns does Burger King get from the workers at the counter? Graph your answer (customers served on the vertical and number of counter workers on the horizontal).

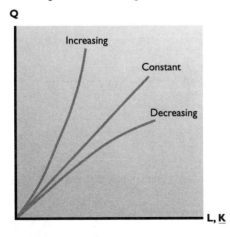

FIGURE 5.3 Returns to labour: constant, increasing and decreasing returns

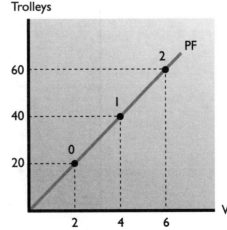

FIGURE 5.4 The checkout production function

The long-run

In the long-run the organisation can change some or all of its fixed factors. *The returns the firm obtains from changing fixed factors are known as returns to scale.* Changing fixed factors is the same as changing the scale of production. The firm attempts to change the scale of production in order to achieve increasing returns to scale. This is the long-run equivalent of the short-run increasing returns to labour.

Changing the capital structure can lead to the workers experiencing increasing returns. I have been teaching at the same college for the past 19 years (bankrobbers serve less time!). When I started teaching in 1980 seminars had six students in a small room. Over the years, the size of seminar rooms has increased. The original building has been refurbished and new buildings have been introduced: the fixed factors have changed over the years. The size of the seminar group has increased from six, to eight and then ten, up to 12, increasing to 15, then 17 and, finally, 20. Sometimes the group exceeds 20. My efficiency has increased each time the size of the seminar room has increased. The college has achieved returns to scale. Figure 5.5 shows how increases in room size have increased the returns to scale the college receives from my teaching.

Practice 5.6

In economics and other seminars, ask your teachers to share their experience of taking seminar groups over the years. Are their experiences similar to mine?

FIGURE 5.5 Seminar group and room size

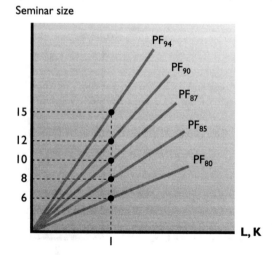

Paying for the factors

The factors of production have to be paid for. This moves the analysis from production to costs. Just as we had fixed and variable factors, we now have fixed and variable costs.

Total factors of production = fixed factors + variable factors

Total costs (TC) = total fixed costs (TFC) + total variable costs (TVC)

Obviously, **the total fixed costs (TFC) pay for the fixed factors and the total variable costs (TVC) pay for the variable factors.** For example:

✓ Fixed costs: The insurance premium to insure the delivery vehicles for Asda. This cost is a fixed cost. It does not vary with output.

✓ Variable costs: The hiring of part-time workers is a variable cost. When demand is high, such as at Christmas, more workers will be hired and the variable cost of employing the workers will increase. Thus, variable costs and output move together. There is a positive relationship.

Practice 5.7

You run a car. The car costs you money to run. There is the petrol, insurance, MOT, annual service and membership of a breakdown organisation. Separate these costs into fixed and variable costs. Remember that variable costs increase with output and fixed costs do not vary with output.

The production possibility curve

The production possibility curve shows the maximum level of production possible. Unfortunately, there is a limit on what can be produced. Production, as we have seen, depends on inputs. The inputs – labour and capital – are in limited supply. They are scarce. The maximum possible production is constrained by the resources available. If all the resources available are used, this sets an upper limit on the level of production possible.

The production possibility curve is shown in Figure 5.6. It is a two-dimensional diagram and only allows for the production of two goods. We will use the classic butter or guns approach. An economy can use its factor inputs to produce butter and guns. If more guns are required in order to fight a war then butter production must be sacrificed. Factor inputs must be transferred from butter production to the production of guns. The cost to society of producing guns is the butter foregone.

The opportunity cost of extra guns is the butter not produced. (We will return to a detailed discussion of opportunity cost in Chapter 7.)

If all factors are used in the production of butter then 100 tonnes can be produced. Alternatively, if all resources are directed at gun production then 50 rifles can be produced. Society would like to be able to produce 60 rifles but 50 rifles are all that is possible with the resources available. Society can produce on the production possibility curve or inside the curve but not outside (at point A). This is impossible. If society produces inside (at B) the production possibility curve then some resources are not used. If society produces on the production possibility curve (at C) then all available resources are used.

The shape of the production possibility curve can be a source of difficulty. The easy way to deal with the shape is to think of what you would do in a war. The need is to produce guns so you transfer resources from the production of butter. What resources would you transfer? Those that are best at producing guns or those that are worst at producing guns? I think the answer is obvious. Each time you transfer resources to the production of guns you select the group that is the best at producing guns of those available. The first group transferred is the most efficient gun producers. The second group transferred is the second most efficient gun producers and so on.

Imagine that it is peacetime once more and that only butter is produced. Total production is 100 tonnes of butter and no guns. Now the threat of war emerges. Inputs are transferred to the production of guns. The best gun-producing resources are taken. Butter production falls by 20 to 80, while gun production rises by 20 to 20 (at point C). The war effort increases and more resources are transferred to gun production. Butter production again falls by 20 to 60 and gun production rises by 15 to 35 in total (at point D). This is the key to the shape of the production possibility curve. For equal falls in butter production (20 each time) the increase in gun production is less than previously. First it was 20 and then only 15. The

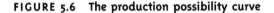

FIGURE 5.6 The production possibility curve

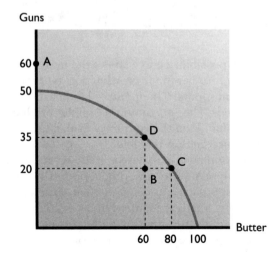

only way we can draw a curve consistent with this information is to draw a concave slope.

Practice 5.8

You are at point D in Figure 5.6. The war is not going well and even more guns must be produced. If butter production falls to 40 then is it possible to increase gun production to 50?

Practice 5.9

What has been the cost to society of producing the increase in guns from zero to 20? What is the cost to society of each of the extra 20 guns?

What has been the cost to society of producing the increase in guns from 20 to 35? What is the cost to society of each of the extra 15 guns?

Summary

You are reading this book. Presumably you are reading it in a room. Is it possible to change the size of the room today? No. The room is one of the fixed factors you require to read the book. It provides comfort and security. You could switch the light on or off. This is a variable factor. Switching the light on would increase the electricity bill! There would be an increase in the usage of this variable factor and an increase in the cost of electricity.

✓ Production analysis helps to show the firm where output can be changed in the short- and the long-run.

✓ Changing the factors employed can change output.

✓ More output in the short-run requires more variable factors such as raw materials and labour.

✓ Long-run increases in output require changes in the fixed factors.

✓ Changes in the short- and long-run can be analysed to see what types of returns (returns to labour in the short-run and returns to scale in the long-run) are experienced by the firm.

✓ The production possibility curve shows the maximum a society can produce. The production possibility curve can be used to calculate opportunity cost.

Understanding production is very important for what follows in the next chapter on cost analysis.

Answers for Chapter 5

Answer 5.1

In my opinion, the factors can be separated into:

Variable	Fixed
Wage staff	Checkout stations
Food	Management
Electricity	Building

The above is an indicative list. What have you listed?

Answer 5.2

✓ In the short-run the supermarket will increase output by purchasing more variable factors, such as part-time staff, electricity, overtime and extending opening hours.

✓ In the long-run the supermarket can increase output by purchasing more of all factors. In the long-run, all factors are variable. The supermarket could increase the size of the capital structure or change the computer technology.

Answer 5.3

This is a long-run adjustment to the production process. In my experience, it takes 18 months to renovate a teaching building. Whatever it takes the change is not an adjustment to short-run variable factors.

Answer 5.4

The graph, with output on the vertical axis, will look like a stretched out S. The figure is:

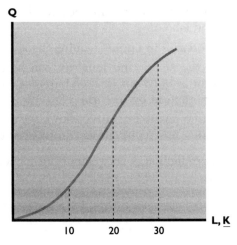

Answer 5.5

I believe that the returns will be constant. Each worker will do approximately, if not exactly, the same as the others. Management supervision, the length of queues (which one do you join?) and the workers will bring this outcome about. The figure looks like:

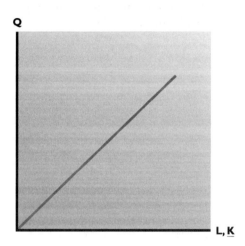

Answer 5.6

I offer no answer, but would be intrigued to hear your lecturers' replies.

Answer 5.7

The fixed and variable costs of running a car can be divided into:

Variable	Fixed
Petrol	Insurance
	MOT
	Annual service
	Cost of car

Answer 5.8

No. If butter production falls by 20 again, then the increase in gun production must be less than the previous increase of 15. The increase in gun production could not be 15. The concave shape of the production possibility curve prevents this.

Answer 5.9

The cost to society of increasing gun production from zero to 20 is the lost butter. Each of the extra guns costs society one tonne of butter (20 tonnes of butter ÷ 20 guns). This is the opportunity cost of each extra gun.

The cost to society of increasing gun production from 20 to 35 is the 20 tonnes of butter lost. The opportunity cost to society of each of the extra 15 guns is 1.33 tonnes of butter (20 tonnes of butter ÷ 15 guns). The opportunity cost of guns is rising.

COST ANALYSIS

How much?

This will help

If you have read Chapter 5 on production then you will have realised the close relationship between production and costs. Production leads to costs. If you have not read Chapter 5 you are advised to read it now. Chapter 5 is quite brief but it does introduce terms and concepts that will be used in this chapter. Knowledge of Chapter 4 on the supply curve would also be an advantage. The story of this chapter is that factors of production have to be paid for. These payments are the costs of the firm.

Introduction

Have a look around you. You can see many products. Focus on just one. This product has been produced using fixed and variable factors. These factors need to be paid for. If the firm aims for profits it must produce the product at an average cost that is less than the price charged to the consumer. Cost control is of vital importance, therefore, to the health and survival of the firm. The firm must examine its costs of production. To do this it needs to know:

✓ how efficient its fixed and variable factors are
✓ what happens when it changes the fixed and variable factors
✓ what all this means for their cost structure.

This is the story of costs and by the end of this chapter you will understand:

✓ the cost structure of firms
✓ total cost and its separation into fixed and variable costs
✓ average cost, average fixed cost and average variable cost

✓ marginal cost
✓ the importance of cost information
✓ the sources of economies of scale.

Identifying total fixed and total variable costs

Total cost is the sum of total fixed cost and total variable cost. Total fixed cost does not vary with output. This is why it is known as fixed cost. Total variable cost *does* change or vary with output. More variable factors (labour, raw materials) are employed to produce more output.

Examining the accounts information of any organisation allows the economist to separate the cost information into fixed and variable cost. The following is real cost information obtained from the annual accounts of Colchester United Football Club. The data are for the 1988/89 season and are based on the club playing 30 revenue-generating matches. The total fixed and total variable costs cover the cost of output, in this case playing football matches. The variable costs vary as more matches are played, while the fixed costs do not vary with matches played. The fixed and variable costs are shown in Table 6.1.

Table 6.1 Colchester United: fixed and variable costs, 1988/9

Fixed costs	£s	Variable costs	£s
Playing staff	261 979	Travelling Expenses	109 667
Non-playing staff	112 012	Officials and police	22 465
Pension costs	1 849	Laundry/Outfits	10 043
Social security	35 864	Heat/light/water	9 193
Depreciation	12 751	General expenses	21 859
Ground maintenance	20 662	Advertising	39 999
Accountancy	3 400	Consultancy	1 000
Rates and insurance	14 965	Termination pay	23 720
Interest	92 586		
Totals	591 457		203 226

Source: Colchester United company accounts, 1989

The cost structure for this football club in the season 1988/89 was:

Total fixed costs	£591 457
Total variable costs	£203 226
Total costs	£794 683

The separation into fixed and variable costs is in the eye of the beholder. It is clear that travelling expenses are a variable cost. The more games played the more travelling involved. All the costs listed under the 'variable costs' heading vary with the number of games played. Is 'playing staff' of £261 979 a fixed or variable cost? The answer depends on whether more playing staff members have to be hired as more matches are played. The same squad of players is used. There are transfers in and out of the club but the club does not purchase more players as it plays more games. Look at your favourite club and see whether it used roughly the same players over the length of the season. Playing staff and non-playing staff (the manager, the coaching staff and the administrators) are, in the main, fixed costs.

Analysing the components of total cost

We know that total cost is the sum of total variable cost and total fixed cost. This section looks at the relationships between output and the components of total cost. Understanding these relationships allows us to understand total cost.

Total fixed costs and output

Total fixed costs pay for the fixed factors of production. Total fixed costs are a short-run concept. There is no relationship between total fixed cost and output. Total fixed cost does not change as output changes. Look at a supermarket early on a Saturday morning when demand is low and again on a Saturday afternoon when demand is high. The fixed factors stay constant. The relationship between total fixed cost and output is a horizontal line. This is shown in Figure 6.1.

FIGURE 6.1   Total fixed costs and output

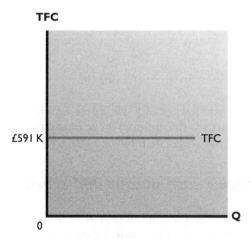

Figure 6.1 shows that total fixed cost is positive when output is zero and stay at the same level even when output increases. In the case of Colchester United, the total fixed cost is £591 457 although no games have been played, and it is still £591 457 after 40 games have been played.

Practice 6.1

Colchester United is an example of an organisation in which fixed costs dominate variable costs. List two other organisations where fixed costs dominate variable costs.

Total variable costs and output

Total variable costs are the costs of employing the variable factors of production. **Total variable cost always equals zero when output is zero.** With zero output, there is no need to employ variable factors. The firm will have only fixed factors. For this reason, **the total variable cost curve always starts from the origin.**

The relationship between total variable cost and output depends on the efficiency of the variable factors, primarily labour. The *three types of returns to labour are increasing, decreasing and constant returns.* If there are increasing returns to labour then each extra worker can produce more output than the previous worker can. Each of the three types of returns will produce a different relationship between total variable cost and output. Table 6.2 shows constant, increasing and decreasing returns to labour in the short-run.

Table 6.2 Returns to labour in the short-run – constant, increasing and decreasing					
Constant returns		*Increasing returns*		*Decreasing returns*	
Output	*Labour*	*Output*	*Labour*	*Output*	*Labour*
0	0	0	0	0	0
5	1	5	1	5	1
10	2	11	2	9	2
15	3	18	3	12	3
20	4	26	4	14	4
25	5	35	5	15	5

Labour is paid a wage of £100. Total variable cost is calculated by multiplying the wage (£100) by the number of workers (labour). This allows us to convert workers into total wages or total variable cost.

Total variable cost, output and returns to labour

Table 6.3 shows the total variable cost of different levels of production under the three different types of returns to labour that can be experienced by firms.

Table 6.3 Total variable costs and returns to labour

Constant returns		Increasing returns		Decreasing returns	
Output	*TVC*	*Output*	*TVC*	*Output*	*TVC*
0	0	0	0	0	0
5	100	5	100	5	100
10	200	11	200	9	200
15	300	18	300	12	300
20	400	26	400	14	400
25	500	35	500	15	500

The three returns relationships must produce three different total variable cost and output figures. The three figures, with total variable cost on the vertical axis and output on the horizontal axis, can be seen in Figure 6.2.

FIGURE 6.2   Total variable cost, output and returns to labour

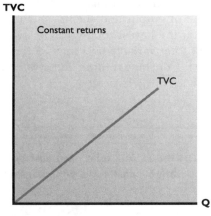

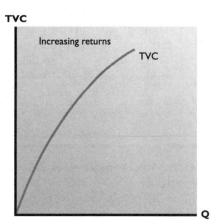

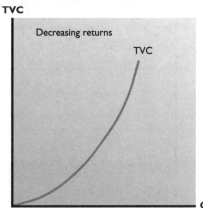

The total variable cost and output figure with constant returns shows a positively sloped straight-line relationship. The positively sloped straight line indicates a constant relationship between total variable cost and output. In the constant returns situation, total variable cost increases by £100 each time output increases by five units. The relationship is a constant one. If you drive a car at a constant speed of 60 mph then the distance you cover each hour will increase by 60 miles.

Increasing returns to labour produces a total variable cost curve that gets flatter as output increases. This flattening of the total variable cost curve is an indication of greater labour efficiency or productivity. The first worker costs £100 and produces five units. The second worker also costs £100 but produces six units. Efficiency is improving. The fifth worker again costs £100 but produces nine extra units. Output is increasing at an increasing rate but the cost of employing the extra worker (£100) stays constant. The result is a total variable cost curve that gets flatter.

Decreasing returns is obviously the opposite of increasing returns. Decreasing returns show a fall in efficiency or labour productivity. The total variable cost curve becomes steeper and steeper. The first worker costs £100 and produces five units, while the fifth worker again costs £100 but only produces one extra unit. Would you be happy to own this firm?

All three total variable cost curves are shown in Figure 6.3. The efficiency of labour is measured by selecting a level of output and seeing which of the three returns to labour produces the output at the lowest total variable cost. Obviously increasing returns produces the lowest total variable cost and decreasing returns produces the highest total variable cost. Constant returns lie between the two.

An easy way to remember the three returns is to view:

FIGURE 6.3 Total variable costs and returns to labour

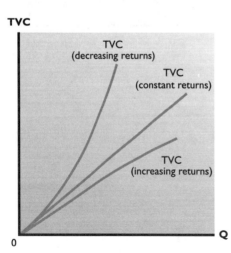

FIGURE 6.4 The total fixed cost curve and the total variable cost curve with constant returns

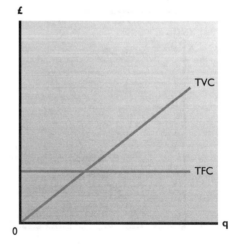

✓ decreasing returns leading to soaring total variable cost
✓ increasing returns producing a flattening of the total variable cost curve
✓ constant returns generating a straight total variable cost and output relationship.

Practice 6.2

Your employer gives you the following production data:

Output	Labour
0	0
10	1
25	2
42	3
60	4

You are asked to examine the data and state the type of returns to labour experienced by the firm. You could plot the two variables using a spreadsheet. Workers are paid £500 per week. Your boss would like to see the resulting total variable cost and output figure.

Total cost: a review

This section attempts to summarise what has been said before concerning total cost and its components, total fixed cost and total variable cost. There is some repetition but this is to reinforce the importance of understanding total cost.

✓ Total cost is the sum of total fixed cost and total variable cost. If we understand total fixed cost and total variable cost then we can understand total cost.

✓ Total fixed cost has no relationship with output. This sounds strange but remember that total fixed cost is fixed and does not vary with output. Thus, total fixed cost cannot vary with output. The local leisure centre has fixed costs. It has these fixed costs whether it is open or closed. Your car insurance is a fixed cost. It does not vary with the number of miles you travel. We know that the total fixed cost and output figure shows that the total fixed cost curve is a horizontal line. Now we need to add the total variable cost curve to the horizontal total fixed cost curve.

✓ The total variable cost curve depends on the type of returns generated by labour, our representative variable factor. The total variable cost curve can take on three different shapes depending on the returns to labour. We simply have to add the total variable cost curve to the total fixed cost curve and this will produce the total cost curve. If we take the example of constant returns to labour then we get the total variable cost curve with a positively sloped straight line. Graphing the two figures (TFC and TVC with constant returns) shows the two cost concepts we need to add together to produce total cost. Figure 6.4 shows these.

✓ The important thing to recognise about the two graphs in Figure 6.4 is that the total fixed cost has a positive intercept. There are total fixed costs when output is zero. Total variable costs are zero when output is zero. The total variable cost curve intercept is therefore zero, and total variable cost only increases with increases in output.

✓ We can now bring the two graphs together and produce the total cost curve. When output is zero the firm has costs. These are the fixed costs. Thus the firm has a total cost which is positive when output is zero. To repeat, the firm's total cost equals total fixed cost when output is zero. As output increases, the firm needs to pay for variable factors. The firm now adds the total variable cost of production to the total fixed cost and the result is total cost. This is shown in Figure 6.5.

✓ The total cost curve is simply the total variable cost curve with the total fixed cost curve added on. The difference between total cost and total variable cost is total fixed cost. Using data for total variable cost and total fixed cost against output makes it possible to see how total cost comes about. This is shown in Table 6.4.

FIGURE 6.5 The total cost curve

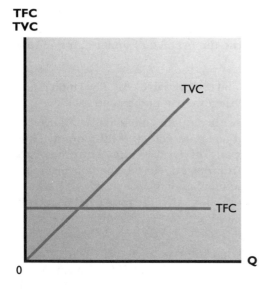
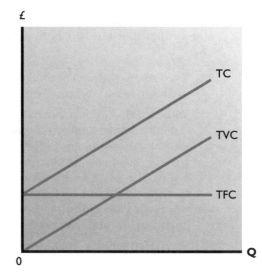

Table 6.4 Total cost is total fixed cost plus total variable cost

Output	TFC	TVC	TC
0	100	0	100
1	100	10	110
2	100	18	118
3	100	23	123
4	100	28	128

Practice 6.3

Using the data in Table 6.4:

✓ graph the TFC curve
✓ graph the TVC curve
✓ graph the TC curve.

What type of returns does the firm experience? Be careful. Look at the shape of the total variable cost.

Averages and marginal

Numbers are not that difficult (hem, hem). We have successfully dealt with the three totals. Now it is on to the three averages and marginal. We can cope with these as well.

Firms clearly have fixed and variable costs. Added together these two costs give the firm its total cost. The three cost concepts – total fixed cost, total variable cost and total cost – can be manipulated to produce averages: average fixed cost (AFC), average variable cost (AVC) and average cost (AC). The definitions of these three averages are:

✓ average fixed cost (AFC) = total fixed cost/output = TFC/Q
✓ average variable cost (AVC) = total variable cost/output = TVC/Q
✓ average cost (AC) = total cost/output = TC/Q

These three average concepts play a very important role in the decision-making process of firms.

In addition, marginal cost (MC) is calculated by analysing the change in either total variable cost or total cost, but not total fixed cost, as output changes. Thus:

✓ marginal cost= change in TVC/change in Q = $\Delta TVC/\Delta Q$
✓ marginal cost= change in TC/change in Q = $\Delta TC/\Delta Q$

The three average measures and marginal cost can be calculated using data. Table 6.5 shows the complete cost information schedule.

Table 6.5   The complete cost schedule

Q	TFC	TVC	TC	AFC	AVC	AC	MC
0	100	0	100				
1	100	10	110	100	10	110	10
2	100	18	118	50	9	59	8
3	100	23	123	33.3	7.7	41	5
4	100	28	128	25	7	32	5

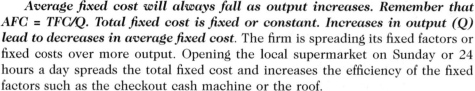

Average fixed cost will always fall as output increases. Remember that AFC = TFC/Q. Total fixed cost is fixed or constant. Increases in output (Q) lead to decreases in average fixed cost. The firm is spreading its fixed factors or fixed costs over more output. Opening the local supermarket on Sunday or 24 hours a day spreads the total fixed cost and increases the efficiency of the fixed factors such as the checkout cash machine or the roof.

Average variable cost depends on the type of returns generated by the variable factors, primarily labour. If average variable cost is falling then the firm is experiencing increasing returns to labour. If average variable cost is constant then returns to labour are constant. If average variable cost is rising then the firm has decreasing returns to its variable factors. In the data given the firm experiences increasing returns to labour.

AC is the sum of AFC + AVC. This follows from:

$$TC = TFC + TVC$$

$$\frac{TC}{Q} = \frac{TFC}{Q} + \frac{TVC}{Q}$$

$$AC = AFC + AVC$$

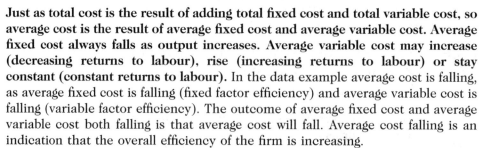

Just as total cost is the result of adding total fixed cost and total variable cost, so average cost is the result of average fixed cost and average variable cost. Average fixed cost always falls as output increases. Average variable cost may increase (decreasing returns to labour), rise (increasing returns to labour) or stay constant (constant returns to labour). In the data example average cost is falling, as average fixed cost is falling (fixed factor efficiency) and average variable cost is falling (variable factor efficiency). The outcome of average fixed cost and average variable cost both falling is that average cost will fall. Average cost falling is an indication that the overall efficiency of the firm is increasing.

For average cost to rise average variable cost must be rising (decreasing returns to labour) and average variable cost must be rising by more than the amount average fixed cost is falling. As always an example helps to explain – see Table 6.6.

Table 6.6 What happens to average cost?

Q	TFC	TVC	TC	AFC	AVC	AC
4	100	40	140	25	10	35
5	100	80	180	20	16	36

Average cost rises because the fall in average fixed cost of five (increasing returns to the fixed factors) is overturned by a rise in average variable cost of six (decreasing returns to the variable factors). The inefficiency of the variable factors (the rise in average variable cost) dominates the efficiency of the fixed factors (the fall in average fixed cost) and the result is that average cost increases. As long as the firm is experiencing increasing or constant returns to labour then average cost will fall and the firm will gain from firm wide efficiency as shown by a fall in average cost.

Marginal cost shows the change in total variable cost (TVC) or total cost (TC) as output changes. The change in output is usually a change of one unit. Marginal cost shows the cost of producing one more unit of output. **It is important to note that marginal cost happens between and not at the output levels.** The marginal cost of producing the second unit of output is £8. This happens between an output of one and an output of two. This is why the marginal cost is plotted or placed between the unit quantities. The marginal cost of £8 is placed or plotted at 1.5 units of output. It happens in between one and two. It does not happen at an output of two. The marginal cost of £8 is the change in total cost or total variable cost. The marginal cost of the fourth unit is £5. Marginal cost is the supply/production equivalent of marginal revenue (MR). Table 6.7 shows the relationship between marginal cost and total variable cost or total cost.

Table 6.7 Marginal cost

Q	TVC	TC	MC
0	0	100	
0.5			10
1	10	110	
1.5			8
2	18	118	
2.5			5
3	23	123	
3.5			5
4	28	128	

If marginal cost is below average cost then average cost will fall. The relationship between marginal cost and average cost is shown in Table 6.8.

Table 6.8 **Marginal cost and average cost**

Q	AC	MC
0		
1	110	10
2	59	8
3	41	5
4	32	5

At an output of one, average cost is 110. The marginal cost of producing the first unit is 10. Clearly marginal cost is less than average cost and average cost will fall if production is increased. Indeed average cost falls to 59. At the output level of two, marginal cost is eight and average cost is 59. Again, average cost will fall if production increases. Average cost falls to 41, as the marginal cost of five is less than the previous average cost of 59.

Practice 6.4

A firm plans to increase its output from five deliveries per day to six. The total cost will increase from £1500 to £1800 per day. What is the marginal cost of the sixth delivery? What is the average cost of five deliveries? What is the average cost of six deliveries? What has happened to average cost?

The relationship between marginal cost and average cost

The relationship between marginal cost and average cost should become a song that you sing. It always turns up in examinations. The song goes like this:

- ✓ If marginal cost is less than average cost then average cost will fall.
- ✓ If marginal cost equals average cost then average cost will be unchanged.
- ✓ If marginal cost is greater than average cost then average cost will rise.

The reason for this relationship is best explained by using the example of your exam marks. In your first module on statistics you get a B grade with a mark of 65. After one module your average is 65. If you want to improve your average then you need to get a marginal mark in excess of 65 in your next module. In your second module on microeconomics you get 75. It must have been through reading this book! Your marginal grade is 75. Your average is now 70. You can calculate the average by dividing the total marks by the number of modules taken. Again, the change in your total marks shows the marginal mark. Your marginal mark of 75 in microeconomics exceeded your previous average of 65. The result is an increase in your average. As long as your marginal exceeds your previous average your new average will increase. In your third module on leisure you get 70. This is your marginal mark. It is equal to your previous average so your average stays at 70.

Unfortunately, in your fourth module on skills you get 50. This is your marginal mark. It is less than your previous average of 70 so your new average drops to 55. Table 6.9 shows the relationship between your marginal mark and what it does to your all-important average mark.

Table 6.9 The relationship between average and marginal marks

Module	Mark	Total marks	Average	Marginal
1 Statistics	65	65	65	65
2 Microeconomics	75	140	70	75
3 Leisure	70	210	70	70
4 Skills	50	260	55	50

Practice 6.5

From the following data, calculate TC, AFC, AVC, AC and MC for an output range of zero to ten. Total fixed cost equals 50. The total variable cost schedule against output is:

Output	TVC
0	
1	10
2	16
3	19
4	20
5	25
6	33
7	42
8	51
9	63
10	75

Average and marginal cost curves

Just as it is possible to graph the total fixed cost, total variable cost and total cost curves from the given information, it is also possible to use the information to graph the average fixed cost, average variable cost, average cost and marginal cost curves. We will use the cost schedule information of Table 6.10 to allow us to graph the average fixed cost, average variable cost, average cost and marginal cost curves.

Q	TFC	TVC	TC	AFC	AVC	AC	MC
0	40	0	40				
1	40	10	50	40	10	50	10
2	40	20	60	20	10	30	10
3	40	30	70	13.3	10	23.3	10
4	40	40	80	10	10	20	10
5	40	50	90	8	10	18	10
6	40	60	100	6.7	10	16.7	10
7	40	70	110	5.7	10	15.7	10
8	40	80	120	5	10	15	10
9	40	90	130	4.4	10	14.4	10

Table 6.10 **Another complete cost schedule**

Practice 6.6

Why is the firm's average cost in Table 6.10 falling over their entire production run?

The average fixed cost (AFC) curve

Average fixed cost falls as output increases. The firm is spreading its fixed factors and costs over higher levels of output. The firm is generating fixed factor efficiency. Average fixed cost falls from a high of 40 when output is one to a low of 4.4 when output is nine. The resulting average fixed cost curve is shown in Figure 6.6. **The average fixed cost curve is always downwards sloping.**

In technical terms, the average fixed cost curve exhibits the property of being a rectangular hyperbola. All this means is that the area under the curve is the same size at any average fixed cost and quantity. We know that total fixed cost is a constant. In our example, it is 40. The area under the average fixed cost curve at AFC = 40 and Q = 1 is 40. It is also 40 when AFC = 8 and Q = 5.

Practice 6.7

What does $Q \times AFC$ always equal?

The average variable cost (AVC) curve

The shape of the average variable cost curve depends on the type of returns to variable factors experienced by the firm. In Table 6.10 the firm is experiencing constant returns to labour. Average variable cost is constant. The average variable cost curve is horizontal at 10. Average variable cost does not fall (increasing returns to labour) nor rise (decreasing returns to labour). The resulting average variable cost is shown in Figure 6.7.

The average variable cost curve will be downward sloping if returns are increasing (greater efficiency) and upward sloping with decreasing returns (reduced efficiency). In our example with constant returns (constant efficiency) it is a horizontal line.

Practice 6.8

Why does AVC = MC in the cost schedule in Table 6.10?

The average cost (AC) curve

The shape of the average cost (AC) curve depends on the type of returns to labour experienced by the firm. The average fixed cost curve is always downward sloping so the average fixed cost curve has no role in making the average cost curve upward sloping. The average variable cost curve determines the shape of the average cost curve. Table 6.11 shows the relationship between average cost and average variable cost.

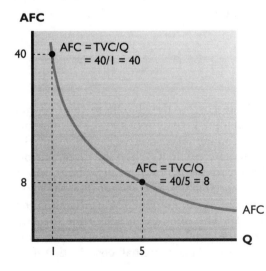

FIGURE 6.6 The average fixed cost (AFC) curve

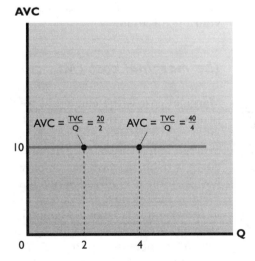

FIGURE 6.7 The average variable cost (AVC) curve

Table 6.11 The relationship between average cost and average variable cost

AVC	Resulting AC curve
Increasing returns to variable factors AVC curve downward sloping	Downward sloping
Constant returns to variable factors AVC curve horizontal	Downward sloping
Decreasing returns to variable factors AVC upward sloping	Downward sloping if AFC fall dominates AVC rise Horizontal is AFC fall equals AVC rise Upward sloping if AFC fall is dominated by AVC rise

In the example the firm experiences constant returns to labour, so the average cost curve is downward sloping. The average cost information shows that average cost falls from a high of 50 to a low of 14.4. This average cost curve is shown in Figure 6.8.

To repeat, the shape of the average cost curve depends on the type of returns experienced by the variable factors.

Practice 6.9

Your firm experiences increasing returns to labour as production starts. Unfortunately, as production increases, decreasing returns set in due to poor supervision of the workforce by management. Eventually the decreasing returns become serious. Your boss asks you to sketch the AFC, AVC and AC curves for your organisation.

The marginal cost (MC) curve

Marginal cost is the change in total variable cost or the change in total cost of producing one extra unit of output. The marginal cost curve shows the marginal efficiency of the firm's variable factors. If the marginal cost curve is falling then the firm has employed extra variable factors that are efficient. When the marginal cost curve is rising the firm has employed extra variable factors, usually labour, which has given the firm marginal inefficiency. If marginal cost is constant then the extra variable factors have been constantly efficient at the margin. This is the situation in the example schedule. Marginal cost is 10. This shows that each time the firm attempts to increase output by one unit the total variable cost and total cost schedules increase by 10, the marginal cost. This marginal cost is therefore horizontal at 10 as shown in Figure 6.9.

Again, remember that marginal cost happens in between, and not at, the output levels. This is the reason why marginal cost is plotted in between the units.

Practice 6.10

Marginal cost increases to 12 at all levels of output in Figure 6.9. What type of marginal returns to labour is the firm experiencing? What will this mean for average cost and average variable cost?

The importance of cost information

Students tend to find the coverage of costs boring. This is a pity as cost information can generate fascinating insights into the working of firms. I hear you yawn!

The totals

Total cost is made up of total fixed cost and total variable cost. Our example of Colchester United showed that the total cost structure was dominated by their total fixed cost. The total fixed cost was £591 000 and the total variable cost was £203 000. This domination of their total cost structure by the total fixed costs can be a problem if the firm, Colchester United, cannot spread its total fixed

FIGURE 6.8 The average cost (AC) curve

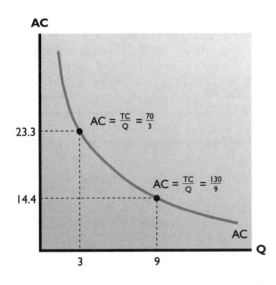

FIGURE 6.9 The marginal cost (MC) curve

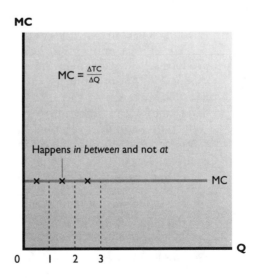

costs over a large enough production run. If the club played 25 games then average fixed cost per game would be £23 658 and average variable cost would equal £6 774, with an average cost of £30 432 per game. If the club were able to increase the number of matches played by having a successful cup run then this would have favourable implications for their average cost and average fixed cost. If the club played 30 games then average fixed cost per game would be £19 715 and average variable cost £6 774, with an average cost of £26 489 per game. The increased utilisation of the club's fixed factors from the extra five games has lowered average cost and average fixed cost by nearly £4 000. The message is clear. Firms with total cost structures dominated by total fixed cost need to make sure that they use their fixed factors as often as possible. Table 6.12 summarises this information.

Table 6.12   Spreading total fixed costs

Games played	AFC	AVC	AC
25	23 658	6774	30 432
30	19 715	6774	26 489

This explains why organisations dominated by total fixed costs such as Asda, Tesco, the local leisure centre, Wembley Stadium, Manchester United, BT, Granada Television with 'Coronation Street', and the BBC with 'EastEnders' attempt to use their fixed factors – the supermarket, the gymnasium, the stadium and players, the BT technology and the television studios – as often as possible. Has 'Coronation Street' increased to four showings per week? Is 'EastEnders' given an omnibus on Sunday afternoon? If organisations cannot spread their total fixed costs sufficiently then they need either to share them or get rid of them. Examples of organisations sharing total fixed costs are the ground-sharing arrangement of Crystal Palace and Wimbledon football clubs, and the New York Mets baseball team and the New York Giants American football team sharing Shea Stadium in New York. Shea Stadium is also used for pop concerts. The Madejski Stadium in Reading is used by Richmond rugby team and Reading football club.

The 1980s and 1990s have seen organisations employing other firms to produce services for them. An example is refuse collection by local authorities. If the local authority produced the service in-house then it would be required to own fixed factors such as the vehicles and depots. Local authorities can convert the fixed factors and costs into variable costs by tendering the contract for refuse collection out to the lowest bidder. The lowest bidder now owns the fixed costs and the local authority no longer has the responsibility for organising and paying for the fixed costs.

Other examples of firms changing fixed factors into variable costs are:

✓ the tendering out of food and laundry provision by the National Health Service

✓ the contracting out of bus and train services by London Transport and British Rail respectively

✓ Monkey Business in Palmers Green.

Monkey Business? Yes, Monkey Business is an indoor play area for young children. It tends to specialise in birthday parties. The menu revolves around burgers, chicken nuggets and chips but, amazingly, Monkey Business has no kitchen or cooks. Monkey Business tenders the supply of the party food to a local restaurant. This enables it to avoid the fixed factors and costs of producing the food. In addition, the cost of the food is now variable for Monkey Business as it can order the amount required. If it feels the cost is too high, then it can go to a cheaper supplier.

Practice 6.11

Examine the programme schedule for Sky Sports 1. Does this channel repeat programmes? Are the repeats shown on the same day? What is the benefit to Sky of repeating programmes?

The averages

The three total concepts – total fixed cost, total variable cost and total cost – can be manipulated to produce the three average concepts: average fixed cost, average variable cost and average cost. The three average measures tell a story about the business.

The short-run

Average cost shows the unit cost of production. Average cost is important because it shows the efficiency of the firm's fixed and variable factors. In the short-run the fixed factors cannot be changed, so the firm can only change the level of output by varying the variable factors. In the short-run, the period in which some factors are fixed, the firm moves along its short-run average cost curve. If output is to be expanded then the firm moves along its short-run average cost curve. More variable factors are hired. The new level of production yields an average cost. This average cost movement shows whether the new level of output is efficient (average cost falls) or inefficient (average cost rises). If average cost stays constant following the output increase then the firm's total factors have generated constant efficiency. Knowing what happens to your average cost following a change in output is important for pricing and management control. If average cost has fallen following the output increase then the firm can reduce its prices. The lower average cost allows the firm to reduce its price and still make profits. The lower average cost indicates that the firm is either experiencing increasing returns or constant returns to its variable factors. Managers are avoiding inefficiency in their control and organisation of the variable factors, essentially labour.

If average cost rises following the increase in production then the firm has two potential problems. Clearly the firm is operating with decreasing returns to labour. The average variable cost curve is increasing, maybe sharply. This inefficiency needs to be investigated. There are problems within the managerial organisation and control of the variable factors. In addition to this problem, the firm will need to examine its pricing policy. The rise in average cost may require an increase in price.

If demand for the firm's product falls then the firm will again experience a movement along the short-run average cost curve. Output has fallen and the firm must react to this drop in demand. Fixed factors cannot be changed as the firm is in its short-run. The firm reacts by reducing its variable factors, mainly labour. For most firms the fall in demand will mean a rise in average cost. The firm may need to increase its price but obviously this could be risky.

Practice 6.12

Graph the average variable cost curve for a firm which increases production and finds that its average cost has fallen.

Practice 6.13

A firm reduces its output following a fall in demand. The average cost of the firm's product does not change following the production fall. What type of returns to labour is the firm experiencing? Graph the average fixed cost, average variable cost and average cost curves.

The long-run

In the long-run, the firm can change all of its factors. A supermarket can change the outlay of the pizza counter, the design of the restaurant and the entrance. A football club can rebuild one of its stands. London Transport can replace a lift in one of its underground stations. The firms are attempting to change their scale of production. The size of the firms fixed factors is being changed. Usually they are being increased. The firm is shifting to a new scale of production. The firm is shifting to a new short-run average cost curve. This may sound confusing so let us look at an example.

The University of North London Business School is located at Stapleton House on Holloway Road. In the mid-1980s the lecture and seminar rooms in Stapleton House had a maximum capacity of 70 and 15 students respectively. Stapleton House was in a short-run. The fixed factors (room capacity) could not be changed in the short-run. It was necessary to empty the building of students and staff for 18 months while the building was refurbished. On return to Stapleton House, the number of lecture rooms had increased, the seating capacity of the lecture rooms had also increased and the seminar rooms had increased seating capacity of 20. Stapleton House was again in the short-run. It was not possible to change the seating capacity of the lecture and seminar rooms without changing the existing fixed factors. The new short-run had the potential to educate more students. The University of North London had increased its scale of production. If the increase in scale was efficient then the new average cost should be lower than the previous average cost. The university has shifted from its 1985 short-run average cost curve to its 1987 short-run average cost curve. This long-run journey is shown in Figure 6.10.

In Figure 6.10 the 1985 and the 1987 short-run average cost curves are shown as downward sloping. The long-run average cost (LRAC) curve is the summation of the two short-run average cost curves. The long-run history of the Clinton Presidency is made up of the short-run hours, days and months of his term of office. Similarly, the long-run average cost curve is simply the points on the short-run average cost curves where the firm would be happy to operate. The long-run average cost is simply an envelope or cover of those points on the short-run average cost curves where the firm would wish to operate. The 1985 short-run average cost curve is preferable to the 1987 short-run average cost curve at seating capacity up to 700 students. The 1987 short-run average cost curve lies above the 1985 short-run average cost curve at seating below 700. The university should stay with the 1985 short-run average cost arrangements if students are expected to number fewer than 700. If student numbers are expected to be greater than 700 then the 1987 short-run average cost curve is preferred as it lies below the 1985 short-run average cost curve. The university planned to expand beyond 700 students, so the 1985 short-run average cost curve was reaching the end of its working life. The expansion required a shift to a new short-run: the 1987 short-run average cost curve. The shift has been efficient as the 1987 short-run average cost curve is below the 1985 short-run average cost curve for student numbers above 700. The 1985 and 1987 short-run average cost curves make up the long-run average cost curve.

The movement down the long-run average cost curve is an example of an economy of scale. The scale of production has been increased and there has been movement down the long-run average cost curve. The increase in the scale of

FIGURE 6.10   The long-run average cost curve

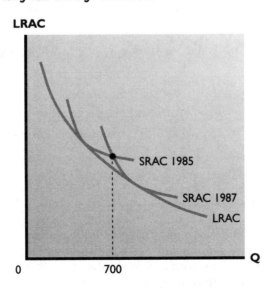

production has been efficient or has resulted in an economy. If the increase in the scale of production had resulted in a movement up the long-run average cost curve then it would have resulted in a diseconomy of scale. The change would have been inefficient. The efficient movement down the long-run average cost curve is the result of good management decision making. This is an example of managerial economies of scale. Bad management decision making or managerial diseconomies would lead to the long-run average cost curve turning upward.

Practice 6.14

Why would a student intake below 700 make the 1987 Stapleton House layout inefficient compared with the 1985 structure?

Marginal cost

Marginal cost, as we know, is the change in total cost or total variable cost as output changes. The change in output is usually one, so marginal cost is the additional or incremental or extra cost of the extra unit of output. Marginal cost is important for a number of reasons:

✓ It shows the marginal efficiency of the firm.

✓ Marginal cost can be compared with marginal revenue to see if extra production will be profitable.

We will only deal with marginal cost as an indicator of efficiency in this section as the role of marginal cost in the pricing and profit decisions of the firm are dealt with in later chapters.

Quite simply, if marginal cost is falling as output increases, then the firm is able to produce extra production more efficiently. The firm is marginally efficient. A firm's variable costs are shown in Table 6.13.

Table 6.13 Marginal cost and production efficiency

Output	TVC	MC
0	0	10 first unit
1	10	5 second unit
2	15	1 third unit
3	16	

The firm has marginal cost falling as output increases. The firm is able to produce each extra unit of production at a lower marginal cost. The marginal efficiency of the firm is improving and will continue to improve as long as marginal cost falls. The firm should be very happy with this outcome, as it is not at all common in the real world. Indeed, it is very difficult to find examples of marginal cost falling as output increases.

Firms typically experience either constant marginal efficiency or decreasing marginal efficiency. A classic example of the former, when marginal cost is constant over the output range, is trains. Virgin runs trains on the West Coast line of England between London and Manchester. Each train journey gives rise to marginal costs. These include the fee paid to Railtrack for the use of the line and the electricity used to power the train. Given that the journeys use the same type of engine and number of coaches, it must be the case that the marginal cost of the journey is constant across the day, week, month, etc. The crucial decision for Virgin is deciding which of the constantly efficient journeys generate cashflow. If the marginal cost of each journey is the same, then Virgin can decide which of the journeys is best in terms of cashflow. Cashflow will be positive if marginal revenue, the extra revenue from running the train, exceeds the marginal cost of providing the service. This provides Virgin with information they can use to remove trains from the timetable. (We examine this issue in more detail in a later chapter.)

If marginal cost is rising then the firm has a serious problem. With marginal cost increasing as output increases the firm is experiencing decreasing marginal efficiency. Each additional unit of output is costing more at the margin. The firm needs to discover the source of this marginal inefficiency. The typical cause is the failure of management to supervise the production process. As output is expanded, more variable factors are employed. Management allows slack to enter the system. An example could be workers taking longer breaks and thus increasing marginal cost. Managers are not supervising the workers and productivity falls.

Practice 6.15

In one figure, graph the marginal cost curve for increasing marginal efficiency and constant marginal efficiency.

Economies of scale

Economies of scale can be generated internally or externally. Economies of scale occur if average cost falls or the average cost curve is falling. Diseconomies happen when average cost is rising or the average cost curve has a positive slope. Internal economies of scale are the result of actions taken by the firm which result in a fall in the long-run average cost of the firm's output. The Stapleton House refurbishment was an example of an internal economy of scale.

External economies of scale result from favourable economic events that are outside the firm's sphere of influence. External economies of scale cause the short-run average cost and long-run average cost curves to shift downward. An example of an external economy of scale would be a local further education college that provides training courses for local workers. The training improves the productivity of the workforce and both short- and long-run average costs fall. The short-run average cost and long-run average cost curves shift downwards.

Another example of an external economy of scale is the opening of a local road network that improves the delivery time of the firm's transport division and hence the productivity of the firm's transport division. Both of these economies lie outside the direction of the firm. Both internal and external economies of scale are shown in Figure 6.11.

An internal economy of scale would be a movement from point a to point b on $LRAC_1$. While an external economy of scale would be shift from point a on $LRAC_1$ to point c on $LRAC_2$.

The LRAC curves are U-shaped and are indicative of internal diseconomies of scale setting in beyond point b on $LRAC_1$. The only reason for the increase in $LRAC_1$ is managerial diseconomies of scale. The managers plan to increase the scale of production but unfortunately they are not able to control and organise this increase efficiently. The result is an increase in long-run average cost. The workforce is not managed productively. It is the world of Fawlty Towers.

Practice 6.16

What is the principal reason for the long-run average cost curve being U-shaped?

Sources of internal economies of scale

If firms are to lower their long-run average cost they must generate internal economies of scale. Changes in scale simply indicate that the firm is attempting

---

FIGURE 6.11   Internal and external economies of scale

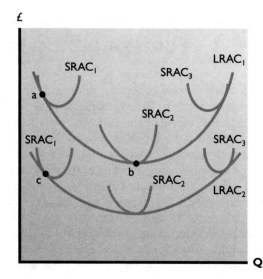

to increase its production. It must use the opportunity to increase output efficiently. To do this the firm take advantage of the sources of internal economies of scale.

The principal sources of internal economies of scale are size of infrastructure, buying power, minimum requirements and operating costs.

Size of infrastructure

Firms gain economies by spreading their overheads or, put more simply, the fixed cost structure can only be built at a certain size. It is not possible continually to increase the size of a railway station as passenger numbers increase. The station is built to accommodate expected usage. It is not increased on a daily basis. It is fixed. An example will help. The cost of the construction of any container increases with its surface area, whereas the capacity increases with volume. An example is a pipe. The pipe is used to pump water. The pipe is simply a sheet of metal that is then shaped into a cylinder. The cost of the pipe is the area of the sheet of metal used. The cost will be for the number of square metres of metal purchased. The volume or efficiency of the pipe will be the amount of water pumped through it. The amount of water pumped will be in cubic metres. This is a power above the cost of the squared metres. This relationship has given rise to the '60% rule of thumb'. This rule of thumb states that on average a 100 per cent increase in capacity will lead to an increase in total cost of 60 per cent. This must lead to a fall in average cost. Capacity or output doubles but total cost does not double. An example proves the point – see Table 6.14.

Table 6.14   The 60% rule of thumb

Output	Total cost	Average cost
100	100	1
200	160	0.8

Output doubles from 100 to 200. The average cost is given by TC/Q. Average cost falls from 1 to 0.8. The firm has experienced an internal economy of scale. This type of economy can be generated in the building of office blocks, warehouses, supermarkets, leisure centres and factories.

Buying power

Larger organisations purchase more raw materials than smaller organisations. The larger organisation should be able to use this to advantage by securing discounts. Japan car producers, such as Nissan, use the size of their orders for raw materials as a way of lowering the cost of production.

Minimum requirements

All organisations require a purchasing department, an accounts department, a personnel department and so on. London Zoo needs a publicity department. This department does not grow as attendance at the zoo increases. London Zoo will generate internal economies of scale from using the publicity department efficiently.

All departments are required when the firm is operating at low levels of output. As the firm increases its output (employing more workers, buying more raw materials and dealing with receipts and payments) it does not need to increase the size of the personnel, accounts and purchasing departments in proportion to the increase in output. It has achieved internal economies through the efficiency of the need to have minimum-sized departments when output is low. The firm is generating organisational economies.

This is similar to your computer. You buy a system with speed, memory and hard disk capacity. The system is expensive if the specification is high but you get returns or economies as you increase the number of software applications you can run on your system.

Operating costs

The major source of economies is specialisation by labour and management. The specialisation of tasks leads to large increases in output with the need for few additional workers. The gain in output is caused by the learning effect when a worker is associated with a single piece of capital equipment. An example would be the checkout station at the local supermarket. Practice at the checkout makes the worker more efficient. The worker, like the student, learns by doing. Table 6.15 provides a summary of the economies of scale information.

Table 6.15 Economies: a summary

Type of scale	Short-run	Long-run
Internal	Movement along SRAC Results from returns to variable factors, mainly labour	Movement along LRAC Results from internal economies of scale, e.g. buying power
External	Shift of SRAC Results from external economies of scale, e.g. fall in ferry prices for containers	Shift of LRAC Results from external economies of scale, e.g. better transport network

Practice 6.17

McDonald's carries out a new staff training programme. What type of economies is the firm aiming for?

McDonald's benefits from cheaper electricity. What type of economies is the firm experiencing?

Summary

This has been a long chapter. The important points to take from this chapter are the differences between the short- and long-run and the cost definitions.

✓ In the short-run there are fixed factors, an example being the size of the building.

✓ In the long-run, firms can change their short-run fixed factors, again the size of the building.

✓ It is also important to understand and then memorise total fixed cost, total variable cost and total cost.

✓ From this base it is possible to come to terms with average fixed cost, average variable cost, average cost and marginal cost.

✓ All these cost measurements have importance for the running of businesses.

✓ In the short-run the firm concentrates on using its variable factors efficiently to move along the short-run average cost curve.

✓ In the long-run the firm concentrates on productive changes in its fixed factors.

✓ The firm attempts to exploit economies of scale. Internal economies cause movement along its long-run average cost curve.

✓ External economies cause the short-run average cost and long-run average curves cost to shift.

Answers for Chapter 6

Answer 6.1

Two organisations that are dominated by fixed costs are BT and Manchester United.

Answer 6.2

We can discover the returns to labour by looking at the change in output as extra units of labour are employed. This is shown in the third column ($\Delta Q/\Delta L$).

Output	Labour	ΔQ/ΔL
0	0	10
10	1	15
25	2	17
42	3	18
60	4	

1. The firm experiences increasing returns to labour. The ΔQ/ΔL column shows each worker producing more than the previous worker.
2. Using the previous table, we can derive the relationship between total variable cost and output.

Output	Labour	TVC
0	0	0
10	1	100
25	2	200
42	3	300
60	4	400

The total variable cost and output figure looks like the 'r' letter and shows that increasing returns occur. The figure is:

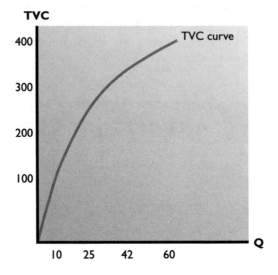

Answer 6.3

The figure looks like:

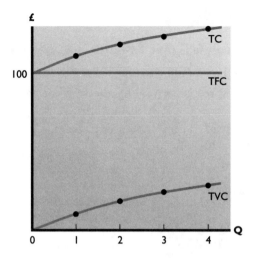

The firm experiences increasing returns to labour up to the third unit of output and then constant returns to labour.

Answer 6.4

A spreadsheet will help us to answer the questions.

Output	Total cost	Average cost	MC
5	1500	300	300
6	1800	300	

Average cost has stayed constant at £300, as the MC of £300 equals the average cost of five deliveries.

Answer 6.5

Again, a spreadsheet will help us to answer the questions.

Q	TFC	TVC	TC	AFC	AVC	AC	MC
0	50	0	50				
1	50	10	60	50	10	60	10
2	50	16	66	25	8	33	6
3	50	19	69	16.7	8.3	23	3
4	50	20	70	12.5	5	17.5	1
5	50	25	75	10	5	15	5
6	50	33	83	8.3	5.5	13.8	8
7	50	42	92	7.1	6	13.1	9
8	50	51	101	6.3	6.4	12.7	9
9	50	63	113	5.6	7	12.6	12
10	50	75	125	5	7.5	12.5	12

Answer 6.6

The average cost falls over its entire range because:

1. The firm has a falling average variable cost.
2. The firm spreads its total fixed cost as more is produced and so average fixed cost falls.
3. The result of (1) and (2) is that average cost falls. This is due to fixed and variable factor efficiency.

Answer 6.7

An easy one. Q multiplied by AFC always equals total fixed cost. This is a tautology (look it up!). Total fixed cost is a constant amount, say £100. So AFC *Q must always equal £100.

Answer 6.8

AVC = MC because:

1. The firm is experiencing constant returns to its variable factors.
2. AVC = TVC/Q = 10 and MC = ΔTVC/ΔQ = 10. If AVC is a constant then it must equal MC.

Answer 6.9

1. AFC will continue to fall as output increases.
2. Increasing returns will cause AVC to fall. This, and the falling AFC, will produce a downward sloping AC curve.
3. The emergence of decreasing returns will cause the AVC curve to rise. This will cancel out the benefits of the falling AFC curve. The AC curve will stop falling, at some point it will flatten and then eventually it will start to rise when the decreasing returns become significant.

Answer 6.10

1. MC has increased to 12 at all levels of output. This could be due to an increase in wages. The firm is still experiencing constant marginal returns to its variable factors but at a higher MC. MC is constant but at 12 and not 10.
2. AVC will now be 12 rather than 10. The AVC curve will shift upward.
3. AC will be higher than the previous AC. The AC curve will shift upward by the change in AVC and MC, in this case it will shift upward by 2 at all levels of output.

Answer 6.11

1. Obviously, Sky Sports 1 does repeat programmes even on the day of original transmission. A classic example is the live Sunday afternoon football game. This is shown again later the same day and the next morning.

2. The benefit to Sky is that it is increasing its output without increasing its costs. The MC of showing the repeat is close to zero. This must cause its average cost to fall. It is identical to the 'Brookside' omnibus and the Sunday afternoon repeat of 'Eastenders'.

Answer 6.12

Clearly, the firm's AVC firm must not be rising. This would eventually cause the AC curve to turn upwards. As long as AVC is either flat or falling then AC will fall. The fall will be greater with a falling AVC. The AVC curve can be either of:

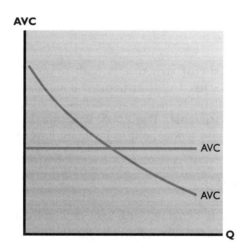

Answer 6.13

1. With a fall in output AFC will rise.
2. AC has stayed constant, so AVC must compensate for the rise in AFC to keep AC the same.
3. If AFC is rising then AVC is falling. The firm is experiencing increasing returns to its variable factors. The fall in AVC equals the rise in AFC. The AC, AVC and AFC curves look like:

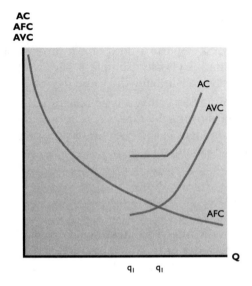

Answer 6.14

The 1987 fixed cost structure is built to accommodate larger student numbers than the 1985 fixed cost structure. If numbers fall below 700 then the 1987 structure is relatively inefficient because the higher fixed costs have to be spread across fewer students. The 1985 structure is more efficient at lower student numbers because it was built to facilitate fewer than 700 students.

Answer 6.15

Marginal cost is constant with constant marginal efficiency and is falling with increasing marginal efficiency. The figure looks like:

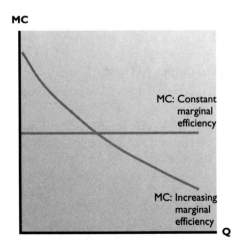

Answer 6.16

The principal reason for the long-run average cost curve being U-shaped is managerial diseconomies. The levels of output increase but managers are unable to manage this increase efficiently. They are overwhelmed and average cost increases due to managerial diseconomies.

Answer 6.17

1. The staff training programme hopes to achieve internal economies.
2. The cheaper electricity is an external economy.

PROFITS AND CONTRIBUTIONS

7

Dad, I want to be a prophet.
No, son, you want to make a profit.

This will help

You need to have prior knowledge of price and costs, so it would be useful to read Chapter 2 on demand and Chapter 6 on costs before you tackle this coverage of profits and contributions. This chapter should be quite straightforward but there will be numbers. If firms are to' make profits then they need to know how much they have spent on costs and how much they have raised in revenue. This is the equivalent of your being happy at the end of the month; there is money in your bank account. As you know your bank account is all about numbers, money in and money out. There is no need to be frightened by the numbers or, indeed, the figures. They are used to help you understand and not hinder you.

Introduction

All private sector organisations aim to make profits. Look at the negative press coverage when a firm makes a loss. A classic example of a firm making a loss and receiving negative press coverage was Laura Ashley in early 1998. BT make profits and everybody seems to be happy with this profit performance. Public sector organisations such as leisure centres are increasingly being required to produce profits. Therefore, it seems as if making profits is an important part of business activity.

Another important part of business activity is the desire and need to make positive contributions to fixed costs. When firms start production they may be unable to generate sufficient demand and production to obtain full economies. They will have a relatively high average or unit cost. It may be difficult to price above average cost. The firm will make losses but it is in its interest to make sure that it makes contributions to the fixed costs. It cannot cover average cost but must ensure that it covers average variable cost.

Profits and contributions are the two concepts we will look at in this chapter and by the end of it you will understand:

✓ what profits are
✓ what contributions are
✓ how profits are maximised
✓ entrepreneurial opportunity cost
✓ the difference between the economist's and the accountant's definition of profits
✓ how contributions are achieved.

Profits

The definition of profits is the difference between the firm's total revenue and total cost. Thus:

Profit (Π) = total revenue − total cost
= TR − TC
= p*q − ac*q
= q*(p − ac)

where Π = profits
p = price
q = quantity or output
ac = average cost.

The firm produces an output of 20 (q = 20), the price the 20 units are sold at is 5 (p = 5) and the average cost of producing the output of 20 is 3 (ac = 3). Therefore:

Profit (Π) = total revenue − total cost
= TR − TC = 100 − 60 = 40
= p*q − ac*q = 5*20 − 3*20 = 40
= q*(p − ac) = 20*(5−3) = 20*2 = 40

Practice 7.1

If price and average cost both equal ten, then what would total and unit profits equal?

Total profits

Total profits are the difference between total revenue and total cost. The firm makes a total profit of 40. The total revenue of 100 exceeds total costs of 60 by the level of profits. The total revenue is made up of price times quantity sold (p*q). The price is 5 and the quantity sold is 20, total revenue is 100. Total cost is average cost times quantity produced (ac*q). Average cost is 3 and with quantity produced equalling 20 then total cost is 60 (ac*q). Total revenue (TR = 100) less total cost (TC = 60) equals total profits of 40 (Π = 40).

Unit profit

Unit profit is price minus average cost. The firm prices at 5 and has an average cost of 3 so the firm makes a unit profit of 2. **The unit profit is the difference between price and average cost (p − ac).** The firm makes and sells 20 units so the total profit is the unit profit of 2 (p − ac =2) times the number of units (q = 20) and equals 40 (Π = 40).

Practice 7.2

Your firm produces and sells an output of 200. The price charged is 8 and average or unit cost is 6.5. Calculate total profits and unit profit. Show that unit profit multiplied by output equals total profits.

Maximising profits

Firms need to make profits. Shareholders require dividends and profits help firms to finance investment and future expansion. The question is 'Do firms maximise profits?'. Increasingly firms are under pressure to maximise profits. This pressure comes from shareholders and pension funds. If firms are to profit maximise then they need a technique. Microeconomics provides that technique.

Students enjoy the idea of firms maximising profits but find the technique difficult to understand. We will go through the technique step by step.

Marginal revenue and marginal cost

The profit-maximising technique uses marginal revenue (MR) and marginal cost (MC). **Marginal revenue** comes from the demand side and is the change in total revenue as output changes. **Marginal cost** comes from the cost side of the firm and is the change in total cost or total variable cost as output changes. The change in output is normally a unit change of one. As a reminder:

✓ marginal revenue (MR) = change in TR/change in q
✓ marginal cost (MC) = change in TC or TVC/change in q.

The firm maximises profits when marginal revenue equals marginal cost (MR = MC). The example in Table 7.1 will help to explain that profits are maximised when the extra or additional revenue (MR) equals the extra cost of production (MC).

Q	P	TR	MR	TC	MC	Π	MΠ	
0	10	0		5		−5		
			9		5		+4	MR>MC
1	9	9		10		−1		
			7		2		+5	MR>MC
2	8	16		12		4		
			5		1		+4	MR>MC
3	7	21		13		8		
			3		3		0	MR=MC
4	6	24		16		8		
			1		4		−3	MR<MC
5	5	25		20		5		

Table 7.1 Profit maximisation

The next three sections examine marginal revenue, marginal cost and profit maximisation. Before you read the next section on marginal revenue and output, attempt the following.

Practice 7.3

Marginal revenue equals marginal cost. Therefore:

a. total profits are zero,

b. marginal profits are zero.

Which of the following is a correct statement?

1. Both answers are correct.
2. Both answers are wrong.
3. a is correct and b is wrong.
4. b is correct and a is wrong.

Marginal revenue, total revenue and output

The first two columns in Table 7.1 give us information on price and quantity. This information can be used to get total revenue (TR = p*q), which is shown in the third column of Table 7.1. When price is 8 and demand is two then total revenue is 16.

Changes in total revenue are shown in the fourth column. This is marginal revenue. When price is 8 and demand is two then total revenue is 16. Now price falls to 7 and demand rises to three. Total revenue is now 21. The change in total revenue is 5 . This is the marginal revenue. Total revenue has increased by 5. The firm sell the third unit of output and their total revenue climbs by 5, from 16 to 21. We can read off the marginal revenue by looking at the information in the fourth column. (Note that the price and demand information of the first two columns indicate that the firm's demand curve is downward sloping).

It is vitally important that you remember and understand that price happens **at** the quantity, while marginal revenue happens **between** the quantities. For instance, the price of 8 happens at the quantity of two, while the marginal revenue of 5 happens between the quantity of two and the quantity of three. Marginal revenue is known as a marginal concept because it happens **between** and not **at**.

Practice 7.4

Plot the demand curve and the marginal curve information of Table 7.1 on the same figure. Remember that marginal revenue happens between, while price happens at. Therefore, you should plot the first marginal revenue of 9 at a quantity of 0.5 and not a quantity of 1.

Marginal cost, total cost and output

This section is very similar to the earlier discussion except that we now focus attention on the cost side of the firm. The first and fifth columns of Table 7.1 show output and total cost information. The sixth column shows the marginal cost data. Marginal cost is the change in total cost. As output increases from two to three units (a change of one unit), total cost increases from 12 to 13. The change in total cost is 1. This is the marginal cost of producing the third unit of output. Again, note that marginal cost happens **between** the output levels. In this case, it happens at an output of 2.5 and not two or three.

Practice 7.5

What is the marginal cost of the fifth unit demanded? At what level of output would you plot this marginal cost?

Total profits, again

As stated previously total profits are the difference between total revenue and total cost. The firm has total fixed costs of 5 and no total revenue when output is zero. The firm makes losses of 5 at this output of zero. When output increases to one, total profits are −1 or total losses are 1. This shows that total cost exceeds total revenue and, again, losses are made. The loss is 1. This is better than the previous loss of 5. The improvement is +4. If you had lost money would you prefer it to be

£5 or £1? What is the difference? The improvement of 4 is the difference between the marginal revenue of 5 and the marginal cost of 1. The firm receives an extra five units of total revenue from selling the first good. The extra cost of producing the first good is 1. The marginal profit on the first unit is 4. This is shown in the eighth column.

Marginal profit (MΠ) is the change in total profits. Total profits have improved and marginal revenue exceeded marginal cost by the improvement in total profits.

Output increases to two units. Total profits are 4. This is an improvement of +5 from the previous level of output. The marginal revenue is 7, while the marginal cost is 2. The marginal profit is 5. Again, marginal revenue exceeds marginal cost and total profits have increased. Is there a relationship emerging? Yes, as long as marginal revenue exceeds marginal cost then profits will increase.

Total profits are maximised at a high of 8 when output is three and four. Amazingly, the marginal revenue as we go from the third to the fourth unit is 3 and equals the marginal cost. To repeat, marginal revenue = marginal cost and thus the marginal profit is 0. There is no change in total profits. Total profits are 8 when output is three and four. So, when marginal revenue = marginal cost total profits are at their highest. All the profitable output opportunities have been exhausted. Profitable output opportunities exist as long as marginal revenue is greater than marginal cost.

If marginal revenue is less than marginal cost then total profits will fall. With marginal revenue less than marginal cost the marginal profit is negative and total profits will fall by the marginal profit (MΠ). Total profits fall by 3 as output increases from four to five units. Marginal revenue is 1 and marginal cost is 4. The marginal profit is -3 and this is the amount by which total profits fall.

To summarise:

✓ If marginal revenue is more than marginal cost then total profits increase.
✓ If marginal revenue is less than marginal cost then total profits decrease.
✓ If marginal revenue equals marginal cost then total profits are maximised.

Practice 7.6

You work as the manager of a local leisure centre. A parent who wishes to organise a swimming party for his daughter, Alice, approaches you. Alice's mother has set a spending limit of £200. You must organise all aspects of the party. What is the highest marginal cost you would tolerate?

Profit maximisation and diagrams

Like other topics in microeconomics, such as indifference analysis and demand, profit maximisation can be explained using diagrams. The concepts used in these diagrams are the demand curve, the marginal revenue curve, the marginal cost curve and the total profit profile.

Profit maximisation, price and quantity

The firm maximises profits when marginal revenue equals marginal cost. The demand curve and the marginal revenue curve are linked. If the demand curve is straight and downward sloping then the marginal revenue curve has the same intercept as the demand curve but the slope of the marginal revenue curve is twice that of the demand curve. Profits are maximised when marginal revenue equals marginal cost. The price and quantity that maximises profit is shown in Figure 7.1.

Marginal revenue equals marginal cost at point a. The profit maximising output is immediately below point a at the output level q_Π. The profit maximising price is p_Π. To get to this price you go immediately up from point a to point b on the demand curve. Price is found on the demand curve. From point b, you go across to p_Π.

Practice 7.7

Profits are maximised when marginal revenue = marginal cost but where do you get the profit-maximising price from?

Marginal revenue, marginal cost and marginal profit

Profits are maximised when marginal profits are 0. All profitable output opportunities have been exhausted. When marginal profit equals 0, then marginal revenue equals marginal cost. The relationship between marginal revenue, marginal cost and marginal profit is shown in Figure 7.2.

FIGURE 7.1 Profit maximisation: price and quantity

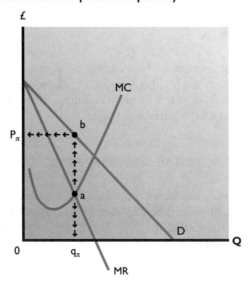

Figure 7.2 can be split into two sections. The first section lies to the left of q_Π. In this section marginal revenue is greater than marginal cost and marginal profit (MΠ) is positive. As output increases towards q_Π profits increase. The second section lies to the right of q_Π. In this section marginal revenue is less than marginal cost and marginal profit (MΠ) is negative. As output increases beyond q_Π profits fall. At the output level q_Π, marginal revenue equals marginal cost and profits are at their greatest.

Practice 7.8

If the profit-maximising firm can sell an extra unit of output, with a marginal cost of £60, and receive an increase in total revenue of £55, would you advise it to take the order?

The total profit profile

When marginal revenue is greater than marginal cost profits are rising and when marginal revenue is less than marginal cost profits are falling. In the short-run the firm has fixed costs so the firm will start with a loss. The loss, when output is zero, will equal the total fixed cost. This information allows us to generate the total profit profile. This profile is shown in Figure 7.3.

When output is zero the firm is making losses equal to the level of their total fixed costs. This is why the firm makes losses when output is zero. Again, the figure has two sections. To the left of q_Π MR is greater than MC and profits grow. To the right of q_Π MR is less than MC and profits fall. Profits are maximised at q_Π where MR equals MC.

FIGURE 7.2 Profit maximisation and the marginals

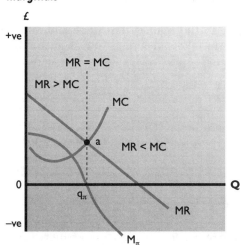

FIGURE 7.3 The total profit profile

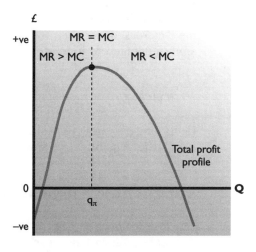

Practice 7.9

Use the total profit profile to identify the two output levels at which the firm breaks even, which is when total revenue equals total cost.

What happens to profits if . . .?

Profit maximisation occurs when marginal revenue equals marginal cost. Changes in marginal revenue and marginal cost will produce changes in output and price for the profit-maximising firm. We now look at the price and output responses of changes in marginal revenue and marginal cost. In addition, changes in average fixed cost will also be analysed.

A shift of the marginal revenue curve

If the marginal revenue curve shifts to the right it is because the demand curve has shifted to the right. Remember that the demand curve and the marginal revenue curves are linked. A shift of demand curve leads to a shift of the marginal revenue curve in the same direction. Figure 7.4 shows a shift of the demand curve and the marginal revenue curve. The marginal cost curve is horizontal.

The original demand and marginal revenue curves are D_0 and MR_0. The profit-maximising output is q_0. This output level is obtained by finding where MR_0 equals MC. This is at point 0. Immediately below point 0 is output level q_0. The profit-maximising price is p_0. This is obtained by going up from point 0 to the demand curve D_0 and moving across to price p_0.

Now the demand curve shifts to D_1. This could be due to an increase in income. As the demand curve shifts to D_1 a new marginal revenue curve results. The new marginal revenue curve is MR_1. MR_1 equals MC at point 1. The profit-maximising output is q_1. The new price is p_1.

The result of the demand curve shifting to the right is that price and output have increased and the profit-maximising firm takes advantage of this favourable shift in demand to increase price and output.

Practice 7.10

Using a figure, show what happens to the price and output of a profit-maximising firm if the demand curve shifts to the left.

A shift of the marginal cost curve

The firm is forced to pay the workforce a higher wage. This leads to an increase in the firm's total variable cost, average variable cost and marginal cost. To keep the analysis simple, we will use a horizontal marginal cost curve. The firm experiences an increase in wages and the marginal cost curve shifts upwards. What will be the reaction of the profit maximising firm to this increase in marginal cost? Figure 7.5 shows what happens following the shift of the marginal cost curve.

The original marginal cost curve is MC_0. The profit-maximising output is q_0 and the firm prices at p_0. The new marginal cost curve is MC_1. The firm equates MR with MC_1 at point 1, the new output is q_1 and the new price is p_1. The firm has reduced output and increased price. The increase in price ($p_1 - p_0$) is less than the increase in marginal cost ($MC_1 - MC_0$). The firm does not pass all the cost increase onto their customers. The firm is still profit maximising but their profits are lower at q_1 than at q_0.

Practice 7.11

Using a figure, show the implications of a fall in marginal cost for the profit-maximising firm.

An increase in average fixed cost

A firm receives the annual renewal for its contents insurance. To its horror the premium has increased. This is an increase in the firm's total fixed costs and with no change in output it is also an increase in the average fixed cost of production. Will the firm pass this increase in average fixed costs onto the customers in the

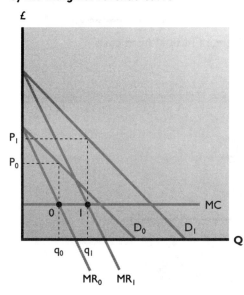

FIGURE 7.4 Price and output changes: shift of the marginal revenue curve

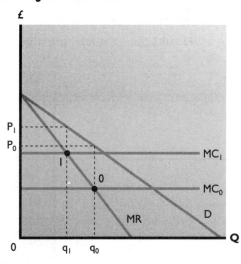

FIGURE 7.5 Price and output changes: shift of the marginal cost curve

form of a higher price? If the firm is a profit-maximising firm then the answer is 'No'. The answer is 'No' because the profit-maximising firm equates marginal revenue with marginal cost and fixed costs have no impact on either of these marginal concepts. The increase in total fixed costs and the subsequent increase in average fixed costs do not lead to an increase in marginal cost. Marginal cost stays the same. All that happens is that profits are reduced by the increase in total fixed costs. Profits are maximised at the same level of output. A figure will help to explain this. The old and new total profiles are shown in Figure 7.6.

Figure 7.6 shows that the increase in total fixed costs simply leads to the total profit profile shifting downward by the amount of the increase in total fixed costs. Profits are, and were, maximised at q_Π. If this is puzzling, think about the top half of a car tyre. The highest point of the tyre on the thread side is also the highest point on the rim side.

Practice 7.12

'If a firm is a profit maximiser then it cannot pass on increases in fixed costs to its customers.' Discuss.

The economist, the accountant and profits

The definition of profits depends on the assumptions made about total revenue and total cost. There is no controversy between the economist and the accountant concerning total revenue. The controversy between the economist and the

FIGURE 7.6   The total profit profile and an increase in total fixed costs

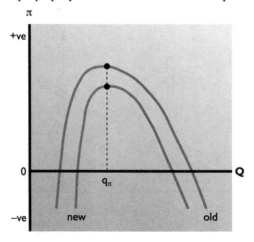

accountant relates to total cost. The debate revolves around what is and is not included in total fixed cost. For the economist, total fixed cost should include entrepreneurial opportunity cost. Accountants do not include the intangible entrepreneurial opportunity cost in their definition of costs. First of all, we will define, explain and examine opportunity cost.

Opportunity cost

I am writing this book. I could be doing something else. You probably think I should have done something else! My best alternative to writing the book is watching the sports coverage on television. The opportunity cost of working on the book for one hour is that I cannot watch the sports coverage during the hour I am doing that work. Opportunity cost can be defined as the value of the best forgone option. The opportunity cost of working on the book for one hour is the value I place on watching sport on the television. This value reflects the money I have to pay for the television coverage plus the value of my time. When I am watching sport the value of my time is high, even though the price of watching the television coverage is low. Therefore, the opportunity cost of writing this book is high. It is because I am a sports nut and can only be prised away from sport by important events. I do not do the washing up when there is football on the television. I leave it until there is a soap on the television. The soap reduces my opportunity cost of washing up.

Students are wonderful people. My experience suggests that lecture attendance is high at the beginning and end of the lecture programme. Attendance is at its lowest in the middle of the term. The students turn up at the beginning to get the lecture programme and return at the end in the hope of getting exam hints. The opportunity cost of missing the exam hints is very high so students turn up. In the middle of the term some students feel that the opportunity cost of missing lectures is not that great. There are people to see and places to go, so some students do not attend lectures.

What is the opportunity cost of buying this book? Obviously it includes the price you pay for this book. You could have bought a CD. In addition, there are the benefits (I hope) of reading, understanding and practising. If you think the price too high and the benefits too low it is unlikely that you will purchase the book. The opportunity cost of not buying the book is low. If the opportunity cost of not buying the book were high then you would purchase it.

Practice 7.13

You are reading this book. What is the opportunity cost of reading the book? Why are you reading the book? Are you finding microeconomics difficult? Oooh ...!

Entrepreneurial opportunity cost

Entrepreneurs organise the combination of the factors of production. A classic example of an entrepreneur is a film producer such as Lord Puttnam, who produced the Oscar-winning film *Chariots of Fire*. He organised the factors of production: director, actors, camera crew, and so on. Presumably somebody as able as Puttnam could earn a living in other occupations. His best alternative salary is Puttnam's entrepreneurial opportunity cost. Puttnam must be paid an income at least equal to this entrepreneurial opportunity cost. This entrepreneurial opportunity cost is a fixed cost. Puttnam must be paid this entrepreneurial opportunity cost. It does not change with output. The entrepreneur is a fixed factor. Accountants do not include entrepreneurial opportunity cost in their definition of fixed costs. Accountants' measure of total costs is lower than that of the economist. Consequently, accountants' profits are higher than economists' profits.

Practice 7.14

Your local home help computer company is run by Sheree. She is a self-employed, one-woman business. If she were salaried, she could earn £40 000 a year working as a computer programmer. Unfortunately, business has not been good and Sheree paid herself only £22 000 a year. What is the minimum Sheree should be paid in her company? Is this a cost to her firm? What is Sheree's entrepreneurial opportunity cost? What is the opportunity cost of Sheree's time?

Calculating entrepreneurial opportunity cost

Accountants do not include entrepreneurial opportunity cost in their definition of fixed costs. Economists do.

Michael runs his own building firm. His previous income was £30 000 a year. Michael's firm had total revenue of £100 000 and total cost of £70 000. He drew a salary of £20 000 that is included in his total cost. The entrepreneurial opportunity cost of his work time was £10 000. He could have earned £30 000 but only earned £20 000. Table 7.2 shows the different approaches.

Table 7.2 Profits: the accountant and the economist

The accountant's profits

	£
Total revenue	100 000
Accountant's costs	70 000
Total profit	30 000

The economist's profit

	£	£
Total revenue		100 000
Accountant's costs	70 000	
Entrepreneurial opportunity cost of working	10 000	
Economist's cost		80 000
Total profit		20 000

The economist has profits £10 000 lower than the accountant does. The difference is the entrepreneurial opportunity cost. Despite this Michael should remain as his own boss as he is making a positive profit of £20 000. His total income (drawings of £20 000 and profit of £20 000) is £40 000 and exceeds his next best employment salary of £30 000.

Should business people wait until the end of their business year to discover if they have made a living, or should they include their entrepreneurial opportunity cost of work in their pricing structure to ensure that they make a living? Do plumbers include all their costs, including their entrepreneurial opportunity cost, in the price they ask you to pay for servicing the central heating?

Practice 7.15

Michael finds that his accounting cost has increased to £85 000. Everything else stays the same. Should Michael give up being his own boss? Should Michael become an accountant?

Making contributions to total fixed cost

Profits are achieved if total revenue exceeds total cost. If price is greater than average cost then unit profit is positive and again profits are achieved. This is what business wants. Unfortunately, there are times when business cannot secure total revenue greater than total cost. Should they close down? Not necessarily. It depends on two factors:

✓ Is price greater than average variable cost?
✓ Are there funds available to finance loss-making operations?

Price and average variable cost

If price is greater than average variable cost then it is the same thing as total revenue exceeding total variable cost. A firm has yet to start production. Its total revenue and total variable cost are both 0. The total fixed cost is £1000. The firm is making losses of £1000. It starts the production run. Total revenue is £50 and total variable cost is £49. This information is shown in Table 7.3.

Table 7.3 Price, average variable cost and contributions

Q	P	TR	MR	TFC	TVC	TC	MC	Π
0	50	0		1000	0	1000		−1000
			50				49	
50	50			1000	49	1049		−999

The price is £50 and average variable cost is £49. The firm makes a contribution of £1 towards paying their total fixed cost. The profit situation is a loss of £1 000 before production starts and losses of £999 when output is one. They improve their loss position by £1. They pay for their variable costs and have £1 over to pay towards their total fixed cost. The total revenue of £50 exceeds total variable cost of £49 by £1. This is the positive contribution to the total fixed cost of £1 000 and takes the total loss to £999. I think I can hear you say 'But it's only a pound'. Right, give the next person you see £1. So, £1 is worth having!

As long as price (total revenue) exceeds average variable cost (total variable cost) then the firm makes positive contributions to their total fixed costs. The firm still makes losses, as total revenue is less than total cost. Should the firm remain in business? It depends simply on whether the loss can be funded. If the bank or backers are happy with the long-term prospects of the firm then they may be happy to finance the loss as long as they see progress. Evidence of progress would be increases in sales and contributions to total fixed cost.

Practice 7.16

Colchester United plays 20 games. Average variable cost per game is £6774. What price do they have to charge per spectator if they anticipate a crowd of 1100 in order to make contributions to their total fixed costs of £591 457?

How long can the losses continue?

Summary

If you want to make economic profits then total revenue must exceed total cost, or price is greater than average cost:

✓ To maximise profits the firm produces output at which marginal revenue equals marginal cost. The price is obtained from the demand curve.

✓ Entrepreneurial opportunity cost is a very important concept in microeconomics. The economist includes the reward the entrepreneur expects in total fixed cost. The accountant does not. Profits will be higher for the accountant than for the economist. When the plumber hands you the bill it should include entrepreneurial opportunity cost.

✓ There are occasions when the firm cannot price above average cost and losses result. Should the firm cease to trade? If positive contributions to total fixed cost are being made, there are funds available to finance the losses and the future looks hopeful, then the firm should stay open. Positive contributions to total fixed cost are made if total revenue is greater than total variable cost. This is the same thing as price exceeding average variable cost.

The next chapter looks at elasticity. But have a rest before moving onto elasticity. It is a concept students find puzzling. I hope that we can remove the confusion.

Answers for Chapter 7

Answer 7.1

Both unit and total profits equal 0. The firm is breaking even.

Answer 7.2

1. Total revenue (TR) equals 1 600 and total cost (TC) is 1 300.
2. Total profits (Π) are 300.
3. Unit profit is price minus average cost, or 1.5.
4. The unit profit of 1.5 multiplied by output of 200 yields 300, which is the total profit.

Answer 7.3

The correct answer is 4. If MR = MC then marginal profits are 0. If MR $-$ MC = 0 then total profits are maximum.

Answer 7.4

1. We only have a price range for 10 to 5 but we can still plot the demand and marginal revenue information in the same figure.
2. The demand information is given by the price and quantity columns.
3. The marginal revenue information is given by the change in total revenue.
4. We plot the demand information at the price and quantity but we plot the marginal revenue information between the quantities.

Answer 7.5

The marginal cost of the fifth unit of output is 4 and it is plotted at 4.5, halfway between outputs 4 and 5.

Answer 7.6

The marginal revenue is £200. If you want to increase your firm's level of profits then MR must exceed MC. Therefore, the highest marginal cost is £199. This would increase total profits by £1.

Answer 7.7

You always get price from the demand curve. It is tempting to move across from where MR = MC onto the price axis but this is not the demand curve. If you want price and the corresponding quantity demanded then go to the demand curve.

Answer 7.8

No. This would reduce total profits by £5, as MR is less than MC.

Answer 7.9

The two points where total profits are 0 and the firm breaks even are the two points on the horizontal axis of the total profit profile. At these points profits are 0.

Answer 7.10

The figure looks like:

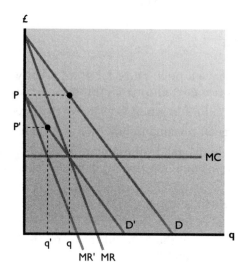

The profit-maximising firm will reduce both output and price.

Answer 7.11

The figure looks like:

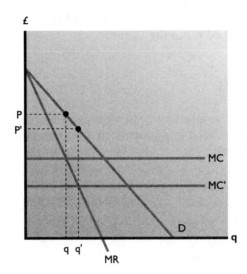

The profit-maximising firm will increase output and reduce price.

Answer 7.12

This is an essay question. See Chapter 14 for help on planning and writing answers to questions of this nature. The answer to this question requires:

1. a definition of profit maximisation
2. the profit-maximising condition (MR = MC)
3. what happens to MC when TFC and AFC change
4. a discussion of why a profit maximiser will not change price or output when fixed costs increase
5. diagrams
6. summary and conclusion.

Answer 7.13

1. What is the opportunity cost of reading this book? The opportunity cost of reading this book is the best foregone alternative use to which you could put your time. It might be watching Oprah or going for a run. As the examination approaches you will spend more time reading economics. Why? Does it have anything to do with opportunity cost?

2. Why are you reading the book? Presumably, because you find economics difficult and the opportunity cost of understanding economics is proving to be a major problem. You are spending a lot of time on economics but are getting nowhere.

3. Are you finding microeconomics difficult? With any luck, not now. You can contemplate watching Oprah!

Answer 7.14

1. What is the minimum Sheree should be paid in her company? It is £40 000. This is her best foregone alternative. She should be paid the opportunity cost of her time.

2. Is this a cost to her firm? Yes, as she is not using her time efficiently. Gaps in efficiency are a cost to all firms.

3. What is Sheree's entrepreneurial opportunity cost? It is £18 000. This is the difference between the £40 000 and the £22 000.

4. What is the opportunity cost of Sheree's time? As previously argued, her opportunity cost is £40 000.

Answer 7.15

No. Michael should remain self-employed. His economic profits have fallen to £5000 but he is making an income of £35 000 in total and this exceeds his best alternative. The total income is the £20 000 is pays himself plus the £10 000 entrepreneurial opportunity cost of working included in his costs plus the £5000 profits. Michael should contemplate returning to the wage of £30 000 only when economic profits are negative.

Answer 7.16

1. To make a contribution price must exceed the average variable cost of £6774.

2. The price comes from each of the crowd of 1100.

3. Therefore, price must be greater than £6774 ÷ 1100 or £6.16.

4. If the average admission price were £6.17, then Colchester would make a contribution of £13 towards their fixed costs. It is not a lot but it is something, and something is better than nothing.

PRICE ELASTICITY OF DEMAND — MOVEMENT ALONG THE DEMAND CURVE

If I stay in the sun for even a short period of time, I get
sunburnt. It is because I have sensitive skin. A small amount
of sun produces a big change in my skin colour.

This will help

This chapter is long. It is best read in sections. Do not attempt to read the chapter in one go. You will get bored. Use the chapter as a collection of information sets and select the set you require. The chapter covers what price elasticity of demand is, the factors which influence price elasticity, the benefits of understanding price elasticity and the calculation and application of price elasticity. Elasticity is a difficult topic but with practice it can be conquered. Read Chapter 2 on demand before you start this chapter. Good luck!

Introduction

Students do not like the topic of elasticity. They find it very theoretical and difficult to remember, let alone understand. This is a pity, as the concept can generate a series of insights into the world of business decision making. An example of the insights to be gained is understanding why placing Tony the Tiger on the front of Kellogg's Frosties makes the demand for the cereal price insensitive. If the price of Kellogg's Frosties increases by quite a lot then the quantity demanded will not change by much at all.

By the end of this chapter you will understand

✓ the concept of price elasticity of demand and the factors influencing elasticity
✓ the benefits of understanding price elasticity
✓ the calculation and application of price elasticity.

Price and demand

Chapter 2 on demand showed that price changes can change the quantity demanded by moving consumers up and down the firm's demand curve. The firm's demand curve is shown in Figure 8.1.

Clearly, it is possible to lower price to increase demand. This is because people are generally more inclined to buy a greater quantity if the price is reduced. While this is generally the case a firm needs to know by how much its total revenue will change following a price reduction. Managers need to know whether total revenue will rise or fall. The concept of price elasticity of demand provides the answer to this vitally important business question. Understanding elasticity and the factors determining elasticity equips the manager with powerful information. This allows the firm to engage in superior decision making. As an example of the advantage to be gained from understanding and applying the concept of price elasticity of demand consider the number of organisations, such as Horizon (package holiday firm) and British Rail, which both change their prices for different seasons of the year, times of the day and types of customer.

These organisations include:

✓ holiday firms that price higher in the school holidays. Look at a holiday brochure to see the higher prices charged in the school summer holidays (the end of July to the beginning of September)

✓ telecommunication companies that price lower at the weekend and outside business hours (see the tariff pricing schedule of your telephone company)

✓ theatres that give students and pensioners price discounts.

FIGURE 8.1   Price and quantity demanded

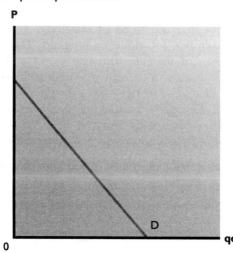

All these organisations seek to combine price changes and information concerning price elasticity to increase their total revenue. The next section defines price elasticity of demand with working examples.

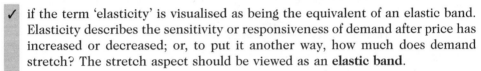

Defining price elasticity of demand

The term price elasticity of demand is used in economics to indicate the responsiveness or sensitivity of changes in demand following a change in the price of the product. The responsiveness or elasticity is measured in percentage terms and seeks to establish the sensitivity of demand following the price change. There are three important aspects to the term elasticity and these need to be understood before proceeding with the rest of the chapter. The concept of elasticity is more manageable:

✓ if the term 'elasticity' is visualised as being the equivalent of an elastic band. Elasticity describes the sensitivity or responsiveness of demand after price has increased or decreased; or, to put it another way, how much does demand stretch? The stretch aspect should be viewed as an **elastic band**.

✓ if the relationship between the two variables under inquiry is stated at the outset. Consumers normally respond to an decrease in price by purchasing more of the good or service. An example of this was the reaction of the newspaper-reading public to a decrease in the price of *The Times* during 1994 by increasing their demand for the paper. Chapter 2 on demand has shown that the relationship between quantity demanded and price is negative. If price increases, quantity demanded would be expected to decrease. Understanding the relationship between the two variables under investigation will make elasticity a much easier concept to manage and understand.

✓ if it is remembered that the elasticity measurement is about percentage changes and not absolute changes. Consider a situation where a student's grant increase from £3000 to £3300. The absolute increase is +£300 whereas the percentage change is +£300/£3000 or 10 per cent.

Practice 8.1

A local bakery increases the price of a loaf of bread from 50p to 52p. What is the percentage increase in price?

Elastic, inelastic and unitary

Bearing in mind the three hints offered it is time to introducy the concept of elasticity explicitly. Elasticity is defined as:

$$\text{Elasticity} = \frac{\text{percentage change in dependent variable}}{\text{percentage change in independent variable}}$$

As far as the relationship between quantity demanded and price is concerned, the dependent variable is demand and price is the independent variable. Remember quantity demanded depends on price. Price elasticity of demand is defined as:

$$\text{price elasticity} = \frac{\text{percentage change in quantity demanded}}{\text{percentage change in price}}$$

Demand is price elastic

Assume that price increases by 10 per cent. This increase in price should normally lead to quantity demanded falling. The normal relationship between demand and price is negative. The 10 per cent increase in price causes demand to fall by 20 per cent. Using the earlier formula, the result of this information is:

$$\text{Price elasticity} = \frac{-20\%}{+10\%} = -2$$

A number of points can be made concerning this calculation:

✓ The price elasticity value is negative. This is the outcome of the negative relationship between quantity demanded and price. Price elasticity of demand should always be negative.

✓ The value of -2 indicates that demand is price elastic. The term 'price elastic' means that the percentage change in quantity demanded dominates or exceeds the percentage change in price. In the example we have used the percentage changes were:

quantity demanded $(-20\%) >$ price (10%) Elastic

The percentage change in quantity demanded is responsive, sensitive or elastic relative to the percentage change in price. The quantity demanded percentage change $(-20$ per cent) has outstretched the percentage change in price (10 per cent). This stretched-out response of demand to price is, for the economist, evidence of an elastic relationship. An easy way of dealing with elasticity is to use helping hands. The price change was 10 per cent. Place your hands in front of you at a distance apart to represent the 10 per cent change in price. The quantity change was 20 per cent. Have your hands moved outwards or inwards to represent this larger change? The answer is outwards. The relationship is elastic or sensitive or responsive. Figure 8.2 shows the elastic relationship.

FIGURE 8.2   Helping hands

☜ 10% change in price ☞

☜   20% change in quantity   ☞

As long as the change in quantity demanded in percentage terms exceeds the percentage change in price, then the relationship is elastic. If, in the example we have used, the fall in demand had been 11 per cent and not 20 per cent, then the relationship would still be price elastic as:

$$\text{Price elasticity} = \frac{-11\%}{+10\%} = -1.1$$

Again, the percentage change in quantity demanded exceeds the percentage change in price and the relationship is still price elastic.

The key to understanding price elasticity is to look at the number generated. The first elasticity was -2, whereas the second value was -1.1. Price increased by 10 per cent in both cases but the demand response was, respectively, -20 per cent and -11 per cent. Both demand changes are elastic, as the percentage change in demand exceeds the percentage change in price, but the -20 per cent change is relatively more elastic compared with the -11 per cent change. Table 8.1 shows the elastic response of an increase in price.

Table 8.1 Elastic demand

10% increase in price

20% fall in demand Elasticity = -2 Elastic	The 20% fall in demand is more sensitive, responsive or elastic than the 11% reduction Both are elastic	11% fall in demand Elasticity = -1.1 Elastic but less elastic than the 20% change in demand

In both examples, the elasticity number, ignoring the negative sign, is greater than one. The negative sign can be ignored as the relationship between price and demand is normally negative. Nothing is lost from the analysis by ignoring it. The relationship is elastic as long as the number is greater than one. The relationship is more sensitive or elastic, the greater the elasticity value. An example will show how economic theory can be applied to a business problem.

Price elastic demand and total revenue – The Parkside Hotel

The management at the hotel is considering reducing the price of their afternoon cream teas from £5 to £4.75, a 5 per cent reduction. The existing demand at the price of £5 is 50 and the management has estimated from past sales that the new demand will be 55. This is an increase in demand of 10 per cent, thus demand is price elastic. The old revenue situation was £250 (£5 × 50), whereas the new revenue position is £261.25 (£4.75 × 55). Revenue has increased by £11.25 following the price reduction as demand was price sensitive or price elastic. The price reduction has proved to be a good business decision as far as sales revenue is concerned. Table 8.2 shows the price and demand information for the hotel.

Table 8.2 The Parkside Hotel data

	Price	Quantity	Total revenue
Old	£5	50	£250
New	£4.75	55	£261.25
Percentage change	−5%	+10%	Elasticity = −2

In summary, so far we have discovered that:

✓ the price elasticity value is normally negative

✓ for elastic or responsive relationships between demand and price, the elasticity value will always exceed one when the absolute (ignoring the sign) value is examined

✓ the higher the elasticity value the more elastic the relationship is

✓ if price elasticity is elastic then total revenue will increase following a price decrease.

Practice 8.2

Given the information on price and quantity changes in the following table, calculate the percentage changes, the total revenues and the resulting price elasticity of demand subsequent to the price increase.

	Price	Quantity	Total revenue
Old	50p	10	
New	52p	8	
Percentage change			Elasticity =

Demand is price inelastic

There are certain products (such as designer clothes) where an increase in price generates small and insignificant reductions in demand. Examples include Levi Jeans, especially the 501 brand, and Frosties. These products are price inelastic. A firm will want to know what happens if the change in demand in percentage terms is less than the percentage change in price. An example of this would be travel on a city transport system in the rush hour before 9.30am. The transport authorities decide to increase price by 10 per cent and the demand response is −4 per cent. The price elasticity value is:

$$\text{Price elasticity} = \frac{-4\%}{+10\%} = -0.4$$

In this case, the percentage change in quantity demanded is dominated by the percentage change in price. The demand change is not sensitive or responsive. The change is inelastic. The top is now exceeded by the bottom. For an elastic relationship to exist it would have been necessary for the fall in demand to have been at least 11 per cent. Use your hands to see that the elasticity outcome is inelastic. Have your hands moved inwards?

Quantity demanded (-4%) < price (10%) Inelastic

The fall in quantity demanded (-4 per cent) is dominated by the price change ($+10$ per cent). The change in demand is price insensitive or inelastic.

Again, the elasticity value is negative. The increase in price has caused demand to fall. The difference this time, compared with the earlier elastic examples, is that the elasticity value is less than one. It is less than one because the percentage change in demand is inelastic or insensitive relative to the price change. If the fall in demand had been 2 per cent and not 4 per cent following the 10 per cent increase in price, then the elasticity value would have been -0.2.

Again, the relationship is inelastic but even more so than previously. **The more insensitive or inelastic the relationship, the lower the elasticity value.** Splash Swimwear shows the case of price inelastic demand.

Price inelastic demand and total revenue - Splash Swimwear

Splash Swimwear markets its products through the distinctive dolphin logo and possesses a brand-loyal customer base. The company is considering exploiting this competitive advantage by increasing price with the aim of securing extra revenue. Will it work? At present the top of the range men's trunks sell at a price of £20 per pair with weekly sales of 1000. The weekly total revenue is £20 000. Splash proposes to increase the price by 5 per cent to £21 per pair and estimates that demand will decrease by 4 per cent to 960 sales per week. The new revenue position, following the price increase, will be £20 160 (£21 times 960). Splash has exploited the brand loyalty of its price-insensitive customer base to increase total revenue. The demand information for Splash is shown in Table 8.3.

Table 8.3 The Splash data

	Price	Quantity	Total revenue
Old	£20	1000	£20 000
New	£21	960	£21 960
Percentage change	+5%	−4%	Elasticity = −0.8

In summary, so far we know that:

✓ if the elasticity value is less than one, the relationship is inelastic

✓ the lower the elasticity value generated the more inelastic the relationship

✓ if demand is price inelastic then total revenue will increase following a price increase.

Practice 8.3

Use the information in the table to complete it.

	Price	Quantity	Total revenue
Old	£4	10	
New	£5	9	
Percentage change			Elasticity =

Demand is unitary elastic

There will be certain products where price changes do not change total revenue. In such cases there is little incentive to use price as a device for increasing total revenue and the firm should consider non-price attributes, such as advertising, as part of the marketing strategy. Knowing that price elasticity is unitary informs the firm that total revenue is maximised at the existing price and price changes will lower the firm's total sales revenue.

In the examples considered so far, demand has been either elastic (the demand change is sensitive to price changes and the demand change dominates the price change) or inelastic (the demand change is insensitive to price changes and the demand change is dominated by the price change). What is the situation when a 10 per cent increase in price leads to demand falling by 10 per cent? In this case, demand is neither elastic nor inelastic but unitary elastic. The percentage change in price is matched exactly by an equal but opposite percentage change in demand. The elasticity value is:

$$\text{Price elasticity} = \frac{-10\%}{+10\%} = -1$$

The −1 value indicates that:

✓ the change in price leads to an equivalent change in demand. The 10 per cent increase in price is matched by a 10 per cent fall in demand

✓ again, the minus sign shows that increases in one factor – price – lead to a fall in the other factor – demand.

Qantity demanded (−10%) = price (+10%) Unitary

Practice 8.4

The demand curve is downward sloping. Could you have a price elasticity that was positive?

The three price elasticity of demand outcomes

Managers have to be aware of the price elasticity of demand when considering price changes. Knowledge of the price elasticity of demand value will enable the managers to make coherent decisions, which are consistent with economic principles. The principles are that:

✓ demand can normally be one of three elasticity values

✓ a 10 per cent fall in price will usually cause demand to increase. The question is: 'How much will demand increase by?'

✓ if the demand increase is greater than 10 per cent, then demand is price elastic

✓ if the demand increase is less than 10 per cent, then demand is price inelastic

✓ if the increase in demand is 10 per cent, than demand is unitary inelastic.

Table 8.4 summarises the three elasticity outcomes.

Table 8.4 The three elasticity outcomes

Action	Result	Demand type
10% increase in price	9% fall in demand	Inelastic
	10% fall in demand	Unitary
	11% fall in demand	Elastic

Calculating price elasticity of demand

Price elasticity of demand can be calculated using the comparison between the percentage change in price and the resulting change percentage in quantity demand, as in the examples we used earlier. The relationship between price and demand is given by the demand curve and price elasticity can be measured along the demand curve.

Market Research International (MRI) and the calculation of price elasticity

Following extensive consumer research by MRI for a travel company the following data have been prepared. The travel company needs to know how demand reacts to price changes. This example was first introduced in Chapter 2 on demand. The data for the quantity demanded could be thousands or hundreds of thousands.

This could make the analysis more realistic but the price and elasticity implications remain the same. Table 8.5 shows the demand information collected by MRI.

Table 8.5   The demand and total revenue schedule

P	QD	TR	MR
10	0	0	
			+9
9	1	9	
			+7
8	2	16	
			+5
7	3	21	
			+3
6	4	24	
			+1
5	5	25	
			−1
4	6	24	
			−3
3	7	21	
			−5
2	8	16	
			−7
1	9	9	
			−9
0	10	0	

Total revenue (TR) is the result of multiplying the price charged by the resulting quantity sold. Marginal revenue (MR) is the change in total revenue following price changes. From the schedule total revenue can be calculated for the price and respective quantity demanded. If the price is 9, then the quantity demanded is one. The resulting total revenue is 9. If the price falls to 8, then quantity demanded rises to two and total revenue is now 16. The change in total revenue is +7. This is the additional, incremental, extra or marginal revenue.

When price is 3 the corresponding quantity demanded is seven and total revenue is 21. A fall in price to 2 results in quantity demand increasing to eight with total revenue equalling 16. The marginal revenue is −5. This example highlights a dilemma often faced by managers when lowering price. If they do not examine the elasticity value, it is possible to lower price and lower total revenue.

Calculating price elasticity as price falls from 9 to 8 – demand is elastic

The price, quantity demanded and total revenue information of interest in calculating price elasticity, as price falls from 9 to 8 is:

p	qd	TR	MR
9	1	9	
			+7
8	2	16	

This information needs to be converted into percentage changes for quantity demanded and price so that the price elasticity can be calculated. Remember that the formula for price elasticity is given by:

$$\text{Price elasticity} = \frac{\text{percentage change in quantity demanded}}{\text{percentage change in price}}$$

$$= \frac{\Delta Q/Q * 100}{\Delta P/P * 100}$$

The percentage change in quantity demanded (the increase from one to two) is the numerator and is calculated by:

✓ measuring the change in demand $(2-1 = +1)$ relative to the original demand of one. This is the first part $[(2-1)/1]$ of the calculation. It is $\Delta Q/Q$

✓ then multiplying by 100 to measure the percentage change combining these aspects results in a percentage change in demand of 100 per cent.

Quantity demand has doubled. But is demand elastic, inelastic or unitary? To answer this question, the percentage change in price has to be calculated.

The percentage change in price is the denominator and is calculated by:

✓ measuring the change in price $(8-9 = -1)$ relative to the original price of 9. This is the first part of the calculation $[(8-9)/9]$. It is $\Delta P/P$

✓ multiplying this relative change by 100 to generate a percentage change

✓ the result is that price has fallen by 11.1 per cent or -11.1 per cent

This information indicates that the fall in price of 11.1 per cent produces an increase in demand of 100 per cent. The price elasticity of demand is elastic. The percentage change in demand of +100 per cent dominates the percentage change in price of -11.1 per cent. The demand change is highly sensitive change. Demand has experienced a highly responsive change relative to the price change. The price elasticity value equals -9.

$$\frac{\dfrac{2-1}{1} \times 100 = +100\%}{\dfrac{8-9}{9} \times 100 = -11.1\%} = -9 \text{ Elastic}$$

The important features to note regarding the price elasticity of -9 are:

✓ The relationship is elastic as the absolute value is greater than one.

✓ The -9 value shows that an 11.1 per cent fall in price generates an increase in demand nine times the fall in price. Demand increased by 100 per cent, which is 11.1 per cent multiplied by 9.

✓ The −9 can be interpreted as showing the impact on demand of a 1 per cent change in price. A 1 per cent increase in price would cause demand to fall by 9 per cent, or a 5 per cent fall in price would lead to demand increasing by 45 per cent. The ratio between the percentage change in demand and the percentage change in price is − 9.

✓ Most important for business decision makers, **when demand is price elastic a fall in price leads to an increase in total revenue and a rise in price will produce a fall in revenue.** If the objective of the business is increasing or maximising total revenue, then price should be lowered if demand is price elastic. Lowering price when demand is price elastic will always result in more sales and sales revenue increasing.

Practice 8.5

Calculate the price elasticity of demand if price falls from 7 to 6.

✓ Find the quantities demanded at the two prices.

✓ Follow the method used in the worked example.

✓ Calculate the percentage change in price (use a calculator). This is the denominator.

✓ Calculate the percentage change in demand (again, use a calculator). This is the numerator.

✓ Place your answers in the formula and use a calculator. Look at the answer section to see if your answer is correct. If correct, well done! If you have calculated something else then have another try.

Calculating price elasticity as price falls from 3 to 2 — demand is inelastic

The price, quantity demanded and total revenue information required to analyse the price fall from 3 to 2 is:

p	qd	TR	MR
3	7	21	
			−5
2	8	16	

This information shows that reducing price from 3 to 2 results in more sales; demand increases from seven to eight. Unfortunately, however, total revenue falls. The formula for price elasticity is:

$$\text{Price elasticity} = \frac{\text{percentage change in quantity demanded}}{\text{percentage change in price}}$$

Again, it is necessary to calculate the percentage changes in quantity demanded and price.

The percentage change in quantity demanded is:

$$\frac{\Delta Q}{Q} \times 100 = \frac{8-7}{7} \times 100 = 14\%$$

Demand has increased by 14 per cent but what was the percentage decrease in price that produced this 14 per cent increase in demand?

The percentage decrease in price is:

$$\frac{\Delta P}{P} \times 100 = \frac{2-3}{3} \times 100 = -33\%$$

The percentage change in price equals 33 per cent and has produced a 14 per cent increase in demand. Using the two percentage changes and the price elasticity formula yields the elasticity value:

$$\frac{\dfrac{8-7}{7} \times 100 = 14\%}{\dfrac{2-3}{3} \times 100 = -33\%} = -0.42 \text{ Inelastic}$$

The price elasticity value is -0.42. This value shows that:

✓ The relationship between price and quantity demanded is price inelastic. The absolute value is less than one. The price reduction of 33 per cent has produced an increase in demand of only 14 per cent. The demand change has, this time, been unresponsive or inelastic.

✓ The organisation changed price by -33 per cent and demand increased but the increase was inelastic. The fact that the demand responsive was inelastic following the price fall results in total revenue also falling. **If demand is price inelastic, then reducing price will cause total revenue to fall**. If the objective of the organisation is to increase or maximise total revenue, then price should be increased when demand is price inelastic.

Practice 8.6

Calculate the price elasticity as price falls from 2 to 1. Again, follow the hints and method given previously.

Review: Price elasticity, price and total revenue

The foregoing examples have highlighted the clear benefits of understanding price elasticity of demand and its effect on the firm's revenue situation following price adjustments.

In summary:

✓ If demand is price elastic, then a decrease in price will increase total revenue and an increase in price will lead to total revenue falling.

✓ If demand is price inelastic, then a decrease in price will cause total revenue to fall while a price increase will increase total revenue.

Increasing and maximising total revenue using price elasticity

We have reached a number of conclusions concerning price elasticity of demand. We know that if price elasticity is inelastic then a fall in price will reduce total revenue. In addition, a price fall when demand is price elastic will lead to total revenue increasing. The relationships between price elasticity, price changes and the resulting changes in total revenue are shown in Table 8.6.

Table 8.6 **The relationship between price elasticity, price and total revenue**

	Price	
	Increase	*Decrease*
Elasticity		
Elastic	↓TR	↑TR
Inelastic	↑TR	↓TR
Unitary	TR constant	TR constant

The situation where price elasticity of demand is unitary is included and suggests that changes in price do not lead to changes in total revenue. If price elasticity of demand is unitary, this indicates that the percentage change in price leads to an equal but opposite percentage change in demand. **Remember that unitary elasticity yields a value of** -1. The following example, from the demand and total revenue schedules we used earlier, shows the total revenue situation when price elasticity of demand is unitary.

Another way of calculating elasticity: The average approach – the case of total revenue and unitary elasticity

In the Market Research International example total revenue equals 24 at prices of 4 and 6 respectively. The demand schedule showed:

p	q	TR	
4	6	24	The change in TR is zero, thus MR = 0
6	4	24	

Is it correct to argue that demand is unitary elastic between the two prices? The answer is 'Yes', but if elasticity is calculated from a price increase between 4 and 6, then the resulting elasticity value is -0.67. The percentage increase in price is 50 per cent but the fall in demand is only 33.3 per cent. Yet it is clear that the total revenue is unchanged. The problem is that the changes in price and demand are relatively large in percentage terms. The price elasticity calculation would suggest that the relationship is inelastic, while the total revenue information would indicate that the price elasticity is unitary. Which is correct? The answer is that the price elasticity is unitary. The solution to this dilemma is to use the average approach to measuring elasticity.

The formula is given by:

$$E^d = \frac{\text{change in qd}/0.5(qd_1 + qd_2)}{\text{change in p}/0.5(p_1 + p_2)} = \frac{\Delta q/\text{average of q}}{\Delta p/\text{average of p}}$$

This looks frightening but simply attempts to generate an elasticity value that is consistent with the total revenue information. In this example:

$p_1 = 4$ $qd_1 = 6$ The change in p = +2 and the change in q = -2
$p_2 = 6$ $qd_2 = 4$ The average p = 5 and the average q = 5

Using this information and the new average (because the old and new price and quantities are averaged) elasticity formula results in the following elasticity calculation:

$$E^d = \frac{-2/0.5(4+6)}{+2/0.5(6+4)} = \frac{-2/0.5(10)}{+2/0.5(10)} = \frac{-2/5}{+2/5} = -1$$

Using the average formula has produced an elasticity value that is consistent with the total revenue information and produces the same elasticity value for price increases and decreases. It is for this reason that the average formula is deemed to be the most appropriate one for calculation purposes. But remember that economics must provide us with insights and applications to inform our ability to analyse and evaluate, so use the economic information you possess in the most appropriate manner. If your regular journey to college proves to be difficult then you would look for a new route. To reinforce the benefits of using the appropriate technique consider the following example.

Measuring correctly

If we are to get correctly fitting clothes, we must know our measurements. It is the same with elasticity.

We must reduce price, as demand is price elastic

A local, non-league football club is desperate to increase the revenue received from gate receipts. The chairman of the club asks his nephew, who is studying economics, for advice.

The chairman tells his nephew that a 50 per cent price reduction is expected to lead to an increase in demand of 80 per cent. The nephew thinks that these are large percentage changes but his uncle is a fierce character and demands a recommendation. The nephew recommends lowering price as demand is, from his uncle's information, price elastic. It looks as if price elasticity is -1.6. The club lowers price but revenue falls! The uncle stops giving his nephew free tickets to games. The nephew is puzzled and asks his uncle for further information.

The full information is:

p	qd	TR	
4	1000	4000	Marginal revenue is -400.
2	1800	3600	

Given a price fall, this indicates that demand is price inelastic.

The nephew informs the uncle that demand is inelastic. A little knowledge has proved to be a dangerous thing. Using the average measure, the elasticity is -0.86. If we use the old method to measure price elasticity down the demand curve, then the price elasticity is -1.6. If we measure up the demand curve from a price of 2 to a price of 4, then the price elasticity is -0.44. The average measure yields a constant measure up and down the demand curve.

Practice 8.7

p	q
6	4
5	5

Use the average formula to show that price elasticity is the same for a price reduction from 6 to a price of 5 as it is for a price increase from 5 to a price of 6.

The total revenue profile

We can use the total revenue profile introduced in Chapter 2 to consolidate our understanding of price elasticity, price changes and total revenue. Consider the information provided in Figure 8.3.

The elastic region of the demand curve corresponds with the top half of the demand curve, while the inelastic range covers the bottom half of the demand curve. Price elasticity is unitary at the halfway point of the demand curve. At the highest point of the demand curve, price elasticity is at its highest. At the lowest point of the demand curve, price elasticity is at its lowest. At the top of the demand curve elasticity is very elastic, while at the bottom of the demand curve elasticity is very inelastic.

If the concern of the organisation is to obtain the maximum total or sales revenue, then price should be 5. The resulting demand will be five. If price is between 10 and 5.1, the firm is operating in the elastic region and lowering price will result in total revenue increasing. If the price charged is between 0 and 4.9, the firm is operating along the inelastic region of the demand curve and increasing price will cause total revenue to rise.

Price elasticity in the real world

Early morning travel on the London Tube

A practical example of using price elasticity of demand is the pricing policy pursued by London Transport on the London Underground system. Prices are charged according to the time the journey is started. Higher prices are charged during the morning peak demand period. Lower prices are charged from 9.30am when the peak demand has subsided. The higher prices are charged before 9.30am due to the price inelastic nature of the travelling public. The transport system is used by the public in large numbers before 9.30am because it is a reliable mode of transport for workers who must start their working day by no later than 10.00am. These workers cannot travel when they wish. They must travel in the busy period. Not only must they travel in the busy period, but also they are forced to use the underground because of both the lack of suitable alternatives and the cost and inconvenience of using private transport, be it car, bike or foot, due to congestion, time, parking and reliability.

Thus the travelling public, up to 9.30am, is constrained to use the Tube. These demand characteristics make the public price inelastic. If London Transport put prices up, the vast majority of the travelling public has no alternative but to pay the higher prices and continue to use the relatively efficient system. This is not a recipe for increasing prices indefinitely. Price increases will only yield increases in total revenue as long as demand is price inelastic. The maximum price is when demand elasticity is unitary.

The travelling public is separated into groups which start their journey before and after 9.30am. London Underground faces two demand curves. One demand curve is for travel before 9.30am, the other for travel after 9.30am. People who need to travel before 9.30am cannot start their journeys after 9.30am. They are constrained. This is not the case for people who can start their journey after 9.30am. If they wish they can travel before or after 9.30am, as they are not constrained. Not only are they freer to choose their start time, they also have the

FIGURE 8.3 The demand relationship and the total revenue profile

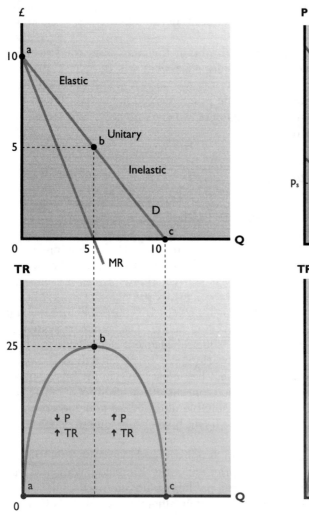

FIGURE 8.4 Peak and off-peak demand curves and the total revenue profiles

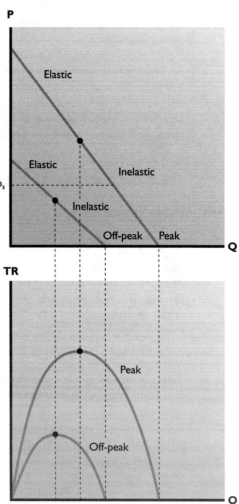

benefit of travelling in relatively nicer circumstances. The roads are less congested and parking restrictions are easier. This makes alternative modes of travel more appealing. The increased choice concerning the time of journey and the increasing number of realistic alternatives make the public more price sensitive after 9.30am. Demand is price elastic after 9.30am and the price charged must be reduced to attract their custom. Thus, price is higher for the inelastic peak-time travellers and lower for the elastic off-peak travellers. Figure 8.4 shows the different prices charged to the two groups and the revenue collected from the two groups.

The peak demand curve lies to the right of the off-peak demand curve. The peak demand curve shows, relative to the off-peak demand curve, that more people travel at any given price in the rush hour period than at other times. Not only does the peak demand curve lie to the right of the off-peak demand curve, but in addition, the peak demand curve is steeper than the off-peak curve. The peak demand curve is steeper due to the relatively price inelastic nature of demand before 9.30am. For any given price increase, the peak demand curve shows a smaller fall in demand than the relatively flatter and price elastic off-peak demand curve.

If the same price (p_s) is charged to both the peak and off-peak users, the peak users are on the inelastic part of their demand curve while the off-peak travellers demand is price elastic. The transport authority can increase its total revenue by charging a higher price to the price insensitive travellers and a lower price to the off-peak travellers.

British Rail pricing

A practical example of price elasticity is the fare charged by British Rail before and after 9.30am for the return journey between Ilford, Essex and Liverpool Street. The return fare in the peak period is £4.80 but only £2.50 after 9.30am. British Rail uses price elasticity of demand to price discriminate between the price-insensitive and price-responsive travellers. The price-inelastic group will always have to pay the higher price. This example concentrates on differing price elasticities according to the time of the day the journey is started but other examples of using price elasticity to generate extra revenue abound.

Eurostar and the English Channel

The price of cross-Channel travel is another example of price elasticity. Table 8.7 shows the pricing structure of cross-Channel travel.

Table 8.7 **Cross-Channel pricing**

	Le Shuttle	Car ferry
Return fare in winter	£220	£126–139
Return fare in summer	£280	£139–220
Return peak holiday season	£310	£289–320

The price elasticity conclusions to be drawn from Table 8.7 are that:

✓ Price elasticity of demand is price sensitive or elastic in the winter for both ferry and Channel Tunnel rail journeys.

✓ Price elasticity is inelastic during the peak holiday season. This season would very closely approximate the school summer holidays from the end of July to the beginning of September. People with children of school age have very little choice as to when they take their summer holiday. They are the seasonal equivalent of the peak-period rail travellers. Their constrained choice makes them price inelastic.

✓ The prices for Le Shuttle and car ferries indicate that users of the Channel Tunnel are relatively price inelastic. They are prepared to pay a higher price to use Le Shuttle. The factors making Le Shuttle relatively price inelastic includes the relatively faster journey time (by one hour) and the increased reliability due to the weatherproof nature of the Channel Tunnel infrastructure plus the novelty factor.

Other real-world examples

Other examples of using price elasticity of demand to generate extra revenue include:

✓ Sporting activities such as the price of tickets for football and cricket games according to the crowd appeal of the fixture and/or opposition. A number of English premier league clubs, Southampton, Wimbledon and Chelsea, adjust their ticket prices to match the attractiveness of the visiting team. Southampton segments visiting clubs into gold, silver and bronze categories. The three categories are priced differently with gold being the highest. Among the clubs in the gold segment are Manchester United, Liverpool, Tottenham, Chelsea, West Ham United, Arsenal and Newcastle United. All these clubs have a large travelling support and, in addition, they have traditionally played to large crowds at away games due to the glamour associated with them. Southampton thus views these clubs as producing price-insensitive games. These price-inelastic games are accordingly the highest priced of all the games played by Southampton.

✓ Clubs outside the English premier league tend to use price elasticity to generate extra revenue during their participation in cup competitions. Clubs such as Aldershot and Oxford have used their success in cup competitions to increase the ticket price as they progress in the cup competitions. The success aspect makes supporters increasingly insensitive to price increases. This is especially the case if the club is drawn at home to one of the big clubs, Manchester United, Liverpool or Arsenal. The clubs use their success and the attractiveness of the opposition to increase their price relative to that charged for a standard league fixture. Stevenage Town increased the admission price for the third round cup tie against Newcastle United in 1998.

✓ Leisure centres take advantage of the differing price elasticities of their customers according to the time of the activity. The price for swimming sessions is varied according to the user group and is shown in Table 8.8.

Table 8.8 Swimmers, time, elasticity and pricing policy

Time	User	Elasticity	Price
Before 9.00am	Serious swimmers with employment, income but restricted choice	Price inelastic	High price
9.00–12.00	Swimmers without employment and unrestricted choice	Price elastic	Low price
12.00–2.00pm	Serious swimmers with employment, income but restricted choice	Price inelastic	High price
2.00–5.00pm	Swimmers without employment and unrestricted choice	Price elastic	Low price
5.00–close	Serious swimmers with employment, income but restricted choice	Choice inelastic	High price

Table 8.8 suggests that the leisure centre prices according to the time of day. The time of the day is indicative of the price sensitivity of the user group and the characteristics of the user group. Is a similar pricing policy operated by your local leisure centre? People who attend the leisure early, late and at lunchtime show themselves to be constrained in their choice, employed and receiving income. They are consequently price inelastic and are charged higher prices. In contrast, people attending the leisure centre mid-morning and mid-afternoon possess greater choice but are usually unemployed and experience low incomes. They are price elastic and can only be attracted to the centre through the enticement of lower prices. The leisure centre practices price discrimination through the different price elasticities of the user groups and the ability of the centre to segment or divide the user groups.

Practice 8.8

Electricity companies charge people for the privilege of switching their lights on. When will the price of switching your kitchen light on be higher: December or June?

Practice 8.9

Why do nightclubs charge males more than females for entrance? Is it because they like women more than they like men? Alternatively, is there an economic explanation?

The factors influencing price elasticity of demand

The factors influencing price elasticity of demand are those factors that influence the demand for the product. They include:

✓ the price of the product
✓ the price and closeness of substitutes
✓ the price of complements
✓ income.

Number and closeness of substitutes

The greater the number of substitutes available the more price elastic demand will be. Substitutes indicate the alternatives consumers are willing and able to turn to. The substitutes need to be close both in the sense of being rivals and in the sense of being available.

I look for a good deal when purchasing a computer. I need there to be rivals and I need them to be able to deliver to me. Serious swimmers would willingly move to the cheaper off-peak prices, but, unfortunately, they are not able to do so.

An example of high substitutability causing price elasticity to be elastic is a single brand of cigarettes. If the price of a single brand increases and other substitute brands do not change their price, there would be a large change away from the relatively higher priced brand. In this case, the relatively large number of close substitutes would make demand price elastic.

Any situation where the demand of the consumer can be satisfied by a number of alternative rival products will make price changes elastic. This could be the case with running shoes. If the consumer views Nike, New Balance, Reebok, Adidas and Puma running shoes as being good substitutes, a price increase by one of the companies will tend to make their products relatively price elastic. The public will switch away from the relatively more expensive running shoe. Obviously, this argument is based on the public's viewing the products of the running shoe companies as being highly substitutable. If the public's perception of running shoes is that they are basically the same, there are real substitutes available. The companies, to counter this competition, attempt to make their shoes unique by creating special features.

The classic examples of this are Nike and Air, the Reebok Pump, the Puma Disc, and Asics and Gel. The firms attempt to make their products price insensitive by creating fairly unique products with limited substitutability. The public becomes brand loyal due to the characteristics of the shoe – Airmax and Gel – and are price insensitive. The introduction of a characteristic reduces the number of substitutes available and with it the price elasticity of the shoe. It is then possible for the companies to increase the price of their shoes without experiencing price elastic responses. The firms usually introduce higher prices when they change the colour and slightly adapt the features of the shoe. An example of this would be the introduction of a new Nike shoe with a bigger air window in the heel in a new colour scheme.

The degree of substitutability, which can be calculated by measuring the cross-price elasticity, covers the extent to which good substitutes exist. The cross-price elasticity of demand is covered in the next chapter. The extent to which good substitutes exist is a geographical issue and depends on the amount of search the public will carry out. If the serious swimmer will not look for information concerning the availability of cheaper alternative pools after 5.00pm, there is very little chance of this swimmer being anything but price inelastic. If there are no rival pools close to the swimming pool, competition is absent and search is futile and the serious swimmer has no alternative but to be price inelastic.

Practice 8.10

Alice, my daughter, tells me that she must have the Teletubby Dipsy for her birthday present. Is my demand for Alice's birthday present elastic or inelastic?

The complementary nature of the product

The greater the extent to which the product acts as a complement to other products the more price inelastic it will tend to be. Perfectly complementary goods are tied in usage and give rise to the term tied goods. An example of tied goods would be the Kodak disk camera and the film used. The two products have no intrinsic value on their own. The two must be used together to produce an output – the picture. If the price of the unique film required for use in the Kodak disk camera is increased, the owner of the camera is forced to purchase the higher priced film as no other alternative exists. Companies with tied goods – the Polaroid camera and film, razors and the complementary razor blades, the Reebok Pump running shoe and the aerosol to inflate the shoe, Gameboy machines and the cartridges, cars and official car replacement parts, Duracell torches and batteries and so on – tend to price the replacement element high relative to its cost, as the repeat purchase component is relatively price insensitive. Companies have an incentive to produce products with tied aspects to generate more revenue from the repeat purchases, and have the ability to increase the price of the repeat purchase component without experiencing price elastic responses. In general, the goods or services that act as complements will tend to be relatively price insensitive. Film processing and shoe repairs will be price inelastic services. The film negative is useless without the final processing service, as is a leaking shoe without a cobbler.

Practice 8.11

BMW produces cars with secured covers over the engine. It is only possible to release the covers with specialist tools. These tools are not on sale to the public and are held only by BMW dealerships. Is this because BMW feels that the public cannot be trusted to tamper with the engines? Alternatively, is there an economic reason for the secured covers?

Income

Demand will be more price inelastic the greater the income of the consumer. The greater the income of the consumer the smaller the share of that income spent on any one item and the less price sensitive the consumer will be. Consider the impact of a price increase for a poor and a rich consumer. The percentage change in the price of the product is the same for both but the impact of the price increase will be greater for the poor consumer. The poor consumer will search for a cheaper substitute, whereas the rich consumer will not. For both the rich and the poor consumer the price increase will be an inconvenience but it will be a significantly bigger problem for the poor consumer whose responsive will be elastic compared with that of the rich consumer. An example of this situation is the pricing of theatre tickets in the West End of London. People with high incomes invariably book their theatre tickets using their credit cards, at the announced price, sometime before the performance. For this group the main concern is obtaining a ticket at the set price and avoiding the risk of missing the performance. The poorer income groups are equally keen to see the performance but their limited income makes the set price unattractive. Therefore, they risk not seeing the performance unless they can secure a cheap standby ticket. The richer income group would not be prepared to forego the certainty of seeing the performance for the risky chance of paying a lower price. This example can also be seen in the aeroplane industry where business people tend to be price inelastic and travel in business or first class, whereas students take the risk of standby tickets due to their price sensitivity.

Practice 8.12

It is more expensive to purchase a British Rail return ticket from London to Liverpool than it is to buy a return ticket from Liverpool to London. Is there an economic explanation for this pricing policy?

Time

Demand is more price elastic the greater the amount of time elapsed after a price change. Chancellors of the Exchequer attempt to raise tax revenue by increasing the tax on goods and services. The goods and services targeted for taxing are the price-inelastic products. These include petrol, alcohol, spirits and tobacco. Members of the public are forced to pay the higher prices following the tax increase and total revenue and tax collect rise as the products are price inelastic. As time elapses after the price increase the public can engage in more search activity and obtain information on the existence of relatively cheaper substitutes. The search activity, if successful, will move the customers away from the relatively expensive product and tends to make it less inelastic. The demand curve will be relatively steep or relatively price inelastic immediately after the price change. After sufficient time has elapsed to allow the consumers to find relatively cheaper substitutes the demand curve will tend to flatten out or be relatively price elastic. Thus demand will be relatively price inelastic in the short-run and increasingly price elastic in the long-run. This is shown in Figure 8.5.

Practice 8.13

The government reduces the rate of VAT on coal to 0. What would you expect to see happen to the demand for coal in the short- and long-run?

Summary

This chapter has been a long journey through price elasticity of demand, so we will keep this summary brief. The topic is one that students find difficult. This is probably due to the combination of percentage changes and numbers above and below one. There is no need for elasticity to be difficult. **The important thing is to use real world examples, such as frequent changes in the style of Arsenal shirts with JVC plastered on the front, as your base.** Arsenal shirts are price insensitive. A 10 per cent increase in the price of these shirts leads to a very small percentage fall in the quantity demanded. It will be only the bravest of parents who will draw the line at buying the shirt. Peer group pressure will win out. Arsenal shirts and Levi 501 jeans are price inelastic. The next chapter covers elasticity resulting from the shift factors.

FIGURE 8.5   Short- and long-run elasticities

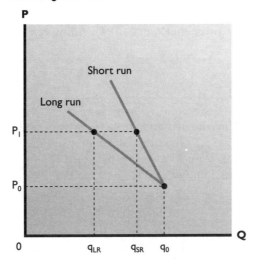

Answers for Chapter 8

Answer 8.1

The percentage increase in price is 4 per cent. This is calculated as follows:

$$\frac{52-50}{50} \times 100 = 4\%$$

Answer 8.2

	Price	Quantity	Total revenue
Old	50p	10	£5
New	52p	8	£4.16
Percentage change	4%	−20%	−5

Demand is price elastic. The 20 per cent change in quantity demanded dominates the 4 per cent change in price.

Answer 8.3

	Price	Quantity	Total revenue
Old	£4	10	£40
New	£5	9	£45
Percentage change	25%	−10%	Elasticity = −0.4

Demand is price inelastic (−0.4). An increase in price leads to an increase in total revenue.

Answer 8.4

No. The fact that the demand curve is downward sloping makes the elasticity value negative. If price falls then demand increases and vice versa. Price elasticity could only be positive if an increase in price lead to an increase in demand, that is, an upward-sloping demand curve.

Answer 8.5

1. The percentage change in price is $-1 \div 7 * 100 = -14.2\%$.
2. The percentage change in quantity demanded is $+1 \div 3 * 100 = +33.3\%$.
3. The elasticity value is -2.3, from using $(+33.3\% \div -14.2\%)$.
4. Price elasticity is elastic.

Answer 8.6

1. The percentage change in price is $-1 \div 2 * 100 = -50\%$.
2. The percentage change in quantity demanded is $+1 \div 8 * 100 = +12.5\%$.
3. The elasticity value is -0.25, from using $(+12.5\% \div -50\%)$.
4. Price elasticity is inelastic.

Answer 8.7

1. To measure the price decrease from 6 to 5 use:

$$E^d = \frac{+1/0.5(5+4)}{-1/0.5(5+6)} = \frac{+1/0.5(9)}{-1/0.5(11)} = \frac{+1/4.5}{-1/5.5} = -1.22$$

2. To measure the price increase from 5 to 6 use:

$$E^d = \frac{-1/0.5(5+4)}{+1/0.5(5+6)} = \frac{-1/0.5(9)}{+1/0.5(11)} = \frac{-1/4.5}{+1/5.5} = -1.22$$

3. Thankfully, the answer is the same and demand is price elastic in both directions. We know this because a price decrease increases total revenue, while a price increase reduces total revenue.

Answer 8.8

Electricity prices are higher in December when demand is higher and less price sensitive. At 4pm on a December afternoon, I need the lights on but not at 4pm on a June afternoon. Have you never been asked to turn lights off, as they are not needed?

Answer 8.9

This is an interesting topic. It could be due to the fact that males, on average and wrongly in my opinion, are paid more than females. Higher earnings reduce price sensitivity.

Answer 8.10

My demand is price inelastic. Alice is Teletubby sensitive and this makes me price insensitive.

Answer 8.11

BMW likes the idea of our buying these cars. The dealerships like the idea of our using them for servicing and repairs. This is the tied or complementary nature of the relationship. By securing the engine BMW dealers possess a monopoly on servicing. I can only take my BMW 320i to a dealership with the specialist tools. I am price insensitive. I would like to take the car to a cheaper garage but it does not have the required tools.

Answer 8.12

Again, it is a question of income. Income is, on average, higher in London than it is in Liverpool. This makes people starting their journey in London less price sensitive. They could choose cheaper substitutes but their higher income makes them price inelastic. The opposite is true of journeys starting in Liverpool. The relatively lower incomes make travellers price sensitive and British Rail must offer lower prices to stop the traveller switching to a rival form of transport.

Answer 8.13

The price of coal will fall. In the short-run, there will be an increase in demand (moving along the demand curve) but the type of heating systems operated will limit it. I have gas central heating and could not convert to a coal-fired system in the short-run. Therefore, the demand for coal will be relatively inelastic in the short-run. In the long-run, I could convert to a coal-fired system. This would increase my demand for coal. The long-run elasticity will be relatively price elastic compared with the short-run elasticity.

ELASTICITY OF DEMAND — SHIFT OF THE DEMAND CURVE

What more elasticities?

This will help

This chapter complements (sorry) the demand and price elasticity chapters. You should read those chapters before you read this one. Managers are not only able to manipulate price to increase total revenue, they can also change their advertising expenditure. In addition, firms can examine and analyse the influence of the action of their rivals and the state of the economy on their revenue position. The chapter covers the demand elasticities of the shift factors. The four shift factors covered are:

✓ the price of complements
✓ the price of substitutes
✓ advertising (tastes)
✓ income.

You will find this chapter much easier than the previous one. This is probably due to your practice.

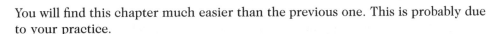

Introduction

In the previous chapter, price elasticity of demand was measured as movement along the demand curve. It is also possible to measure elasticity via shifts of the demand curve. To understand elasticity and shifts of the demand curve, it is necessary to list some of the factors causing the demand curve to shift. The important factors, in terms of elasticity, are:

✓ the price of substitutes and complements
✓ advertising
✓ income.

Each of these factors generates its own elasticity measure with respect to demand. Understanding these elasticity measures allows business decision makers to assess the logic of their policies.

By the end of this chapter you will understand:

✓ three new demand elasticity measures:

   cross-price elasticity

   advertising elasticity

   income elasticity

✓ the benefits of understanding the three elasticity measures for business decision making

✓ the calculation and application of the three elasticity measures.

Cross-price elasticity of demand

The own price elasticity of demand measures the change in quantity demand of product A following a price change in product A. The cross-price elasticity of demand (XED) attempts to measure the relationship between the change in the price of one product (B) and the resulting change in the quantity demanded of another product (A). As usual with elasticity, the analysis uses percentage changes.

The formula for the cross-price elasticity of demand is:

$$XED = \frac{\text{percentage change in the demand for good A}}{\text{percentage change in the price of good B}}$$

The only difference between the own price elasticity and the cross-price elasticity is that the cross-price elasticity looks at the change in the price of product B and the resulting change in the demand for product A.

This elasticity measure can generate powerful insights for business decision makers. The first cross-price elasticity examined is that between substitute products. This is when the cross-price elasticity is positive.

Cross-price elasticity of demand – rivals and substitutes

Business decision makers often find it necessary to examine the behaviour of their rivals. A classic example of this is the relationship between changes in the price of the *Mirror* newspaper and the resulting impact on the demand for the *Sun* newspaper. The managers at News International, the publisher of the *Sun*, would be very interested to know the likely impact on their sales position following price reductions by their rival, Mirror Group Newspapers. Using the cross-price elasticity of demand allows firms to discover:

✓ the identity and closeness of rivals
✓ the impact on their demand and sales revenue from the actions of their rivals.

To repeat, the cross-price elasticity of demand (XED) measures the change in the demand for good A following a change in the price of good B. Again, the analysis is carried out in percentage terms and the formula is given by:

$$XED = \frac{\text{percentage·change in the demand for good A}}{\text{percentage change in the price of good B}}$$

Lacoste (product A) and Kappa (product B) shirts are rivals and compete against one another. Consider a situation where the price of Kappa increases by 10 per cent. The demand for Kappa should normally decrease but what will happen to the demand for Lacoste? Will it increase, decrease or remain constant? The cross-price elasticity of demand will provide the answer to this question.

If the demand for Lacoste increases, then the goods are substitutes. Thus, if the cross-price elasticity of demand is positive (the price of Kappa and the demand for Lacoste have both increased), the two products are rivals or substitutes.

Practice 9.1

We know that Nike and Adidas training shoes are substitutes. If Nike reduces the price of its training shoes, then we would expect to see an increase in the demand for Nike training shoes. What would we expect to see happen to the demand for Adidas training shoes? Is the cross-price elasticity of demand value positive?

$$XED = \frac{\text{percentage change in the demand for Adidas}}{\text{percentage change in the price of Nike}}$$

Measuring the cross-price elasticity of demand

Paps Restaurant and Fresh Fry are two local fish and chip shops. Fresh Fry lowered its prices in the opening week to generate demand and customer loyalty. Paps Restaurant saw demand drop following the price reduction by Fresh Fry. Table 9.1 shows the cross-price elasticity between the restaurants.

Table 9.1 Measuring the cross-price elasticity between Paps and Fresh Fry

Fresh Fry price	Paps restaurant demand
£3	200
£1.50	20
Percentage change = −50%	Percentage change = −90%

The resulting cross-price elasticity of demand is +1.8:

$$XED = \frac{\text{percentage change in the demand for Paps}}{\text{percentage change in the price of Fresh Fry}} = \frac{-90\%}{-50\%} = 1.8$$

The cross-price elasticity of demand is positive (1.8) and shows that the two fish and chip shops are rivals. The value of +1.8 indicates that each time Fresh Fry increases its prices by 1 per cent Paps will see its demand increase by 1.8 per cent. The two fish and chip shops are rivals and the positive cross-price elasticity of demand proves the existence of rivalry between the two. Fresh Fry should be wary of price increases, as it will lead to its rival gaining custom.

Practice 9.2

Calculate the cross-price elasticity of demand when Fresh Fry increases price from £1.50 to £3.

We need to use the averaging approach to produce the same value for price increases and decreases. You can find the averaging measure in the price elasticity chapter.

The implications of positive cross-price elasticity of demand values

The extent to which the demand for good A rises following a 10 per cent increase in the price of good B shows the degree to which the two products are close substitutes. Table 9.2 shows two cross-price elasticity values.

Table 9.2   **Differing cross-price elasticities**

	Price of B	*Demand for A*	*Demand for A'*
	50p	100	100
	55p	107	150
Percentage change	+10%	+7%	+50%
XED		+0.7	+5

The greater the percentage change in the demand for the good following the 10 per cent change in the price of good B, the greater the extent to which the two products are close substitutes or rivals for each other. In the situation in Table 9.2, the cross-price elasticity values are +0.7 (B and A) and +5 (B and A'), and show the three products to be rivals. The greatest competition is between B and A with the cross-price elasticity of +5. The greater the positive cross-price elasticity of demand, the closer the degree of rivalry or substitutability between the two products.

The firm producing good B would have to be careful when considering independent price changes as a cross-elasticity value of +5 shows that for every 1 percentage point increase in price they will find the demand of the rival's product, good A, increasing by 5 per cent. The demand for good B will fall, in percentage terms, in line with their own price elasticity of demand value. With a cross-price elasticity of demand value of +5, the policy implication for the firm producing good B is to decrease its price and capture some of the demand and market share presently held by good A. If the price of good B is decreased by 10 per cent, then the demand for good A will fall by 50 per cent and good B will gain some of the market share lost by A.

To summarise, for firms with high, positive cross-price elasticity values the policy implications are that:

✓ Price increases are dangerous unless the rival is also increasing price.

✓ Price decreases, if not matched by rivals, will generate relatively large changes in demand, market share and extra revenue.

✓ The firm should consider changing the nature of its product to reduce the cross-price elasticity of demand.

✓ The firm should consider changing the way in which consumers perceive the product by manipulating the identity of the brand.

Firms do not enjoy having high positive cross-price elasticity values and attempt to reduce the number and degree of substitutes by creating brand loyalty. Examples of this are heavy advertising (Heinz baked beans), designer labels (Benetton) and product characteristics (Airmax). By reducing the cross-price elasticity of demand, the firm will also reduce their own price elasticity of demand and price increases will not be so painful.

Practice 9.3

Use the data in Table 9.2 to construct a figure showing the response of A and A' to the increase in the price of B. Put the price of B on the vertical axis and the demand for A and A' on the horizontal axis. Are the curves positively sloped? Which curve shows the greater change in demand? Which curve shows the higher cross-price elasticity?

Cross-price elasticity of demand – complements

The previous section covered the cross-price elasticity of demand and looked at the situation when the relationship was positive. The positive value indicated the existence of rivals. We can also use the cross-price elasticity of demand to examine the relationship between complements. A complementary relationship exists when the two products are used together. It could be rowing boats and oars. **The cross-price elasticity of demand for complements is negative.**

Complements or tied goods

To repeat, the formula is:

$$\text{XED} = \frac{\text{percentage change in the demand for good A}}{\text{percentage change in the price of good B}}$$

If the response of a 10 per cent increase in the price of good B is that the demand for good A falls, then goods A and B are complements and not substitutes. The cross-price elasticity of demand will be negative.

Consider the situation of Gameboy machines and the disks required to produce the game. The machine and the disk are complements and increases in the price of the machine will lead to the demand for the disks falling. The relationship is a negative one. If a 10 per cent increase in the price of the Gameboy machine leads to a 50 per cent fall in the demand for the disks, then the cross-price elasticity of demand will be −5. This would be a much more worrying finding for the makers of the machine and the disk than if the cross-price elasticity were −0.7. In this case, the −0.7 value shows that an increase in the price of the machine leads to a fall in the demand for the disks of only 7 per cent (10% × 0.7 = −7%). The producers of the Gameboy machine and the associated disks would have greater power to increase the price of the machine when the cross-price elasticity is −0.7 than when it is −5. Increasing the price of the machine when the cross-price elasticity is −5 has a significant knock-on effect for the demand for disks. Producers who sell tied products would be best advised to examine the cross-price elasticity between the two goods before price increases are considered.

In this last example, the producers of the Gameboy machine have two options:

✓ Decrease the price of the machine and see an increase in the number of machines sold. In addition, with a cross-price elasticity of −5, there would be a significant increase in the demand for the associated product – the disk.

✓ The producers of the Gameboy could examine the cross-price elasticity of demand between a change in the price of the disk and the demand for the machine.

This is the opposite policy to that described earlier. Again, the two products are the same two complements but will the cross-price elasticity be −5? The answer is 'No'. The public will be more concerned with the price of the initial package rather than the price of extra games. Thus, increasing the price of extra games will not lead to the demand for the initial machine package falling significantly. The cross-price elasticity will be negative. The two are complements but increases in the price of the extra games will not lead to worrying falls in the demand for the machine. The policy implication is that the price of the additional games should be increased if the firm wants to obtain additional revenue. Remember that the demand for the extra games is inelastic and, in addition, the cross-price elasticity between an increase in the price of the extra games and the demand for the machine is negative but low.

Another example of the business decision-making logic of negative cross-price elasticity of demand is Clarks' shoes and shoe repairs. The purchase and repair of shoes are complements. Your local shoe repair shop cannot repair Clarks' shoes. I have tried to have my Clarks' shoes repaired locally, only to be told that Clarks makes its shoes in such a manner that shoe repair shops do not possess the necessary technology to repair them. Clarks can repair the shoes but the price is much higher than that quoted for ordinary shoe repairs.

I bought the Clarks' shoes at a high price. Tastes dominated price and I was price inelastic in my demand for the shoes. I thought that I would be price elastic in the repair of the shoes. I would take them to the cheapest repairer but, unfortunately, I cannot do that. The tied or complementary nature of the shoes and their repair means that I have to use Clarks as the repairer. I have two choices. Either I throw the expensive shoes away or I use the expensive shoe repair service. What should I do?

Practice 9.4

BMW produces cars with secured covers over the engine, as we have seen already. It is only possible to release the covers with specialist tools. These tools are not on sale to the public and are held only by BMW dealerships. The ownership of these cars and the servicing of them by the dealerships are complements. Will the cross-price elasticity of demand be negative? If the dealerships increase the price of the service by 10 per cent, what would you except to see happen to the demand for services in percentage terms?

Cross-price elasticity of demand – a summary

In summary, the cross-price elasticity of demand can be either positive or negative:

✓ If it is positive then the two products are substitutes.
✓ A negative value indicates the two to be complements.

However, the situation is not as clear cut as the demarcation into positive and negative values might suggest.

Firms selling in a competitive market need to know their cross-price elasticity of demand so that price changes make sense. Firms selling tied products need to examine the cross-price elasticity of demand between the two tied products. It makes sense for Gillette to sell razors at a competitive price and then sell the razor blades, the complement, at a relatively high price. If the price of the initial product, the razor, were uncompetitive, I would not buy it. I buy it and then discover that replacement razor blades are expensive. I am back to my Clarks' shoes conundrum. Do I throw the razor away and start again? This shows that the cross-price elasticity will differ depending on whether the price change is for the initial purchase or the additional complementary purchases.

Products such as Gameboy and Sega are sold through heavy advertising aimed at particular groups. It is to the issue of the advertising elasticity of demand that the discussion of elasticity now turns.

The advertising elasticity of demand

Advertising is a very powerful tool in a firm's marketing strategy. The amount of advertising on commercial television and in newspapers is testimony to the power of this demand increasing tactic. Firms advertise for many reasons, one of them is to increase demand. It is therefore in the interest of the decision makers to know how successful their advertising strategy is. Knowledge of the advertising elasticity of demand allows decision makers to gauge the correctness of their advertising campaign. It would be futile to increase the advertising budget, which is a cost to the firm, and see the level of demand stay constant or only increase marginally.

The advertising elasticity of demand shows the degree to which demand responds to changes in advertising expenditure. The formula for the advertising elasticity of demand (AED) is given by:

$$AED = \frac{\text{percentage change in demand}}{\text{percentage change in advertising}}$$

The advertising elasticity of demand, also known as the marginal sales effect of advertising, is measured as being either elastic or inelastic and is normally positive. Increases in advertising are expected to increase demand by shifting the demand curve to the right. If this occurs, then advertising is said to be effective. The degree of the effectiveness is measured by the elasticity value. If advertising increases by 10 per cent, in monetary terms, and demand increases by more than 10 per cent, then demand is advertising elastic. Conversely, if the 10 per cent increase in advertising leads to an increase in demand of less than 10 per cent, than demand is held to be advertising inelastic.

Knowing the advertising elasticity of demand will allow firms to make business-relevant decisions. The dilemma facing the business organisation is how to increase demand without sacrificing total revenue. Lowering price and increasing advertising can increase demand. Obviously, lowering price will increase demand but the total revenue situation will depend upon the price elasticity position. Price reductions will only be worthwhile when demand is price elastic.

If an organisation faces a price-inelastic demand curve, then reducing price will generate more demand but at the cost of falling total revenue. The policy implication for this firm is to increase demand through extra advertising. An example of this dilemma, a price-inelastic product, is Heinz baked beans. Heinz can increase the demand for its baked beans not by lowering price but by advertising the product heavily. The advertising campaign seeks to make baked beans synonymous with the Heinz brand via the slogan 'Beanz meanz Heinz'. The unbranded rivals, the baked beans of the supermarkets, do not compete with

Heinz on advertising but, rather, attempt to attract demand by pricing their unbranded baked beans significantly below the price charged by Heinz. The price difference is in the order of 33 per cent. Heinz could take demand from the supermarkets by lowering price but its total revenue would fall. Heinz secures its market share by engaging in heavy advertising expenditure. The supermarkets' advertising elasticity of demand is low or inelastic. Increasing their advertising budget to inform the public of the 'quality' of their baked beans does not produce worthwhile changes in demand. Supermarkets engage in advertising to persuade the public of the competitive value of their products. The supermarkets advertise on price, whereas Heinz advertises on quality or taste and not on price. Heinz has broken free of the price competition of the unbranded rivals. Sainsbury's, however, increases its market share by taking demand away from Tesco and Asda through price competition. Heinz will experience a more elastic advertising relationship than the unbranded supermarket products. If Heinz increases its advertising budget it will produce a significantly greater increase in demand than if the supermarkets concentrated their advertising budget on the 'quality' of their baked beans. Firms with relatively price-inelastic demand will find that advertising is the appropriate policy to use in securing extra demand. Examples of this include not only Heinz but also Kellogg's branded cereals, such as Frosties with the brand spokesperson Tony the Tiger, and branded shampoos including Vosene and Vidal Sassoon. All of them experience heavy advertising, as they are price inelastic and relatively advertising elastic.

The argument can be given a graphical form by considering what effective advertising means for the price elasticity of demand. This is shown in Figure 9.1.

Effective advertising shifts the demand curve to the right. The greater the rightward shift the more effective the advertising is. Consider the following price and demand combinations before and after successful advertising has taken place,

FIGURE 9.1 Effective advertising and price elasticity of demand

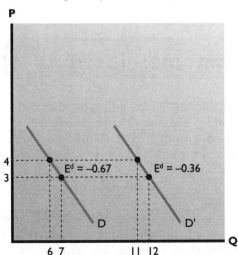

and the resulting price elasticities. Table 9.3 shows the reduced value for price elasticity following the effective advertising campaign.

Table 9.3   Price elasticity and effective advertising

P	QD	Ed	P	QD	Ed
pre-advertising			post-advertising		
4	6		4	11	
		−0.67			−0.36
3	7		3	12	

Successful advertising has shifted the demand curve to the right by five units at all prices. Price elasticity was inelastic, −0.67, before advertising was introduced but following the successful advertising campaign price elasticity, −0.36, is even more inelastic. Effective advertising makes price elasticity increasingly inelastic and firms which are heavy advertisers have relatively price-inelastic demand. People with relatively high incomes tend to be more attracted by advertising than consumers on relatively limited incomes. The latter group tends to be relatively price sensitive and not too responsive to advertising. The issue of income elasticity of demand completes the coverage of demand and elasticity.

Practice 9.5

The next time you visit a supermarket look at the price difference between branded and non-branded products. An example would be Sainsbury's and Kellogg's cornflakes. Are the brandeds more expensive? Are the brandeds more heavily advertised?

Income elasticity of demand

Firms are able to use price and advertising changes as part of their demand strategy but they are not able to manipulate the level of consumer income. Consumer income is probably the single most important factor in determining the level of demand for goods and services, and knowledge of the sensitivity between demand and consumer income can save firms from making disastrous decisions. An example of this is the situation of a recession when incomes are tight and sometimes falling.

Travel firms need to judge the level of future demand. Imagine that the economy moves into a recession. Economic activity declines and unemployment increases. Consumers react to the economic downturn by moving away from luxury expenditure, such as expensive holidays. Travel companies would be very unwise to offer the same type of holiday packages as sold in boom periods. The holiday companies would need to examine the relationship between changes in income and demand.

Income elasticity of demand measures the percentage change in demand emanating from a given percentage change in income. The formula for income elasticity of demand (YED) is given by:

$$YED = \frac{\text{percentage change in demand}}{\text{percentage change in income}}$$

The income elasticity of demand is normally positive and is divided into being greater than one (elastic) and less than one (inelastic). If income increases by 10 per cent and demand increases by more than 10 per cent, then demand is income elastic. Conversely, if income increases by 10 per cent and demand increases by less than 10 percent, then demand is income inelastic. Products with income elasticity between zero and one (inelastic) are described as being necessary products. If income falls, demand for these products also falls but by less than the percentage change in income. Consumers do not respond in a sensitive manner, as they consider these products important for their basic living standards and not totally dispensable. Products falling under this heading in the United Kingdom include food. Table 9.4 shows the income elasticity for various products in the UK.

Table 9.4 Income elasticities

Product	Income elasticity
Dairy products	0.53
Vegetables	0.87
Alcohol	1.14
Foreign travel	1.14
Clothing	1.23
Services	1.75
Recreational goods	1.99
Wines and spirits	2.60

Source: Begg, Fischer and Dornbusch, 1994

Table 9.4 shows that food in general and particular sections of the general food group are income inelastic. In contrast, drink and foreign travel are examples of income-elastic products. These income-elastic products are described as being luxury items of expenditure. If income grows, then these items experience a more than proportionate growth in percentage terms. The income elasticity for foreign travel is 1.14. This indicates that a 1 per cent increase in income will lead to a 1.14 per cent increase in foreign travel. This is good news for package holiday companies and travel agents, provided income is rising. If income is falling, then consumers will protect their basic standard of living by cutting back on overseas travel by more than the fall in their income in percentage terms.

Practice 9.6

The income elasticity of demand for recreational goods, such as tennis equipment, is 1.99. Is it true to say that an increase of 5 per cent in income will lead to an increase in demand of approximately 10 per cent? What will a fall in income of 2 per cent in income mean for the demand for recreational goods?

Growth in national income and business decision making

The United Kingdom has experienced high and low national income growth rates during the 1980s and these growth rates had differing impacts on a firm's demand curves according to the value of the product's income elasticity of demand. Table 9.5 shows the impact of economic growth on the demand for food and foreign travel.

Table 9.5   The impact of UK economic growth on foreign travel and food

Year	Growth	Income elasticity	Change in demand
1980	−2.1%	1.14	−2.4% foreign travel
1980	−2.1%	0.45	−0.95% food
1988	4.45%	1.14	5.1% foreign travel
1988	4.45%	0.45	2.0% food

Sources: Begg, Fischer and Dornbusch, 1994; Eurostats database

Table 9.5 shows that the poor economic growth performance of the United Kingdom in 1980 had a fairly severe impact on the travel industry, whereas the income-inelastic nature of food limited the damage as far as the producers, wholesalers and retailers of food were concerned. In 1980 the public reacted to the severe recession of that year by cutting their expenditure on both food and foreign travel – the demand for both categories of expenditure fell. However, the situation for the travel industry was significantly more difficult than that experienced by the food industry. The boom year of 1988 resulted in the opposite outcome. Both industrial sectors benefited but the travel industry experienced the greater increase in demand due to the income elastic nature of travel and holiday expenditure. The public increased their demand for foreign travel by 5.1 per cent and created a boom situation for the travel industry. Food producers, wholesalers and retailers also gained from the high growth of the late 1980s but less than the travel industry and the economy in general. The public uses extra income to move into luxuries. The policy implications of this are:

✓ Income-elastic goods and services experience favourable growth when income is rising, whereas income-inelastic products are cushioned when income is falling.

✓ Firms should avoid putting all their eggs into one basket. This is especially true in recessions. Firms should attempt to balance the products they sell between income-elastic and income-inelastic products. If firms cannot predict the future course of economic growth, then spreading their risk between income-elastic and income-inelastic goods best protects their trading position. This may explain why Sainsbury's has followed Asda's example of selling food and clothes. Clothes are income elastic and provide a balanced spread when combined with the income-inelastic character of food.

✓ Recreational and leisure service producers seem particularly prone to the cold winds of recession given the income-elastic nature of services and recreational goods. This may explain the severe problems the leisure and tourism industry experienced during the UK recession of the late 1980s and early 1990s.

The reaction of firms in the leisure and tourism sector of the economy to low economic growth should be to:

✓ move into income-inelastic activity (could be difficult given the funding required to start new business)

✓ change their pricing and advertising strategies in accordance with the values of the price and advertising elasticities.

Practice 9.7

Consider the situation facing a national newspaper with a price elasticity of −0.2 and an advertising elasticity of 3.5. What will a 10 per cent decrease in price or a 4 per cent increase in the advertising budget mean for the firm's demand? Which of the two would you recommend the firm implements?

Summary

This chapter has introduced you to the elasticities of the shift factors:

✓ The cross-elasticity of demand looked at substitutes and complements.
✓ If the cross-elasticity is positive then the two products are substitutes.
✓ A negative cross-elasticity shows that the two products are complements.
✓ Businesses have control over the cross-elasticity as well as the advertising elasticity.
✓ The advertising elasticity splits goods and services into advertising-elastic and advertising-inelastic groups.
✓ The final elasticity examined was the income elasticity. Firms have no control over this elasticity but they can change their product range to take advantage of rising income or cushion the effects of falling income.

The coverage of elasticity is now complete. It is time to breathe a sigh of relief! You have suffered the topic most students hate and fear. I hope you now understand elasticity. It will stand you in good stead for the future.

References

Begg, D., Fischer, S. and Dornbusch, R. *Economics* 4 ed. (Maidenhead: McGraw-Hill, 1994)
Eurostat Database for Windows

Answers for Chapter 9

Answer 1

✓ We would expect the demand for Adidas training shoes to fall.

✓ The cross-price elasticity of demand value is positive. Both the top and bottom of the formula are negative. A negative over a negative yields a positive.

Answer 9.2

The formula is:

$$E^d = \frac{\text{change in qd}/0.5(qd_1 + qd_2)}{\text{change in p}/0.5(p_1 + p_2)} = \frac{\Delta q/\text{average of q}}{\Delta p/\text{average of p}}$$

Inserting the relevant data produces:

$$E^d = \frac{-180/0.5(20 + 200)}{-£1.50/0.5(£1.50 + £3)} = \frac{-180/110}{-£1.50/£2.25} = 2.46$$

The cross-price elasticity of 2.46 is higher than the 1.8 value. Again, the relationship between the two is sensitive. Fresh Fry must be wary of increasing price, as it will lose a significant amount of market share and demand to Paps.

Answer 9.3

The figure looks like:

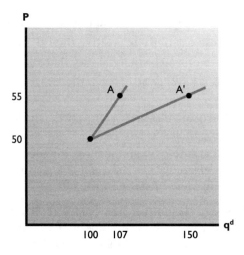

Obviously, both are positively sloped. The curve for A' is the steeper. The relatively flat curve for A shows a large demand response relative to A'. The cross-price elasticities are:

1.   AB = +0.7
2.   A'B = +5.0

Not surprisingly, the curve showing the greater sensitivity also has the higher cross-price elasticity.

Answer 9.4

1.   The cross-price elasticity of demand will be negative. An increase in the price of cars will lead to a fall in the demand for cars. With fewer cars being demanded, there will be a fall in the demand for servicing.
2.   If the dealership increases the price of the service by 10 per cent then you would except to see an inelastic response (less than 10 per cent fall), as there are no good rivals. Some people will miss their service intervals but not many.

Answer 9.5

1.   The brandeds are more heavily advertised. Branded breakfast cereals, such as Frosties, have high television exposure compared to their non-branded rivals.
2.   The branded are more expensive both absolutely and relatively. The percentage differences can be in the order of 30 to 40 per cent.

Answer 9.6

1.   Yes, an increase in economic growth of 5 per cent will lead to an increase in the demand for recreational goods of approximately 10 per cent. The correct figure is 9.95 per cent (1.99 multiplied by 5 per cent).
2.   An economic growth rate of −2% would lead to the demand for recreational goods falling by 3.98 per cent (−2% multiplied by 1.99).

Answer 9.7

1.   A 10 per cent decrease in price will lead to a 2 per cent increase in demand. Demand is price inelastic.
2.   A 4 per cent increase in advertising will lead to a 14 per cent increase in demand. Demand is advertising elastic.

PRICING

*Who makes the price? Is it the market or
the marketing department?*

This will help

Pricing is probably the one thing in microeconomics that directly affects you on a daily, if not hourly, basis. I have recently purchased a computer system. I looked at the specification which includes all the things I struggle to understand such as the amount of RAM and the size of the hard disk. However, most of my attention focused on the price charged. I got a good deal given the price I had to pay. The firm I purchased the computer from made the price and I reacted by taking it and paying the price. This type of decision faces you daily.

You will find this chapter easier if you have prior knowledge of Chapters 2 and 4 on demand and supply. Prior knowledge of Chapter 6 on costs, especially average cost, would be advantageous. However, the crucial thing to bear in mind as you work through this chapter is that you pay prices. Try to decide how the price was determined.

Introduction

This chapter will explain how price is determined. The two competing theories in microeconomics are:

1. market-determined price
2. administered price.

Market-determined price suggests that it is the clash between demand and supply that produces price. The firm is a price taker. The market makes the price and the firm takes that market-made price.

Administered pricing suggests the firm price on the basis of average cost. The firm makes the price and the consumer takes that firm-administered price. We will cover both of these pricing strategies and by the end of this chapter you will understand:

✓ market-determined pricing
✓ how changes in supply and demand affect market-determined pricing
✓ administered pricing.

Market-determined pricing

If we accept that the demand curve is downward sloping and the supply curve is upward sloping, then we can move to the traditional approach to market-determined price. Figure 10.1 shows that a downward-sloping demand curve and an upward sloping supply curve produce a unique market-clearing price.

Figure 10.1 shows that market demand equals market supply at, and only at, the market-clearing price, p_e. The market clearing quantity is q_e. This market equilibrium between demand and supply occurs at point e.

If price is above p_e then supply exceeds demand and there is excess supply. Put your index fingers on point e and move one up the market demand curve and the other up the market supply curve. The distance between your index fingers shows the amount of excess supply. Sx denotes the level of excess supply at price p^+.

If the market works efficiently then the excess supply should lead to price falling back to the equilibrium price p_e. In a situation of excess supply, supply outstrips demand. At the present time, it appears that the supply of computers is greater than the demand for computers. This explains the fall in their price.

FIGURE 10.1 Market-determined price

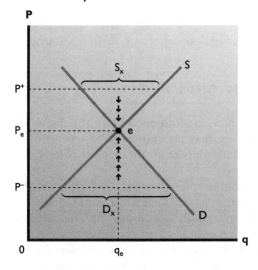

As price falls from p^+ to p_e three things happen. First, the lower price moves consumers down the demand curve and demand increases. Second, the lower price moves producers down the supply curve and supply decreases. Third, the disequilibrium of p^+ (excess supply is not equilibrium, but disequilibrium) becomes equilibrium at p_e. The arrow indicates the direction of the price change. If price is below the equilibrium price p_e at p^- then there is excess demand (D_x). Demand is greater than supply. The fourfold increase in the price of oil in the mid-1970s was caused by the excess demand for oil. Again, there is a movement along the demand and supply curves. The difference between demand and supply reduces to zero (demand equals supply) as the price returns to the equilibrium price p_e. The arrow shows the direction of the price change.

Practice 10.1

p	q^d	q^s
10	0	10
9	1	9
8	2	8
7	3	7
6	4	6
5	5	5
4	6	4
3	7	3
2	8	2
1	9	1
0	10	0

Using these data calculate:

✓ the equilibrium price p_e
✓ the level of excess demand (D_x) when price is 2
✓ the level of excess supply (S_x) when the price is 7

The demand curve shifts

If there is an increase in income then the demand curve shifts to the right. What impact does this increase in income have on the market-determined price? Figure 10.2 shows what happens to the market price following the rightward shift of the demand curve.

The original market-clearing equilibrium price is p_e and the original market-clearing quantity is q_e. These are the outcomes of the interaction of the original demand (D) and supply (S) curves. The new demand curve is D'.

At p_e, with the original supply curve (S) and the new demand curve (D'), there is a situation of excess demand (D_x). Under the pressure of this excess demand, price rises to clear the market. There is a movement along the demand curve from point d to point e'. The higher price chokes off some of the excess demand. In addition, there is movement along the supply curve from point e to point e'. The higher price brings on or encourages more supply. The new market-clearing equilibrium price is p'_e and the new market-clearing equilibrium quantity is q'_e. At all market-clearing prices and quantities demand equals supply. This is true of p'_e and q'_e. The prediction of market-determined pricing is that a shift of the demand curve to the right will cause price to increase. Obviously, a shift of the demand curve to the left will cause price to decrease.

Practice 10.2

Following on from practice 1, the demand curve has shifted to the right and demand is now two units higher at each price. Supply is unchanged.

p	q^d	q^s
10	2	10
9	3	9
8	4	8
7	5	7
6	6	6
5	7	5
4	8	4
3	9	3
2	10	2
1	11	1
0	12	0

FIGURE 10.2 Market-determined price: a shift of the demand curve

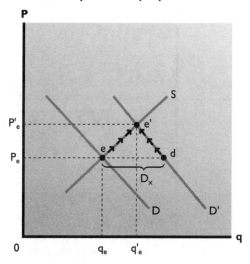

Calculate:

✓ the new equilibrium price and quantity
✓ the level of excess demand at the old equilibrium price.

Graph on one figure:

✓ the old demand curve
✓ the new demand curve
✓ the supply curve.

Use the figure to show:

✓ the original equilibrium
✓ the new equilibrium
✓ the level of excess demand with the new demand curve and the original supply curve at the old equilibrium price.

The supply curve shifts

Just as we can analyse the market price response of a shift of the demand curve, so we can inquire into the implications of a change in market supply. Figure 10.3 shows what happens to the market price following an increase in the number of firms supplying the product in the market.

Figure 10.3 shows that the rightward shift of the supply curve leads to a lower price p'_e and an increase in output q_e. These are the new market clearing price and quantity as the market moves to point e'. This rightward shift of the supply curve is

FIGURE 10.3 Market determined price: a shift of the supply curve

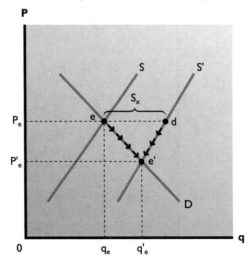

an example of the computer market. There appears to have been an increase in the number of suppliers. Look at the adverts in local and national newspapers. The result of this increase in supply is the new supply curve S'.

Using the original demand curve D and the new supply curve S' there are two outcomes. There is the disequilibrium outcome at price p_e when supply outstrips demand and the level of excess supply is equal to the distance d–e. This excess supply leads to a fall in price to p'_e. This price is the new market-clearing equilibrium price where the original demand (D) equals the new supply (S').

The predictions of market-determined pricing are that:

✓ a rightward shift of the supply curve leads to a lower price and an increase in output

✓ a leftwards shift of the supply curve leads to a higher price and a decrease in output.

Practice 10.3

The number of firms in the market declines. The market supply **falls** by two units at all prices. Using the new market information:

p	q^d	q^s
10	0	8
9	1	7
8	2	6
7	3	5
6	4	4
5	5	3
4	6	2
3	7	1
2	8	0
1	9	0
0	10	0

Calculate:

✓ the new market-clearing price
✓ the level of excess demand at the old market-clearing price
✓ the level of excess supply if price was 9.

Price floors and price ceilings

Occasionally governments do not like the outcome of the market. The price may be too high or too low. Governments are usually worried about high prices when they believe that people cannot afford one of life's essentials, such as rented accommodation. Governments become concerned with low prices when they are worried about the income of the recipients of the low prices.

Price floors

Price floors are also described as minimum price legislation. Governments are worried that the market-determined price is too low and introduce legislation to place a floor or minimum on price. A classic example of a price floor was the attempt by the Roosevelt Administration in America in the 1930s to protect and increase the income of the farming community by guaranteeing a minimum price in excess of the market-determined price. Farm income was thought to be too low due to the low prices received by farmers. During the Great Depression, American farmers were finding their total revenue did not cover even their total variable cost let alone make contributions. The result was that large numbers of farmers defaulted on their mortgages, which made them leave the rural economy. The rural economy was being destroyed. Figure 10.4 shows the income received by farmers before and after the introduction of the guaranteed minimum price.

The farmers' income is p_e multiplied by q_e before the introduction of the price floor. Their income is determined by the market and the intersection of the market demand and supply curves. In an attempt to increase farm income farmers are given a minimum price guarantee of p_f. Farmers now find it profitable to produce an output of qf. This price floor increases farm income to p_f*q_f. Farmers are better off. If the government forces customers to pay price p_f then demand falls along the demand curve. There will be an excess supply of farming produce. This example is similar to the Common Agricultural Policy (CAP) of the European Union.

European farmers are guaranteed a price floor, which results in excess supply or what we hear described as 'butter mountains' and 'wine lakes'. The relatively high prices paid by European consumers are the price we have to pay to support the European farmer. The consumer loses and the farmer gains.

The Net Book Agreement (NBA) is another example of price floors. This agreement attempted to secure an income for book writers. What a great idea! Unfortunately, the NBA no longer exists.

Practice 10.4

What would be the effect of a minimum price being set below the market-clearing price?

Price ceilings

Price ceilings or maximum prices are introduced when governments are concerned about the high prices people have to pay for services, such as private rented accommodation. This concern emanated from the behaviour of so-called 'Rackman' property owners. Peter Rackman was a West London property owner of the 1950s and 1960s. He used the high demand for accommodation and the relatively low supply to force prices up. The proportion of income spent on accommodation was rising and the government introduced a price ceiling on private rent. Figure 10.5 shows the situation before and after the introduction of a price maximum.

The concern is not with the income of the property owner but rather the price paid for the accommodation. The market-clearing price is p_e and the number of flats occupied is q_e. This market-clearing price is too high as far as the government is concerned. It introduces legislation to create a maximum price of p_c. People with lease agreements benefit from this reduction in rent. The longer the lease, the greater the benefit to the leaseholder. As leases expire, the accommodation is withdrawn from the private rental market. There is a movement along the supply curve from point e to point c. The withdrawn property is sold or put to other uses. There is usually an attempt to circumvent the price ceiling legislation by introducing key money or non-returnable deposits. The key money is usually equal to p_e-p_c and the property owner receives the market-clearing price from those able and willing to pay. I think students are familiar with the games property owners play.

Practice 10.5

Draw the short- and long-run supply curves following the imposition of a binding price ceiling for private rented accommodation. Remember that in the short-run people with leases will benefit from the legislation.

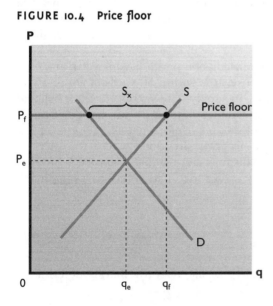

FIGURE 10.4 Price floor

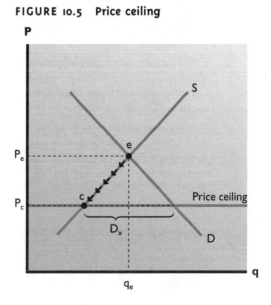

FIGURE 10.5 Price ceiling

Administered prices

The chapter opened with the question 'Who makes the price? Is it the market or the marketing department?'. The answer to this question lies at the heart of whether or not price is market driven or administered. Administered prices are prices made by the firm. Therefore, the theory of administered prices sees the firm as a price maker. The principal price maker in the organisation is the marketing manager. It is the marketing department that is charged with the marketing of the good or service. The marketing department does not have to be populated by a group of smartly dressed young people. The marketing department could be situated in your local garage and the marketing manager the mechanic who services your family car.

Practice 10.6

You have been asked to advise the catering department of your college on pricing policy. Specifically, the catering department requires advice on how to price a cup of tea. What information would you need to know to help the catering department set a price?

The problem with market-determined pricing

Market-determined pricing suggests that a shift of the demand curve to the right leads to an increase in price, while a shift of the supply curve to the right leads to a fall in price. Two real-world examples challenge the predictions of market-determined pricing. The first is the price of fish and chips and Friday. The price of fish and chips should be higher on a Friday than the other days of the week as this is the big demand day of the week. As we know, the price is the same throughout the week.

The second example concerns an increase in competition. A new fish and chip shop has recently opened close to our house. It is within 50 yards of another fish and chip shop. There has been an increase in supply. The supply curve for fish and chips has shifted to the right. Using my understanding of market-determined pricing, I expected the price of fish and chips to fall. Unfortunately, the price of fish and chips has stayed the same. These are two situations where the market-determined pricing model breaks down. This may suggest that firms use a different approach in determining their pricing structure. The alternative approach examined is full-cost pricing.

Practice 10.7

Is the practice of 'happy hours' in pubs consistent with market-determined pricing?

Full-cost pricing

The marketing manager needs to make sure that the firm sell the good or service. The price must be attractive to the buying public. The marketing manager must ensure that the price is a profit making price. **Price must exceed average cost. Average cost becomes the base on which price is made. Thus, price is a mark up on average cost.** A number of assumptions underpin this pricing approach:

✓ The firm is fairly certain of its likely output range. The firm plans its production run and has a very good idea of how much to produce.

✓ Because the firm knows its output range, it organises its cost structure to generate constant returns to labour. The average variable cost is constant. Adding average fixed cost (which is falling over the planned output range) to the constant average variable cost gives the firm its average cost of production. The firm will have good knowledge of average cost of production. Indeed, firms will always have better knowledge of their production side than their demand side. They work within the cost structure on a daily basis. They are aware of the production costs, efficiency and returns.

✓ The firm aims to make a profit. Total revenue must exceed total cost or price must be greater than average cost. The price is some multiple of average cost and is marked up on the basis of average cost. Thus:

$$P = k.AC$$
$$\text{where } P = \text{price}$$
$$AC = \text{average cost}$$
$$k = \text{mark up.}$$

Price and average cost are concepts that we can handle but the mark-up (k) is new. If average cost is £10 and the firm is looking for a unit profit of £5 then the appropriate price to charge is £15. The mark-up (k) is 1.5:

$$P = k.AC = 1.5 \times £10 = £15$$

The mark-up (k) of 1.5 covers the average cost of £10 and produces a unit profit of £5. If the firm's average cost increased to £12 because of an increase in either average fixed cost or average variable cost then the new price would be £18 (1.5 × £12). Of the price of £18, £12 covers the average cost and the remaining £6 is the unit profit. The firm passes all of the increase in average cost, be it average fixed cost or average variable cost, on to customers in the form of a higher price. The increase in average cost is £2 (£12 − £10) and the percentage increase in average cost is 20 per cent. The increase in price is £3 (£18 − £15) and again the percentage increase in price is 20 per cent. All the percentage increase in average cost is passed on to the customer. This is full-cost pricing.

✓ The mark-up reflects the firm's view of demand and competition. If demand is thought to be shifting to the left then the mark-up should fall. If competition is increasing then again the mark-up should fall.

Full-cost pricing suggests that price determination is the outcome of average cost and a mark-up factor. Price always exceeds average cost. This generates profits. The profits may not be at their maximum but profits do emerge from the marketing manager basing price on cost knowledge possessed by the firm. All the firm needs to know is its cost information as opposed to the marginal revenue and marginal cost informational requirements of the profit-maximising model.

The dominant factor in full-cost pricing is cost. There is a role for demand and that is the mark-up (k). Changes in demand or changes in the share of demand (competition) lead to changes in price. The firm adjusts the mark-up value. If the situation is favourable, for example, package holidays in the school summer holidays, then the mark-up will be increased. Price will increase. Despite this, the role played by the mark-up factor is argued to be minor compared with average cost.

We have two competing theories on pricing. One is the market-determined approach of demand and supply curves, and the other one the full-cost pricing method. Which is the correct method? The only way to discover the answer is to examine the evidence. In my opinion, Celtic is the best football team in the world. Unfortunately, the evidence does not support my opinion!

Practice 10.8

The average cost of production is £300. Your firm practices full-cost pricing. The targeted unit profit is 10 per cent on average cost. What price is charged? What would happen to price if there were an increase in total fixed cost? Is your firm a profit maximiser? What is the mark-up factor (k)?

The evidence on pricing

My experience of buying fish and chips supports the full-cost pricing approach. Changes in demand, the 'Friday' factor and competition, have not produced changes in price. Alternatively, my experience of buying a holiday is in line with the market-determined approach to pricing. Package holidays are more expensive during the school holidays than they are in June and September. The holiday firms appear to operate a market-determined pricing method. Changes in demand lead to changes in price. I am sure that you can identify prices that you experience as full-cost price or market-determined price but this is casual empiricism. For Dorward (1987):

> ... different economic/market environments are likely to require different pricing strategies ... Alfred (1972) identified six types of market situation

which may require different pricing strategies, namely: type of product; the nature of the geographic market; the type of competitive market; the age of the product; the nature of production; and the level of production capacity in relation to expected market requirements. (p. 67)

Cost is easily recognised in the costing procedure, while demand plays a nebulous, ill-defined role. (p. 121)

It seems that each good and service has its own pricing method but that cost appears to dominate demand.

Practice 10.9

List two goods or services that you believe are examples of market-determined and full-cost pricing.

Summary

This chapter looked at pricing. There are two approaches, the market determined model of pricing and full-cost pricing:

✓ The principal issue between the two approaches is the role of demand. The market approach gives equal prominence to demand and changes in demand and supply and changes in supply. The market approach sees pricing as the outcome of the demand blade interacting with the supply blade to produce price. The blade analogy is used because just as one blade of a pair of scissors is useless without the other, so the supply curve is useless without the demand curve.

✓ The full-cost approach emphasises cost. There is a role for demand but only in generating changes in the mark-up factor. The calculation of price is easy. The marketing manager simply marks up average cost. Unlike the profit-maximising approach where changes in fixed costs do not influence price, the full-cost approach permits firms to pass on changes in fixed costs. Full-cost pricing is easy but just because it is easy does not make it correct. Students like it because it is intuitively appealing and there are no figures!

The next chapter looks at market structure. The underlying premise is that firms profit maximise so they are price takers, unlike the full-cost approach where firms are price makers.

Reference

Dorward, N. *The Pricing Decision: Economic Theory and Business Practice.* (London: Harper & Row, 1987)

Answers for Chapter 10

Answer 10.1

1. The equilibrium price is 5. This is where supply = demand = five units.
2. When price is 2 the level of excess demand is six. Demand is eight and supply only two.
3. When price is 7 the level of excess supply is four. Supply is seven and demand only three.

Answer 10.2

1. The equilibrium price is 6. This is where supply = demand = six units.
2. At the old equilibrium price of 5, there is excess demand of two. Demand is seven and supply only five.
3. The figure looks like:

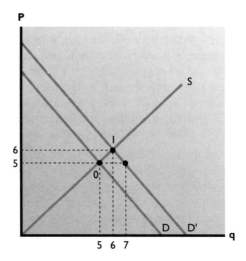

Answer 10.3

1. The equilibrium price is 7. This is where supply = demand = five units.
2. At the old equilibrium price of 6, there is excess demand of two. Demand is six and supply only four.
3. If the price were 9, then excess supply would be four. Supply is seven and demand only three.

Answer 10.4

If a minimum price were set below the market clearing then the price would rise to the market-clearing price. The forces of demand and supply would remove the excess demand. It would be illogical to set a minimum price below the market price. The point of a minimum price is to overrule the market and not reinforce it. The figure looks like:

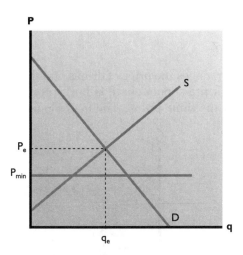

Answer 10.5

The figure looks like:

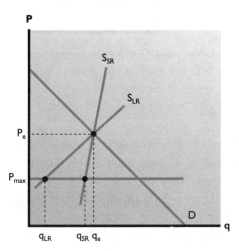

The long-run supply curve rotates towards the north-west as owners take property out of the regulated sector. The short-run supply curve is steep as the property owners are bound by the lease agreements. In the long-run, leases expire and the property is transferred to more profitable uses. The long-run supply curve is flatter that the short-run curve.

Answer 10.6

The answer depends on whether the price is set on a market-clearing approach or an administered approach. If it is the former then information on the supply and demand schedules will be required. In addition, profit-maximising considerations will require data on marginal revenue and marginal cost.

The administered approach requires knowledge of average cost and the mark-up to be charged.

Answer 10.7

Yes. The pub reduces the price of drinks and thus shifts its supply curve downward (I assume that the supply curve is horizontal, as pubs will supply as much as is demanded at the same price). The figure looks like:

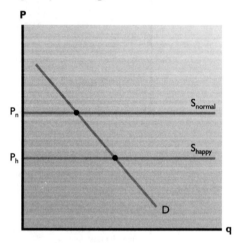

The pub shifts supply from the normal supply curve to the happy hour supply curve. Consumers are moved along their happy hour demand curve.

Answer 10.8

1. Price equals £330. Average cost is £300 and unit profit is £30.
2. An increase in average fixed cost (AFC) leads to an increase in price as AFC increases average cost.
3. The firm is not a profit maximiser as it changes price only if there are changes in marginal revenue or marginal cost.
4. The mark-up factor (k) is 1.1.

Answer 10.9

1. Market determined: package holidays and pop concerts.
2. Administered prices: new cars and McDonald's Big Macs.

MARKET STRUCTURES 1 – PERFECT COMPETITION AND MONOPOLY

Free to choose?

This will help

There are four market structures in traditional microeconomics:

✓ perfect competition
✓ monopolistic competition
✓ oligopoly
✓ monopoly.

We cover perfect competition and monopoly in this chapter. To try to cover the four market structures in one chapter would be too demanding for you and, incidentally, for me.

Analysing a market involves looking at many features of the firm. Firms make up the market structure, so understanding the firm helps us to understand the market structure in which the firm operates. The assumption that firms are profit maximisers is the dominant one in the analysis of market structures. So we need to have knowledge of total revenue, total cost and total profit coverage before starting this chapter. Market structure involves, among other things, price determination. Prior knowledge of supply, demand and price determination would be useful. This is a lot of prior knowledge but we are moving towards the end of the book and market structure encompasses most of the nuts and bolts of microeconomics. In many ways, market structure lies at the pinnacle of microeconomics. The sequential nature of microeconomics is brought to fruition in the coverage of market structure.

You are on holiday in Ibiza. You have taken sterling travellers' cheques and need to exchange them into pesetas. Just think of the fun you have searching out the best deal. 'It's 244 here, but a bloke at the hotel said you can get 246 down the road.' The exchange bureaux in Ibiza are a market structure. Are they a competitive or monopoly market structure? We will answer that question in this chapter.

Introduction

The purpose of this chapter is to examine how two market structures operate. The market structures examined are perfect competition and monopoly. The other two market structures, monopolistic competition and oligopoly, are analysed in Chapter 12.

Perfect competition and monopoly represent the two extreme market structures in microeconomics. Perfect competition is the ideal. It is perfect in terms of its outcomes. If the computer market were perfectly competitive, it would be impossible for consumers to be confused or ripped off. Monopoly is the bad boy of market structures. Consumers are exploited by the power of the single seller. Price exceeds average cost and the monopolist makes supernormal profits.

By the end of this chapter you will understand:

✓ how perfect competition and monopoly operate
✓ why perfect competition is the ideal market structure
✓ how government has used microeconomic theory to form policy.

Perfect competition – the consumer as king

Perfect competition is a theoretical model. There are very few, if any, real-world examples of perfect competition. This market structure produces performance outcomes which economists view as being perfect. Indeed, the privatisation and compulsory competitive tendering programmes of the Conservative government in the United Kingdom during the 1980s and 1990s were based on the teachings of perfect competition. Perfect competition has a number of assumptions. If they can be realised, then a perfectly competitive market should be forthcoming. We can measure the competitiveness of real-world markets by seeing how many of these assumptions exist in reality.

The assumptions

The assumptions of perfect competition can run to pages. We will concentrate on the most relevant ones and explain their importance.

Buyers and sellers

There are many buyers and sellers. Neither buyers nor sellers have any power to influence price. As a purchaser of baked beans, I have no power to influence their price. Most markets have many buyers. The crucial factor is the number of sellers. Think of your search for car insurance. You read the *Yellow Pages*. There are many adverts put there by sellers of insurance. The telephone numbers are 0800 and 0500 so the price of the call is free. The more sellers, the more competitive the market is. In perfect competition, the sellers should be of equal size. If there are 100 firms in the market then each should have 1 per cent of the market. The outcome of many buyers and sellers is that price is determined in the market and is not an administered price. The interaction of the many buyers and their market demand curve with the market supply curve of the many sellers produces the market price. This price is a market-clearing price and is taken by the sellers. The firms are price takers. The price maker is the market. Figure 11.1 shows the price sellers charge and purchasers pay.

Price is determined by the interaction of competition among the many buyers and sellers.

Objectives of the buyers and sellers

Buyers and sellers act rationally. The buyers maximise their utility, while the sellers maximise their profits. Producers have the required information to maximise profits. They have knowledge of marginal revenue and marginal cost. It is in the interests of firms to have knowledge of their revenue and cost as this will allow them to profit maximise.

FIGURE 11.1 The market price

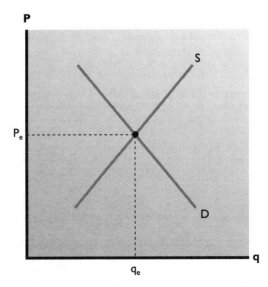

Information

Firms have the freedom to enter and exit the market. There are no barriers to entry or exit. Firms can obtain the necessary factors of production at the prices paid by the other firms in the market. The markets they purchase their factors of production in are also competitive.

Firms know the most efficient method of production. They operate on the lowest average cost and marginal cost curves. All firms in the market have knowledge of the most efficient production method and thus they all produce the same level of output. If there are 200 firms in the market, each firm will have a market share of 0.5 per cent.

Consumers also have perfect knowledge of the market. They cannot be fooled by the gimmickry of advertising.

The product

The product is homogeneous. This means that the product sold by one firm in the market is the same as the products sold by the other firms in the market.

This is not the world of product differentiation, branding and Nike or Microsoft. The homogeneous product has no need for advertising. Consumers possess the necessary information to make rational purchases. The firms cannot advertise effectively as the product is known to the consumer and the homogeneous product cannot be differentiated. Advertising would be a waste of money and would reduce profits.

Practice 11.1

Select a market – it could be the market for personal computers – and measure the extent to which that market is perfect.

Use the assumptions of perfect competition as the base for gauging the extent to which the market is perfect.

Perfect competition and the short-run

In the short-run, the firm makes either supernormal profits or losses. The firm does not make normal profits in the short-run. Normal profits are an indication that the long-run has arrived. Table 11.1 shows what happens to profits in different time periods in perfect competition.

Table 11.1 **Perfect competition: profits and time periods**

Supernormal profits	P > AC	Short-run	Firms enter
Losses	P < AC	Short-run	Firms leave
Normal profits	P = AC	Long-run	Number of firms unchanged

The firm makes supernormal profits if price exceeds average cost or total revenue is greater than total cost. In the short-run, knowledge that supernormal profits can be earned attracts new firms to the market. Alternatively, firms make losses if price is less than average cost. Some of the existing firms decide to leave the market. In the long-run, normal profits are made. Normal profits are earned when price equals average cost or total revenue equals total cost. This can be puzzling but remember that average cost includes entrepreneurial opportunity cost. Entrepreneurial opportunity cost is the reward for organising the factors of production and facing the risk. If all the costs of production, including the expected normal reward or return, are covered by the price received then normal profits are made. Normal profit provides a return to the firm. It is easy to think that total revenue equal to total cost means that there is no reward for the entrepreneur. This is not true, as the normal return is included in total cost in the form of entrepreneurial opportunity cost.

Practice 11.2

A firm has total revenue of £100 000 and total cost of £70 000. The firm's owner includes her entrepreneurial opportunity cost of £20 000 in the total costs. What type of profits has the firm earned? What profits are earned according to the accountant and the economist?

The firm, the market and the shortrun

The firm is a price taker. It takes the price from the market. The market is the price maker. The firm can only sell at the market-given price. The firm cannot sell above the market price as its demand would collapse to zero. Selling below the market price would reduce profits. The firm can therefore only sell at the single market price. The firm's demand curve is horizontal at the market price. If the market price were £10 then the firm would sell at this price. It would sell the profit-maximising quantity. Therefore, the firm is a price taker and quantity maker. It takes the price and makes the quantity to profit maximise.

The result of the firm's demand curve being horizontal at the constant market price is that marginal revenue equals price. An example will explain why a constant price yields marginal revenue equal to price.

Price	Quantity	TR	MR
10	0	0	
			10
10	1	10	
			10
10	2	20	
			10
10	3	30	

The firm takes the market price of £10 and each time it sells one extra unit total revenue increases by £10. This is the firm's marginal revenue. Thus, price equals marginal revenue when price is constant.

The firm maximises profit by equating marginal revenue and marginal cost. The level of profits can be measured by looking at price and average cost. If price exceeds average cost then supernormal profits are earned. We can see the behaviour of the firm and the market in Figure 11.2.

The firm takes the market price p_e. This price is made in the market at the intersection of the market demand and supply curves. The firm's demand (D) and marginal revenue (MR) curves are the same. The firm equates marginal revenue with marginal cost (MC) at output level q_f. This is the firm operating as a quantity maker. We now turn to examining the level of profits. In order to measure profits, we look at price (P) and average cost (AC). The average cost curve is U-shaped and is at its minimum when average cost equals marginal cost. The firm produces output of q_f at an average cost of AC_f. We know the firm's average cost curve and simply run a finger along this curve until we get to output q_f. Price exceeds average cost so the firm is making supernormal profits. The size of the supernormal profits is the shaded area. If price is £10, the average cost of output is £8 and the profit maximising output is 30, then the firm is making supernormal profits of £60. Remember that the average cost of £8 contains the normal reward.

The knowledge that supernormal profits can be earned acts as a signal to entrepreneurs outside the market. They enter the market to get their hands on the supernormal profits. The number of firms in the market increases and the market supply curve shifts to the right.

FIGURE 11.2 **Perfect competition: short-run equilibrium**

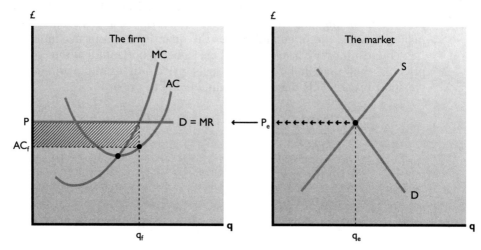

Practice 11.3

Draw a figure of the firm earning supernormal profits. Now lower the price slightly. What happens to the level of supernormal profits? Has the price reduction increased sales?

Perfect competition and long-run equilibrium

The existence of short-run supernormal profits acts as a signal to firms outside the market to enter the market. The market supply curve shifts to the right. The market price falls because of the increase in supply and competition. The firm has to take the lower price and its demand and marginal revenue curves shift down. Price continues to fall until all the supernormal profits have been competed away. Freedom to enter the market and secure the required factors of production leads to price falls and the elimination of supernormal profits.

The market is in long-run equilibrium when firms are earning normal profits. This happens when price equals average cost. The market price falls to a price at which only normal profits are earned. The firm's demand and marginal revenue curves touch the average cost curve at its minimum or lowest point. In technical terminology, the demand and marginal revenue curves are tangential to the average cost curve. Figure 11.3 shows the market price taken by the firm that eliminates supernormal profits.

The old market price was p_o but has fallen to the new and lower price of p_n. This price reduction was the result of the shift of the supply curve to the right (S'). The increase in market supply was due to the existence of supernormal profits at the old price p_o. The new market-clearing quantity is q_n.

FIGURE 11.3 Perfect competition: long-run equilibrium

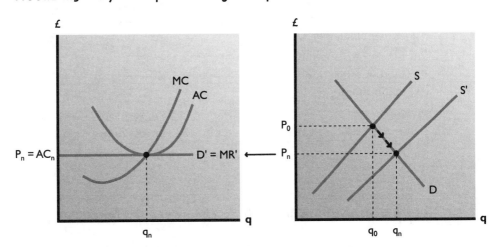

The firm take the new market price p_n and their demand (D') and marginal revenue (MR') curves shift down. The firm is a profit maximiser and equates the new marginal revenue (MR') and marginal cost to make the profit-maximising output q_n. The average cost (AC) of producing the profit-maximising output q_n is at its lowest. Supernormal profits have been eliminated as price p_n now equals average cost AC_n. The firm is making a return equal to entrepreneurial opportunity cost. Firms are unhappy to see the elimination of supernormal profits but they are content to stay in the industry, as the price covers all their average costs including the reward or risk required to operate in this market. There is no incentive to enter as no supernormal profits exist. There is no incentive to leave as normal profits are being made. The market is in long-run equilibrium as the number of firms is unchanged. There is no incentive to enter or exit.

Practice 11.4

In the short-run firms are making losses. What will happen to the market and firm figures in the long-run?

Perfect competition is perfect

The outcomes generated by the firm and the market give the market structure its perfect status. The outcomes concern the behaviour of price and costs and can be seen in the short- and long-run figures. Table 11.2 summarises the outcomes.

Table 11.2 Perfect competition: the outcomes

	Short-run	Long-run
Allocative efficiency P = MC	Yes	Yes
Production efficiency AC is minimum	No	Yes
Profits P and AC	Supernormal or losses	Normal
Supply and demand in the market S = D	Yes S = D	Yes S = D

Supply and demand – does the market clear?

The short- and long-run market figures show that the market always clears, as supply always equals demand. The mechanism that produces the market-clearing behaviour is competition and price flexibility. Price flexibility ensures that the market clears. If there is excess supply then price falls to clear the market. Supply equal to demand is the desire. The requirement is price flexibility. An analogy is a bowl into which you drop a marble. The marble eventually comes to rest at the bottom of the bowl. This is equilibrium. If you shake the bowl then the marble rotates away from equilibrium. The force of gravity restores the marble to equilibrium. This is the law of gravity. Price flexibility brings supply and demand into equality. There is market equilibrium and the law of markets. If governments want market-clearing behaviour then they have to put in place policies to promote price flexibility.

Practice 11.5

Is the market for telephone calls a market-clearing one in the United Kingdom?

Allocative efficiency – does price equal marginal cost?

Allocative efficiency occurs when price equals marginal cost. This is the firm's equivalent of supply equalling demand in the market. Price equals marginal cost in both the short- and long-runs just as supply equals demand in both time periods. Allocative efficiency means that resources or factors of production are being allocated to their best use. If price exceeds marginal cost then society can gain if output is increased. Price reflects the benefit we get from the good and marginal cost indicates the cost of extra production to society. If price is below marginal cost then society is overproducing the product. The benefit, as shown by the price, is less than the cost to society, as shown by marginal cost. The point of maximum benefits to society is shown in Figure 11.4.

FIGURE 11.4 **Benefits to society: price and marginal cost**

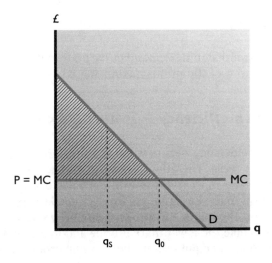

Price reflects the value we place on a product. It indicates or values the benefits we derive from consuming the product. Marginal cost shows the cost to society of producing an extra unit of the product. The difference between price and marginal cost shows the net benefit to society of producing the product. Society should produce the product up to the point where price equals marginal cost or the net benefit is zero. If output is q_s then output is sub-optimal as price exceeds marginal cost. The area of net benefit is the shaded area. This area could be increased if production were at q_o. This is the optimal output level as price equals marginal cost.

An example may help to explain this. In the United Kingdom the price of a local telephone call is 3.2 pence a minute. The marginal cost of the local call per minute is zero. Yes, 0. You rent the line and probably own the telephone. Both are fixed factors. All the other factors used in the production of the one-minute call are fixed – cables, BT vans, telephone exchanges – with the exception of the electricity used to generate the call. The price of the electricity for a one-minute call is low but you pay it in your quarterly electricity bill. Society would benefit if the price of telephone calls were to fall. More calls would be made. The price of a one-minute local call should be free. This is the pricing tariff in the United States. The Federal Communication Commission requires telephone companies to follow the allocative-efficiency pricing method of perfect competition where price equals marginal cost. If the telephone market were perfectly competitive then price would equal marginal cost. If the telephone market is not perfectly competitive then the government should regulate to force the telephone companies to price at marginal cost. This should bring the telephone market into market clearing.

Practice 11.6

Is the market for telephone calls a market-clearing one in the United Kingdom? This is not a mistake. It is the same question as the previous one. Has your answer changed?

Practice 11.7

Use a downward-sloping demand curve and a constant marginal cost curve to show that the output of the profit-maximising BT is sub-optimal.

Production efficiency – is average cost minimum?

Production efficiency occurs when the firm produces at the minimum point of its average cost curve. The firm is exhausting all economies and is operating at its most efficient. In the short-run, the firm does not operate at the minimum point of its average cost. In the long-run, the firm is forced to operate at minimum average cost. Competition eliminates supernormal profits by forcing market price down. The firm is forced to take the lower market price and move along its average cost curve. The firm is in long-run equilibrium when normal profits are earned, price equals average cost and average cost is at its lowest. If, and it is a big if, firms possess U-shaped average cost curves then they could be forced to produce efficiently by being exposed to competition. This may well have been the rationale for the introduction of compulsory competitive tendering into the provision of publicly produced goods and services such as refuse collection and leisure during the 1980s.

Practice 11.8

If the average cost curve is L-shaped can competition make for productive efficiency?

Profits – does price equal average cost?

In the short-run the firm can make supernormal profits or losses. The key to understanding that supernormal profits are being made and the size of those supernormal profits is to look at price and average cost. **If price exceeds average cost then supernormal profits exist. The firm profit maximises when marginal revenue equals marginal cost.** This gives us the quantity to be made. The quantity produces an average cost. Run your finger along the average cost curve until you get to the profit-maximising quantity. In the short-run this is at qf (see Figure 11.2). The average cost of producing q_f is AC_f. Price exceeds average cost, so supernormal profits exist. The size of these supernormal profits is price minus average cost times the quantity produced. The area is $(P - AC_f) \times q_f$. The total revenue of $P \times q_f$ exceeds the total cost of $AC_f \times q_f$. Total revenue exceeds total cost by the shaded area.

Supernormal profits can only be made in the short-run. The firm is making a return more than that necessary to keep the firm in the market. The firm would be happy with price covering all costs including their entrepreneurial opportunity cost. The firm makes a supernormal profit at the expense of its customers. The customers are being ripped off. Competition will eliminate these supernormal profits.

In the long-run, the firm only makes a return on all its factors of production that is normal and not excessive. The firm makes normal profits. Competition removes the supernormal profits. The shift of the supply curve leads to a lower price and this price equals average cost. Only normal profits exist. The customer is no longer exploited.

Perfect competition leads to the elimination of supernormal profits through the freedom of firms attracted by supernormal profits to enter the market. We now turn to the monopoly market structure. Perfect competition is seen as being good, while monopoly is bad. We shall see why.

Practice 11.9

Do the water companies in the United Kingdom make normal or supernormal profits? What was the position of the UK government in the late 1990s towards the prices charged by the water companies? What does this suggest for the government's view of the type of profits made by the water companies?

Monopoly

In traditional microeconomics, monopoloy is a market with one firm. This was the situation with the telephone market in the United Kingdom before it was opened up to competition. The telephone market was completely under the supply control of British Telecommunications. BT monopolised it, as it was the sole domestic supplier. The definition of monopoly, therefore, is one firm in the market. When you play the board game Monopoly, the aim is for one person to own everything.

Monopoly: good or bad?

There are at least two ways to analyse monopoly. We can see what would happen if a perfectly competitive market were monopolised. To do this we would use the cost structure of the U-shaped average cost curve. We can then compare the outcomes of monopoly with those of perfect competition and see why monopoly is considered bad. Alternatively, we can take a more realistic approach to monopoly by using an L-shaped average cost curve. Monopolists usually exist in markets where only one or a few firms are able to exploit the natural economies of scale. These natural economies relate to the high fixed costs required to set the market working. However, before we analyse these alternative cost structures, we will look at the monopolist's demand structure.

The monopolist's demand and marginal revenue curves

The monopolist is the market supplier and as such faces the market demand curve. The market demand curve is the monopolist's demand curve. This curve is downward-sloping. Refer to either of the perfect competition figures. With a downward-sloping demand curve, the monopolist has a marginal revenue curve that is also downward-sloping. Figure 11.5 shows the relationship between the downward-sloping demand curve and the marginal revenue.

The demand curve starts at a price of £50 on the vertical axis and finishes at a quantity of 20 on the horizontal axis. Marginal revenue also starts at the price of £50 on the price axis but cuts the quantity axis at the halfway point. The halfway point is a quantity of ten. This is halfway between a quantity of zero and a quantity of 20. If the demand curve is a downward-sloping straight line then the marginal revenue curve starts at the same price as the demand curve and cuts the horizontal quantity axis at the halfway point. The monopolist is argued to be a profit maximiser and equate marginal revenue with marginal cost. Profits can be measured by looking at the relationship between price and average cost.

Practice 11.10

p	q
5	0
4	1
3	2
2	3
1	4
0	5

Using these data, plot the demand curve and the resulting marginal curve. Remember that marginal happens **between** while price happens **at**.

Monopoly and perfect competition

We will look at the monopolist in the long-run. It makes little sense to look at the monopolist in the short-run and the long-run. If the monopolist exists in the long-run then it is because it existed in the short-run and protected its monopoly status into the long-run. The reason why the monopolist existed into the long-run as a monopoly and did not come under competitive pressure is due to barriers to entry. Unlike perfect competition, where firms are free to entry or exit, the monopolist survives into the long-run by preventing entry. The monopolist bars entry by

FIGURE 11.5 The monopolist's demand and marginal revenue curves

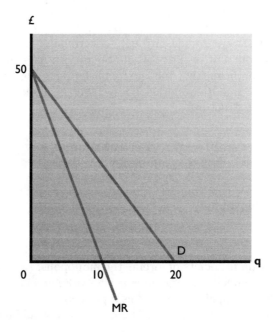

setting up barriers. The barriers to entry include high costs of set-up, advertising, patent rights, control over wholesale or retail outlets, exclusive ownership or rights to an important factor of production. If the monopolist can maintain barriers to entry then it will survive into the long-run as the single supplier in the marketplace.

The monopolist profit maximises just as the perfectly competitive firm does. Marginal revenue is equated to marginal cost. The behaviour of the two in the long-run can be see in Figure 11.6.

The monopoly profit maximises when marginal revenue equals marginal cost; this is at the output q_M. The monopolist prices at p_M. The average cost of producing q_M is AC_M and this average cost is clearly below the monopolist's profit maximising price, p_M. The monopolist makes long-run supernormal profits given by the shaded area. Is this the only aspect that makes the monopolist bad? No.

Practice 11.11

Is BT's marketing strategy of Friends and Family a barrier to entry? Why?

Allocative efficiency

The firm is an efficient allocator of resources when price equals marginal cost. The market is an efficient allocator when supply equals demand. In the long-run, the perfectly competitive firm produces at price p_{PC} and output q_{PC} (see Figure 11.7). Price p_{PC} equals marginal cost so the firm is an efficient allocator of resources. It is using society's scarce resources efficiently. Does the monopolist use resources efficiently? The answer is 'No'. The monopolist prices at p_M and produces q_M. The marginal cost of producing q_M is MC_M. The monopolist does not price at marginal cost but the perfectly competitive firm does. Society would benefit if the monopolist were forced through government regulation to act as if it were perfectly competitive. Price would be lower at p_{PC} and output would be higher at q_{PC}. The profit-maximising monopolist prices higher and produces less than a perfectly competitive market does. Table 11.3 summarises the behaviour of the two market structures.

Table 11.3 **Perfect competition and monopoly, allocative efficiency and price and marginal cost**

Perfect competition	Price = marginal cost	Efficient allocator
Monopoly	Price > marginal cost	Inefficient allocator

The gain to society of forcing the monopolist to behave in accordance with the perfectly competitive outcomes is shown Figure 11.7.

If the monopolist operated as a perfectly competitive firm does, then the gain to society is the shaded area. The monopolist would price at p_{PC} and produce q_{PC}.

Society would gain units of output. Price reflects the benefit to society of having the good while marginal cost indicates the cost to society of producing the good. Production is allocatively inefficient if price is greater than marginal cost. I, like you, would enjoy lower BT prices. I would make more telephone calls. Society would benefit. One of the reasons why the Internet has been taken up by a higher percentage of Americans than Britons is the fact that local telephone calls are free in the United States. If the information superhighway is important for education then a lower price for accessing the Net will benefit society. The Americans seem to have it right.

Practice 11.12

The government is keen that every school has access to the World Wide Web. All the hardware and software will be provided free of charge to the schools. What will stop the schools using the Net optimally? What would be your recommendation to the government?

Production efficiency

The definition of production efficiency is that production takes place at minimum average cost. In the long-run, the perfectly competitive firm exhausts all possible economies while the monopolist does not. The monopolist operates at an average

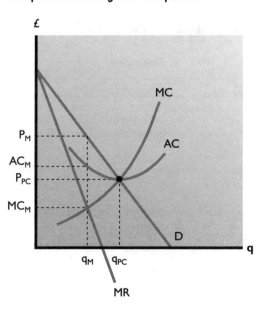

FIGURE 11.6 Monopoly and perfect competition: a long-run comparison

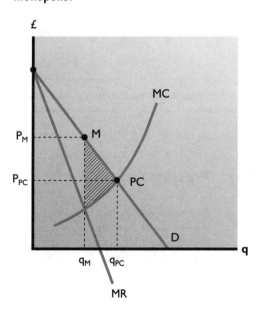

FIGURE 11.7 Gains to society of regulating the monopolist

cost that is above the minimum. Here we are assuming that both market structures have a U-shaped average cost curve. This assumption is relaxed later in the analysis. In Figure 11.6 we saw that the monopolist operates at average cost of AC_M which is clearly above the minimum point of the average cost curve. Table 11.4 summarises the difference between the two market structures.

Table 11.4 Perfect competition and monopoly, productive efficiency and average cost		
Perfect competition	Average cost is minimum	Efficient producer
Monopoly	Average cost is not minimum	Inefficient producer

Profits

In the long-run, the perfectly competitive firm only make normal profits as price equals average cost. There are supernormal profits or losses in the short-run but these are competed away. Price equal to average cost ensures that the firm makes only a normal return. This seems fair.

Monopoly, with its barriers to entry, prices above average cost and supernormal profits are earned in both the short- and the long-run. The firm makes a return more than that necessary to keep it in the market. The supernormal profits are made at the expense of the customer. The monopolist exploits the customer. This may explain the attitude of the Labour government in the late 1990s towards the privatised companies such as water and rail. Table 11.5 summarises the profit performance of the two market structures over time.

Table 11.5 Perfect competition and monopoly and profits		
	Short-run	*Long-run*
Perfect competition	Supernormal profits or losses	Normal profits
Monopoly	Supernormal profits	Supernormal profits

Practice II.13

A nationalised monopolist is privatised. The government required that the nationalised market follow the pricing rules of perfect competition. What changes would you expect to see in pricing and output following the privatisation of the market?

Monopoly, the real world and politics

In the real world, the monopolist exhibits significant economies of scale. The long-run average cost curve is continually downward-sloping and approximates an L-shaped average cost curve. The monopolist's cost structure is dominated by high fixed costs and reaps benefits from these high fixed costs as output increases. An example is the provision of underground rail travel in London. London Transport needs stations, track, trains, computer technology and a management infrastructure before trains can be run. The system is dominated by fixed costs. Variable costs exist but they are insignificant compared with the fixed costs. The marginal cost of production is low and constant. The marginal cost of providing a train journey includes the electricity, some wear and tear on the train and system and wages. The marginal cost of the each journey should be the same. The system experiences constant returns. Marginal cost is low and constant. The cost structure of the monopolist with high fixed costs and low and constant marginal cost is shown in Figure 11.8.

Obviously, the average fixed cost curve falls as more and more output is made. The fixed costs are spread over greater output and are the source of the monopolist's efficiency. The trains, staff and stations are being used time and time again. The marginal cost curve equals the average variable cost curve and shows that the firm experiences constant returns to variable factors. The extra cost of running the train from Cockfosters to Heathrow on the Piccadilly line is the same for morning, afternoon and evening journeys. The average cost curve is simply the average fixed cost curve shifted up by the constant average variable cost curve.

FIGURE 11.8   The monopolist's cost structure: high fixed costs and constant marginal cost

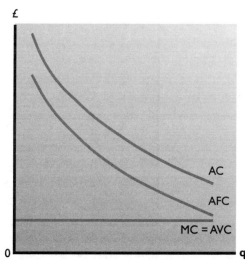

The average cost curve approximates an L-shape as opposed to the U-shape of the perfectly competitive firm. Firms with high fixed costs and constant marginal cost such as water companies, the providers of electricity and gas and car producers, all possess L-shaped average cost curve structures. What should the monopolist do? Should it profit maximise or price at marginal cost? Can it do both? The perfectly competitive firm can.

Practice 11.14

Can a monopoly exist where firms do not experience high fixed costs?

Pricing and profits

The monopolist can either operate in its own interests and profit maximise (MR = MC) or it can work in society's interests (P = MC). The monopolist cannot do both. The dilemma is shown in Figure 11.9.

   The monopolist is a private organisation and acts in its own best interest. The monopolist profit maximises. Marginal revenue is equated to marginal cost, the output level is q_M and price is p_M. The monopolist has an average cost of AC_M (point b). This is less than the monopolist's price and supernormal profits of area $p_M abq_M$ are made. The monopolist prices above average cost and marginal cost. Society would benefit if output increased to the point where price equalled marginal cost. In addition, the monopolist does not fully exploit potential economies by operating at point b on the average cost curve.

FIGURE 11.9   Monopoly: nationalised or privatised?

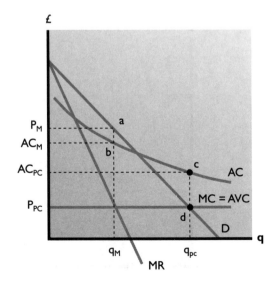

Should the monopolist be nationalised or be regulated to behave as if it were a perfectly competitive market? It is an unfortunate fact that, at this point, politics enters into microeconomics. If the monopolist behaves in the interests of society then it will price at marginal cost. The output level will be q_{PC} and price equals p_{pc}. Price equals marginal cost. Price has fallen and output is higher. So far so good. Now the problem. If the monopolist operates in accordance with society's needs, then losses will result. The average cost of producing q_{pc} is AC_{pc} (point c). Unfortunately, AC_{PC} lies above P = MC. The nationalised monopolist must make losses if it prices at marginal cost. The area of the loss is $AC_{pc}cdP_{pc}$. The nationalised monopolist is allocatively efficient as price equals marginal cost. It is also productively efficient compared with the privatised monopolist. Look at AC_M and AC_{pc}. The nationalised monopolist is efficient but is loss making. Who will pay for the loss?

The loss has to be funded. The loss can be financed in a number of ways. Tax revenue can be given to the loss making but efficient nationalised industry. This has not been the chosen method. Instead, the nationalised industry has apportioned the loss equally to users. Users of the service pay a standing charge that is equal to their share of the loss. This is a fixed payment and its total collection equals the loss. Look at your gas or electricity bill. You see a standing charge. This was introduced when the formerly nationalised industries made losses. They priced at or close to marginal cost and made losses. The loss had to be financed. The users financed the loss through a standing charge. The privatised monopolies appear to make supernormal profits. Price exceeds average and marginal costs. We are still paying the standing charge. Should we? I would refuse to pay a standing charge to my local pub. So why should I pay a standing charge to my electricity company? As I said – politics.

Practice 11.15

An essay question. I think you are ready. If not, read Chapter 14.

'Nationalised industries made massive losses. They were economically inefficient.' Discuss.

Summary

Does perfect competition exist? Probably not, but it does create outcomes against which the behaviour of firms and markets can be measured:

✓ Perfect competition is market clearing as supply always equals demand.

✓ The firm has price equal to marginal cost in both the short- and the long-run and is therefore an efficient resource allocator.

✓ Price equals average cost in the long-run, so the firm makes only normal profits. Customers are not exploited.

✓ In the long-run, the perfectly competitive firm is productively efficient as production is carried out at the minimum point of the average cost curve. Things could not be better.

✓ In contrast, monopoly is a badly performing market structure. The customer is exploited in both the short- and the long-run as supernormal profits can be earned in both periods.

✓ Resources are allocated inefficiently as price exceeds marginal cost.

✓ Using the same cost structure as perfect competition, the monopolist is productively inefficient as output is produced at an average cost above the minimum.

✓ When a comparison is made between a private monopoly and a state monopoly, we can see that the private monopolist profit maximises at the expense of the customer and society. The state monopoly is allocatively efficient and produces at relatively low average cost but is loss making. A conundrum exists of efficiency and loss making.

This chapter asks questions about the way the outcomes of perfect competition should be incorporated into the world of monopoly. In the United States the Federal Communication Commission requires telephone call providers to price local telephone calls at zero price. Should this be the rule in the United Kingdom? The answer must be 'Yes'.

The next chapter looks at the market structures of monopolistic competition and oligopoly. Before moving on, please make a telephone call to Oftel, the telephone market regulator, explaining why the price of local telephone calls should be 0.

Answers for Chapter 11

Answer 11.1

The answer lies in the extent to which the particular market approximates to the assumptions of perfect competition. If the structure is that of a perfectly competitive market then you could expect the conduct and performance to be similar to perfect competition in terms of pricing and profits.

Answer 11.2

1. The firm earns supernormal profits of £10 000, as total revenue exceeds total cost. The total cost is £90 000 (the accounting cost of £70 000 plus the entrepreneurial opportunity cost of £20 000).

2. The accountant's profits are £30 000, while the economist argues that profits are £10 000. The difference is the entrepreneurial opportunity cost of £20 000.

Answer 11.3

1. The figure looks like:

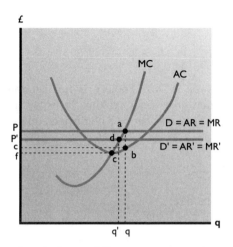

2. The price decrease has led to a fall in supernormal profits, profits were p_{abc} and fell to p'_{def}. The latter area is the smaller.

3. The price decrease does not lead to an increase in output. The reason is that the lower price is the result of an increase in market supply. More firms enter the industry and each firm has less of the market share than was previously the case.

Answer 11.4

The market figure will experience a shift of the supply curve to the left as some of the loss-making firms exit the industry. This will lead to an increase in the market price.

The higher market price will translate into a shift upwards of the firm's demand and marginal revenue curves. The change in price will stop when firms are just covering their average cost. Normal profits are earned and losses have been eliminated. The figure looks like:

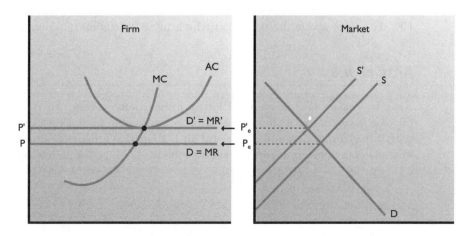

Answer II.5

Unfortunately, the answer is 'No'. Price exceeds marginal cost, so demand cannot equal supply.

Answer II.6

Again, the answer is 'No'. Society is not gaining the maximum benefits as price exceeds marginal cost. Society, that is us, would benefit from lower prices. The maximum benefit would occur when price equals marginal cost.

Answer II.7

The figure looks like:

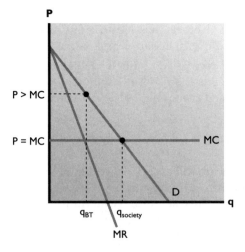

Society is not maximising the benefits of telecommunication provision in the UK. BT prices above the output at which price equals marginal cost.

Answer II.8

No. The reason is that competition requires many sellers. An L-shaped average cost suggests that size offers benefits. It is impossible to measure the size of a firm with a horizontal demand curve and an L-shaped average cost curve. A U-shaped average cost curve presents no such problem. Look at the following figure:

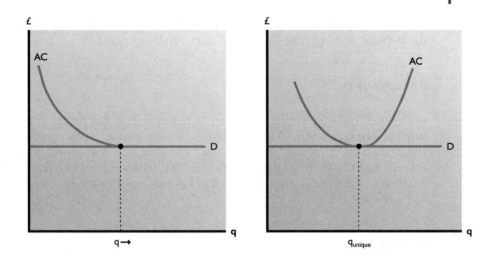

Answer 11.9

I believe that the water companies make supernormal profits. This is the message I get from the media and my water bill. The government appears to agree with me. It is forcing the water companies to reduce their prices. Their total revenue will fall and so will the level of their supernormal profits, *ceteris paribus*.

Answer 11.10

The figure looks like:

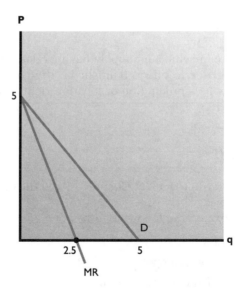

The marginal revenue curve starts at the same point as the demand curve on the vertical and cuts the horizontal at the halfway point.

Answer 11.11

In my opinion, it is a barrier to entry. BT uses its market power to prevent other firms securing a foothold in the market. If they cannot secure sufficient market share then they cannot get economies of scale and cost benefits. BT uses the Friends and Family to stop people moving to rival operators. The rivals are not in a position to offer attractive products like Friends and Family due to the small scale of their operation.

Answer 11.12

In my opinion, it will be the fact that local telephone calls are not free in the UK. This is because school budgets will be stretched if they are to offer open access to the Internet. The government could force BT to price local calls at 0 for all public education institutes. I doubt that this will happen.

Answer 11.13

All things considered, it is my belief that the privatised industry will increase price and thus reduce output. The privatised firm needs to make profits to satisfy the demands of the shareholders. Profits are incompatible with price equals marginal cost and a continually downward-sloping average cost curve.

Answer 11.14

It is difficult to imagine a monopoly having relatively low fixed costs. There would be no cost barrier to entry. It might be the case that the monopoly has other advantages such as production or location rights but costs are the main source of barrier to entry.

Answer 11.15

Again, I advise you to look at Chapter 14 and the coverage on planning and writing an essay answer.
I would expect the following to be covered:

1. Introduction.
2. Definitions of monopoly and efficiency.
3. Normal and supernormal profits.

4. Allocative efficiency.
5. Price and marginal cost.
6. The nature of the monopolist's average cost curve.
7. Price, marginal cost, average cost, allocative efficiency and profits.
8. Summary
9. Conclusion – a loss-making nationalised industry is efficient.

MARKET STRUCTURES 2 — MONOPOLISTIC COMPETITION AND OLIGOPOLY

Do you vacuum or do you hoover?

This will help

Read Chapter 11 before you read this chapter. Perfect competition generates a number of ideal outcomes. Unfortunately, it can be criticised because there are no real-world examples of perfectly competitive market structures. Firms advertise and we react to this advertising. We need models of the firm that include advertising. Firms also change price and we again react to lower and higher prices. We also need models of the firm that allow firms to change their prices. Unfortunately, perfect competition cannot cope with firm's making price changes and advertising. Two market structures that allow the firm to adjust price and advertise are monopolistic competition and oligopoly.

Introduction

This chapter covers monopolistic competition and oligopoly. These market structures can be seen as lying between the extremes of perfect competition and monopoly. In monopolistic competition, there are many buyers and sellers. It is very similar to perfect competition. The essential difference is that the monopolistically competitive firm engages in product differentiation. Oligopoly is the world of a few producers. These firms act and react to the behaviour of their rivals. An example of oligopoly is your local petrol station.

By the end of this chapter you will understand:

✓ the underlying behaviour of monopolistic competition and oligopoly
✓ the importance of advertising, product differentiation and pricing in the decision-making process of the firm.

Monopolistic competition

Do you vacuum or do you hoover? The vacuum cleaner may actually be a Hoover or it may be a Zanussi. You never say that you are going to Zanussi. However, people understand what hoovering means. The term has become part of the language but the word is only recently to be found in the dictionary. In the 1930s products such the Hoover vacuum cleaner were developed and marketed. Part of the marketing strategy was the use of advertising. Firms attempted to differentiate their products through features such as after-sales service, warranties, packaging and advertising. This was the beginning of the marketing department. Firms were also acting as price makers as opposed to taking their price from the market. The firm's demand curve was downward sloping and not the perfectly elastic demand curve of perfect competition. Finally, the 1930s was the decade of the Great Depression with long-term mass unemployment. Firms were operating at less than full capacity. They were not operating at the minimum point of their average cost curves.

Monopolistic competition has, like all market structures, assumptions. We look at these assumptions in the next section.

The assumptions

Many buyers and sellers

There are many buyers and sellers in the market. All markets have many buyers. It is the assumption that there are many sellers that gives the competitive aspect to monopolistic competition. Each firm has an insignificantly small share of the market and its actions are unlikely to affect its rivals to any great extent. When making decisions, monopolistically competitive firms do not have to worry how their rivals will react. The size of the market can be measured by using the cross-price elasticity of demand. The cross-price elasticity shows the relationship between the change in the price of one product and its implication for the demand of another product. If cross price elasticity is positive then the two products are substitutes. If the value is high then it can be argued that the two products are close rivals and may constitute a market. An example could be Hoover and Zanussi washing machines. If the two products are close substitutes then the cross price elasticity will be positive and high.

Product differentiation

 The firm attempts to differentiate its product. An example is polo shirts. Are LaCoste, Kappa, Benetton and Marks & Spencer polo shirts the same? Some of the producers attempt to differentiate their polo shirts by using badges, logos and advertising. The products are differentiated and this gives the monopoly element to monopolistic competition. The firm is creating a barrier to entry. Despite product differentiation, there exist close enough substitutes to allow a market to exist for the product. We talk of a market for polo shirts despite the fact that firms attempt to product differentiate their shirts.

Freedom of entry and exit

It is assumed that there is freedom of entry and exit. This again enhances the competitive aspect. If supernormal profits exist then firms will enter the market. Firms can secure the required factors of production. The assumption of entry clashes with product differentiation. Presumably, firms such as Reebok engage in product differentiation as a barrier to entry. The assumption that entry is easy is questionable.

Profit maximisation

Firms are assumed to be profit maximisers in both the short- and long-run. Profits are maximised when marginal revenue equals marginal cost.

Uniformity

It is assumed that all firms are of the same size. Firms have identical cost and demand curves. This questionable assumption allows one figure to show the behaviour of the representative monopolistically competitive firm.

With these wobbly assumptions in mind, we can examine the short-run profit-maximising behaviour of the monopolistically competitive firm.

Practice 12.1

Are Arsenal football shirts consistent with the assumptions of monopoly or monopolistic competition?

The monopolistically competitive firm in the short-run

The firm is a profit maximiser. The firm engages in product differentiation and has a downward-sloping demand curve. The firm can make supernormal profits or losses in the short-run. Figure 12.1 shows the firm's short-run behaviour.

The firm equates marginal revenue (MR) with marginal cost (MC) to obtain the profit-maximising output level (q_Π). The firm price at p_Π. It makes supernormal profits of $p_\Pi abAC$. In terms of outcomes, the monopolistically competitive firm prices above both marginal and average cost. The firm is neither an efficient resource allocator ($P > MC$) nor productively efficient (AC is not minimised). The firm could exploit existing economies and produce at a lower average cost.

It produces at point b on the average cost curve. The firm is not producing the perfectly competitive output level (pc). There are idle resources. The British economist Joan Robinson argued that the idle capacity (b − pc) was the unemployed workers of the 1930s.

Practice 12.2

Construct the short-run figure for a loss-making monopolistically competitive firm.

The monopolistically competitive firm in the long-run

The existence of supernormal profits or losses acts as a signal. With losses, some of the existing firms exit the market. With supernormal profits, new firms enter the market. We will continue the supernormal profit story.

Firms enter the market and the demand curve of the representative firm experiences two changes. It shifts to the left. The market has increased in size but each firm has a reduced share of the market. The firm's demand not only shifts to the left, it also becomes flatter. The newly entering firms make the demand curve more elastic. There is more choice. The old and new demand curves are shown in Figure 12.2.

The new demand curve D_{new} is flatter than the old demand curve D_{old}.

FIGURE 12.1 Monopolistic competition: short-run equilibrium

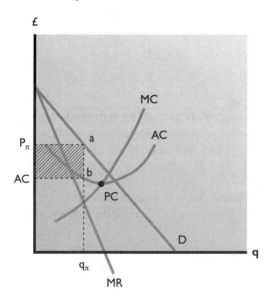

FIGURE 12.2 Demand curves and entry

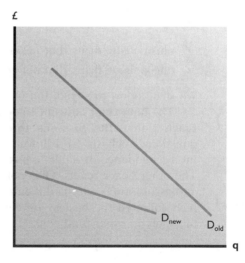

Entry eliminates supernormal profits and the firm's price equals average cost. The firm's demand curve touches or is tangential to the average cost curve. This is shown in Figure 12.3.

The firm's price equals average cost but exceeds marginal cost. The firm is making normal profits but is again neither an efficient resource allocator (P > MC) nor productively efficient (AC is not minimised). Again there is idle capacity.

Practice 12.3

Complete the following table to contrast and compare the long-run behaviour of the perfectly competitive firm and the monopolistically competitive firm.

	Perfect competition	Monopolistic competition
P and MC		
P and AC		
Idle capacity?		
Profits		

Oligopoly

The oligopolistic market structure has a small number of firms. How many firms are there? Few enough firms that the behaviour of any one firm in the market affects market price. Thus, oligopolistic firms are big enough to influence market price. The minimum number of firms in oligopoly is two. This is duopoly. The classic approach to studying the behaviour of oligopoly is to break the analysis into:

 oligopolistic firms that act non-collusively
 oligopolistic firms that act collusively.

We shall follow this tradition in our coverage.

 The important concept to conquer in oligopoly is the fact that firms act and react. Unlike the previous three market structures analysed, oligopolists ask questions such as 'If I lower my price what will my rivals do?'. There is interdependence. It is like a boxing match. One boxer acts by throwing a punch. The other boxer reacts. Oligopolistic models can be very demanding. The figures and assumptions can be difficult to understand. We will keep it simple. Once you have followed the basics you can then move onto the demanding treatments of oligopoly in other textbooks.

Oligopolistic firms act non-collusively

Firms act independently, in that they do not collude with anybody, but there is interdependence between firms. An explanation is required. Petrol companies are an example of oligopoly. They own the petrol stations. Let us look at two petrol stations. They are close to one another. The Chell station decides to increase the price of a litre of petrol. It is acting independently. The rival station, Hesso, decides not to follow the price increase. Some time later Chell decide to lower its price and take it below the Hesso price. Again, Chell has acted independently. This time Hesso decides to follow suit and matches the price reduction. There has been interdependence.

The interdependence relationship of the two petrol stations produces the kinked demand curve. The price increase is unmatched, while the price reduction is matched. If the petrol station increases price and its rivals do not follow then the demand curve for the price increase will be elastic or flat. The petrol station will lose a lot of demand. If the petrol station lowers price and its rivals match the price reduction then the demand curve for the price reduction will be steep or inelastic. The petrol station will only experience a slight increase in demand. The two demand curves are shown in Figure 12.4.

The two petrol stations price a litre of petrol at p'. Chell decides to increase the price above p'. Hesso does not follow or match this price increase. This is

FIGURE 12.3 Monopolistic competition: long-run equilibrium

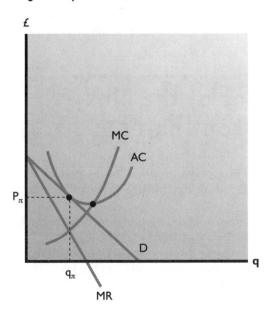

FIGURE 12.4 The kinked demand curve

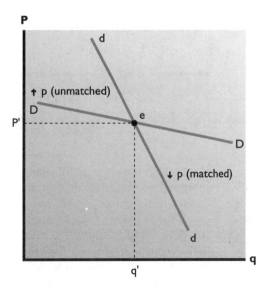

because it can gain some, or all, of Chell's market share. Chell's demand curve for the unmatched price reduction is De. If the price increase had been matched then the relevant demand curve for Chell would be de. However, this has not happened.

Chell decides to lower price below p'. Hesso matches this price decrease and Chell's demand curve for the matched price reduction is ed. This is because the price reduction is matched and so Chell gets none of Hesso's market share. It achieves a slight increase in demand from the lower price, but not at the expense of Hesso. If the price decrease had been unmatched then Chell's demand curve would be eD. Again, this has not happened. The result is that for the unmatched price increase, the demand curve is the flat De and for the matched price reduction, the demand curve is ed. The demand curve with reaction is kinked at point e. The marginal curve for this kinked demand curve is strange. The marginal revenue curve has two sections. One for De, the unmatched demand curve, and the other for ed, the matched price reduction. The kinked demand curve and the resulting marginal revenue curve is shown in Figure 12.5.

This is a difficult figure to draw accurately. Try drawing the marginal revenue curve. Remember that if the demand curve is linear then the marginal curve starts at the same point as the demand curve on the price axis and cuts the quantity axis at the halfway point. The marginal revenue curve for the unmatched demand curve De starts at point D and ends at point a. The marginal revenue curve for the matched demand curve ed begins at point b. Between points a and b immediately below the kink there is a discontinuity in the marginal revenue curve.

Practice 12.4

Practice drawing the kinked demand curve and the resulting marginal revenue curve with the discontinuity. Make sure that you have drawn the marginal revenue curve accurately. It may turn up in an exam and markers check for accuracy.

The implications of the kink and the discontinuity

If the oligopolist is a profit maximiser, the oligopolist produces at the point where marginal revenue equals marginal cost. The profit-maximising price and quantity is shown in Figure 12.6.

If the constant returns marginal cost curve cuts the marginal revenue curve in the discontinuity (between points a and b) then the profit-maximising price is p_Π and output is q_Π. Given that the discontinuity is the largest part of the marginal revenue curve, it is possible for the profit-maximising price to be at the kink. What happens if there is an increase in marginal cost?

Practice 12.5

Draw a kinked demand curve figure in which the oligopolist does not profit maximise at the kink.

The kinked demand curve: price and increases in marginal cost

Will the oligopolist pass an increase in their marginal cost onto customers? The increase in marginal cost is an increase for the oligopolist and for the oligopolist only. The oligopolist's rivals do not experience the cost increase. The increase in marginal cost, due to an increase in wage rates, shifts the marginal cost curve upward. The marginal cost increase occurs in the discontinuity and the outcome is shown in Figure 12.7.

Strangely, the increase in marginal cost (MC_0) is not passed on. The oligopolist fears that passing the cost increase onto its customers would cause a significant fall in demand. Consumers would shift to the cheaper products of rival producers. An increase in marginal cost would always cause a monopolist or a perfectly competitive firm to increase price but not the oligopolist. There appears to be a stable price at p_Π. For this reason oligopolistic market structures have been described as experiencing price stability. The oligopolist tends to use non-price incentives to increase sales. These include Green Shield stamps, gift vouchers and petrol shops that stock milk and bread.

FIGURE 12.5   The kinked demand curve and its strange marginal revenue curve

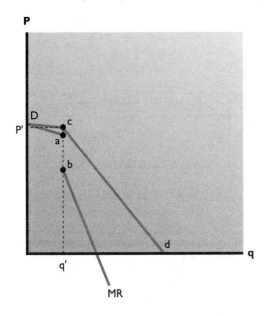

FIGURE 12.6   Oligopoly and profit maximisation

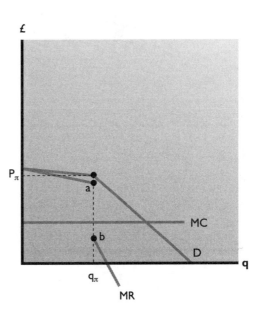

Practice 12.6

Draw a kinked demand curve in which a decrease in marginal cost leads to a fall in price and an increase in output.

A decrease in demand – what happens to price and output?

If demand falls due to a drop in income then the kinked demand curve shifts to the left. This is shown in Figure 12.8.

Not an easy figure to follow, so we will go through the outcomes one at a time. The firm profit maximises with a price of p and a quantity of Q when the kinked demand curve is D. The firm sets marginal revenue (MR) equal to marginal cost (MC). Now demand shifts to the left to the new demand curve, d. The new kinked demand curve, d, also has a new marginal revenue curve (mr). The profit-maximising oligopolist again equates marginal revenue to marginal cost. The profit-maximising quantity falls to q but the price charged stays constant at p. The oligopolist has changed quantity but not price. A fall in demand has not produced a price change.

In the 1930s, during the Great Depression and its resulting unemployment, it was argued that firms were quantity adjusters. Changes in demand led to quantity adjustments but not price adjustments. As the firm reduced its output, it also reduced its demand for variable factors of production. The principal

FIGURE 12.7   **The kinked demand curve: price and increases in marginal cost**

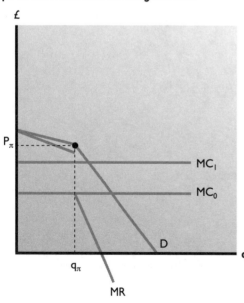

FIGURE 12.8   **The kinked demand curve: a fall in demand**

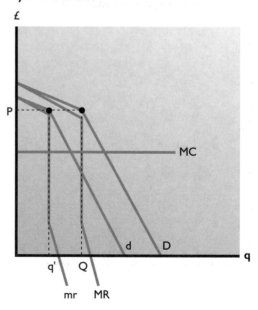

variable factor of production was and is labour. The kinked demand curve appeared to provide an explanation for the high unemployment of the 1930s.

Practice 12.7

Draw a figure for the oligopolist in which supernormal profits are earned. You need to insert an average cost curve.

Oligopolistic firms act collusively

Sometimes it is in people's interests to collude. An example would be a football match. At the end of the 1996/7 season West Ham United played Manchester United at Old Trafford. It is alleged, I repeat alleged, that some West Ham players placed a bet on the time of the first throw-in. You can get bets on the time of the first corner, first goal, number of goals, etc., on spread betting. Interestingly, West Ham kicked off. Was there collusion with Manchester United? Directly from the kick-off the ball was kicked into touch. It is alleged, I repeat alleged, that certain West Ham players won money from winning the spread bet.

It may also be in the interests of firms to collude. The kinked demand curve is based on firms trying to guess the reaction of rivals. There is uncertainty when people are forced to guess. This uncertainty can be removed if firms agree on a pattern of behaviour. In most countries colluding is illegal, as the victim of the collusion is usually a consumer. Oligopolistic firms may overcome legal action by forming trade associations where they meet to discuss issues facing the industry. They may even publish a trade journal that comments on their plans for the future.

There are two forms of collusive behaviour practised by the oligopolist. These are:

1. cartels
2. price leadership.

We will look at an example of each of these practices.

Cartels

Cartels are a form of collusion between firms to suppress competition among themselves. The classic cartel is the Organisation for Petroleum Exporting Countries (OPEC). OPEC tries to set a price for petrol. OPEC has used its cartel power to increase price by controlling output.

Again, there are many models of cartel behaviour. We will cover market sharing through non-price agreements.

Firms within the cartel agree a common price. An example could be the market for trainers. There are a limited number of firms in this market. The leaders appear to be Nike, Reebok and Adidas. Other firms include New Balance, Asics and Puma. The firms agree on a common price for the different shoes in the range. Go to a sports shop, look at a running magazine or www.sportsshoes.com. You will see Nike, Reebok, etc., offering a variety of shoes. All appear to offer and price shoes at the same prices. The mid-range shoe is usually priced at £50, while the top of the range is normally £80.

The colluding firms agree not to sell below the agreed price. The firms are free to use non-price aspects to secure their market share. These non-price aspects include advertising, packaging and product design. All the firms in the market have something unique in the design of their training shoes. Table 12.1 shows the key design feature of a number of running shoes.

Table 12.1 **Sports shoes and key characteristic**

Company	Feature
Nike	Air
Puma	Cell
Asics	Gel

The firms in Table 12.1 use product development as the non-price method for securing market share and growth. You will reply that running shoes are offered at sale prices. This is true. The sports shop pays the firm the wholesale price and sells to the customer at the agreed retail price. If the shop cannot sell the shoes purchased from the wholesaler then it reduces price at their expense. The shop suffers and not the firm.

The local fish and chip shop, Paps, had a monopoly of the market. There were other fast food outlets but no other fish and chip shop. Recently a new fish and chip shop, Fresh Fry, opened not 50 yards from Paps. The economist in me expected this increase in supply to lead to competition and a fall in price. Unfortunately, I was, as usual, wrong. The two shops have identical prices. The competition appears to be non-priced based. I should have read this chapter and practised my microeconomics.

Practice 12.8

How do you think Paps and Fresh Fry engage in non-price competition? What would you do to move demand towards your restaurant?

Price leadership

In this section, we will cover price leadership by the dominant firm in an oligopolistic market structure. Price leadership is a way of co-ordinating price behaviour allowing mutually interdependent firm to secure high profits. There are other forms of price leadership models such as price leadership by a low-cost firm and barometric price leadership, but the dominant firm price leadership model provides a feel for the three.

The dominant firm leads and the other firms follow. This model is also known as leader-follower pricing. Obviously, the leader sets the market price and the followers take this price. The leader has the largest market share. An example could be British Telecom and the followers are the competing telephone call providers such as Cable & Wireless, Mercury, Orange and your local cable firm.

The dominant firm knows the market demand curve and also has knowledge of the cost structure of the followers. Knowledge of the followers' cost structure allows the leader to form an estimate of how much the followers will supply at different prices. This permits the leader to estimate the total supply curve of the followers. From this, the leader can work out the amount of total supply that will be supplied by the followers. This sounds complicated but consider the following. The leader knows that at a price of 10p per minute, total market demand is 20 000 calls. The followers will supply a total of 15 000 calls, so the leader will have the remaining 5 000 as its demand. If the price were 5p per minute then total market demand is 25 000. Followers would supply a total of 10 000 at the price of 5p, so the leader will have 15 000 as its demand. The leader, therefore, estimates its demand curve. This is shown in Figure 12.9.

The total market demand curve (D) and the supply curve of the followers (S_F) are shown in the left-hand figure. If the price is p_0 then the followers take all of the demand. The leader's demand at p_0 is zero. With a price of p_1 the followers have demand share p_1 – a, and the leader has demand share a – b. Therefore at a price of p_1 the leader has demand equal to a – b. Again, at a price of p_2 the followers

FIGURE 12.9 Price leadership: the dominant firm's demand curve

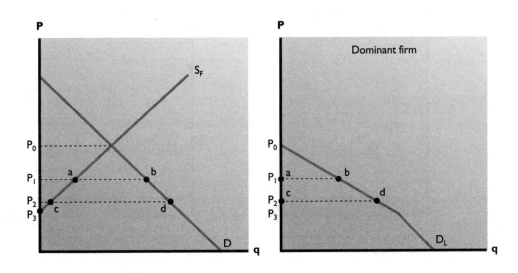

share is p_2 – c and the leader has c – d of total market demand. With a price of p_2 the leader has demand c – d. When the price is p_3 the followers do not supply anything, so from p_3 all the market demand is the leader's demand. The leader's demand curve is the market demand curve from price p_3 and below. This information allows us to construct the dominant firm's demand curve. This is carried out in the right-hand figure and is labelled D_L. The leader's demand curve is kinked. We can now introduce the firm's marginal revenue and marginal cost curves. This is shown in Figure 12.10.

The dominant firm profit maximises and produces quantity q_L and prices at p_L. This is the market price. The total market supply at price p_L is q_M. Of this total supply, the followers produce q_F and the leader produces the rest, q_M – q_F. If the followers step out of line then the leader will take aggressive behaviour towards them. One policy would be a heavy advertising campaign such as Friends and Family. Alternatively, the leader could lower price to p_3. This would reduce the followers' demand to zero. This would cause suffering to the leader as profits would be reduced but the damaged caused to the followers could be disastrous.

Practice 12.9

Another essay question.

'Collusive behaviour is said to be unstable as it is in the interests of firms to cheat and break away from the agreement.' What sanctions, if any, does the dominant price leader firm possess to discipline the followers?

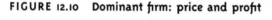

FIGURE 12.10   Dominant firm: price and profit

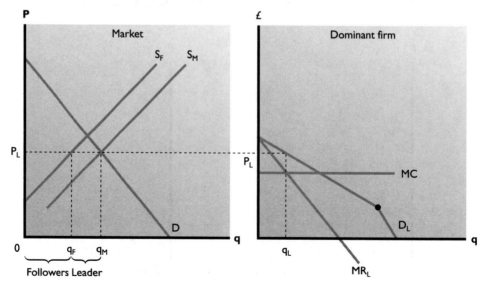

The four market structures
– an overview

This chapter and the last have covered the four market structures of perfect competition, monopolistic competition, oligopoly and monopoly. The four are listed in order of performance as far as society is concerned. Perfect competition generates a number of ideal outcomes. The other market structures can be judged against the golden outcomes of perfect competition. If a market structure's performance is worrying in terms of allocative efficiency or profits, then there is something wrong with the way the market structure conducts itself. The poor conduct is due to problems with its structure. Table 12.2 summarises the performance of the four market structures.

Table 12.2 The market structures and performance

Performance	Percom[1]	Monocom[2]	Oligopoly	Monopoly
Allocative efficiency P and MC	SR[3] Yes LR[4] Yes P = MC	SR No LR No P > MC	SR No LR No P > MC	SR No LR No P > MC
Productive efficiency AC minimum	SR No LR Yes	SR No LR No	SR No LR No	SR No LR No
Profits P and AC	SR P $\neq$ AC LR P = AC	SR P $\neq$ AC LR P = AC	SR P $\neq$ AC LR P $\neq$ AC	SR P $\neq$ AC LR P $\neq$ AC

Notes: 1 = Perfect competition
2 = Monopolistic competition
3 = short-run
4 = long-run

Table 12.2 shows that of the six targets perfect competition hits four, one in the short-run and all three in the long-run. Monopolistic competition only scores one. This is for normal profits in the long-run. Oligopoly and monopoly score zero. (This is based on the comparison being carried out using a U-shaped average cost curve.) This is no surprise. Competition, be it perfect or monopolistic, is better than oligopoly or monopoly. My experience of the local duopoly between Paps and Fresh Fry shows the price stability of oligopoly, whereas the competitive nature of foreign exchange bureaux on Ibiza recommends competition.

Practice 12.10

The next time you are shopping, try to identify examples of competitive and non-competitive behaviour in the high street.

Summary

This chapter has attempted to explain two market structures: Monopolistic competition and oligopoly:

✓ The coverage of monopolistic competition was in the tradition of perfect competition and monopoly in that certain assumptions were cited and performance outcomes generated.

✓ Unfortunately, the assumptions and outcomes of monopolistic competition appear to clash. Monopolistically competitive firms engage in product differentiation to give themselves a competitive edge. It is the world of branding, yet it is assumed that the existence of supernormal profits allows for the free entry of new firms. Presumably, the branding is a form of barrier to entry and is created with the dual intentions of attracting customers and distracting rivals.

✓ The coverage of monopolistic competition is, I believe, a full and fair coverage. I cannot say the same with respect to oligopoly.

✓ Oligopoly features action, reaction and interdependence between firms. The interdependent nature of oligopolistic markets has allowed many models of the action and reaction. These models can be quite demanding.

✓ I have covered one non-collusive model, the kinked demand curve, and one collusive model, the dominant price leader. This is not a definitive coverage. The purpose of this book has been to take the fear out of microeconomics. If I were to cover the plethora of oligopolistic models then I would be putting the fear of microeconomics into you. When you are comfortable with the two oligopolistic models covered here then please venture to the detailed coverage in other textbooks.

The next chapter looks at the market for factors of production. Chapter 13 is the last microeconomics chapter. We are nearly there! Chapter 13 underpins the cost and production coverage of Chapters 5 and 6.

Answers for Chapter 12

Answer 12.1

Arsenal football shirts are a monopoly product. Spurs shirts are not a rival, neither are Celtic shirts.

Answer 12.2

The figure looks like:

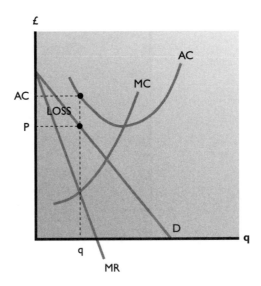

It is a difficult figure to draw so practice is required.

Answer 12.3

	Perfect competition	*Monopolistic competition*
P and MC	Yes	No
P and AC	Yes	Yes
Idle capacity?	No	Yes
Profits	Normal	Normal

Monopolistic competition falls down on allocative and productive efficiency.

Answer 12.4

This is a difficult diagram to draw accurately. The key is practice. Look at the kinked demand curve in the chapter. Remember the relationship between the demand curve and the marginal revenue curve (the marginal revenue curve cuts the horizontal at half the distance the demand curve does).

Answer 12.5

The figure looks like:

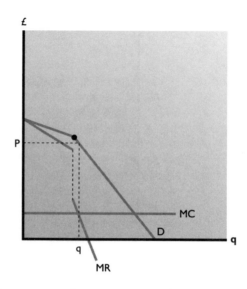

The oligopolist does not profit maximise at the kink because marginal cost does not equal marginal revenue in the discontinuity. Marginal revenue equals marginal cost below the discontinuity.

Answer 12.6

The figure looks like:

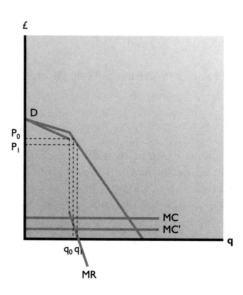

Answer 12.7

The figure looks like:

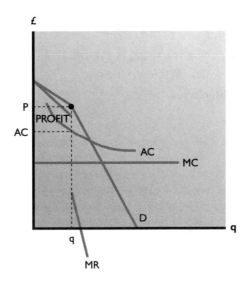

Answer 12.8

Interestingly, Paps has gone upmarket by offering three-course lunches to OAPS, while Fresh Fry has refurbished its restaurant. Prices, however, remain identical.

Answer 12.9

Again, look at Chapter 14 for hints on answering essay questions. The coverage for this question should include:

1. Introduction.
2. Definition of oligopoly and price leadership.
3. An example of price leadership with a figure.
4. Policies used by the price leader to discipline misbehaving followers:
    a. predatory pricing
    b. advertising
    c. barriers to competition.
5. Summary and conclusion.

Answer 12.10

Look at:

1. product differentiation
2. advertising
3. whether the advertising is informative or persuasive
4. brand loyalty characteristics
5. price differences.

THE MARKET FOR FACTORS OF PRODUCTION

Why do workers get what they get?

This will help

This chapter covers the market for factors of production. This topic can be quite demanding and it is for this reason that I have placed it near the end of the book. Do not put the customers off too early! Students tend to find the techniques involved complex. However, this is the last chapter of the microeconomics coverage. I can hear you cheer? Again, we will go through the analysis sequentially and build an understanding of the topic with examples. This chapter complements the previous work of Chapters 5 and 6 on production and costs. You are therefore advised to read those chapters before you start this topic.

Thankfully, workers are paid. The essential question is 'Why do workers get what they get?'. We will try to provide an answer to this question as well as provide other answers.

Introduction

The factors of production include labour, land, capital and the entrepreneur. In combination, the factors of production produce the output. They need rewards. I need a reward to write this book. You require rewards to get out of bed and go to work. The level of the reward earned by each of the factors of production depends on who has power in the market for the factor.

I am a member of a trade union, NATFHE. Collectively, we organise to limit the power of our employer in setting our level of pay. Is the factor market for lecturers competitive? We will look at competitive and non-competitive factor markets. The answers generated are revealing.

By the end of this chapter you will understand:

✓ the reward earned by each factor of production
✓ why the demand for a factor of production is a derived demand

✓ the labour market and wages
✓ the capital market and interest
✓ the difference between competitive and non-competitive factor markets.

The rewards earned by factors of production

Each factor of production needs to be paid a reward to entice it to enter the productive process. Table 13.1 shows the reward earned by each factor.

Table 13.1 Factors of production and their rewards

The factor of production	The factor's reward
Labour	Wages
Capital	Interest
Land	Rent
Raw materials and energy	Prices
Entrepreneurs	Profit

Labour and wages

Workers are paid wages. Wages include salaries. Wages are approximately 70 per cent of total variable cost. Labour is usually the first variable factor to be dropped when demand for the firm's product declines. For employers, wages have to reflect the productivity of the workers.

Capital and interest

Capital is used as a catch-all and includes the plant, machinery, computers, shelves, railway tracks and so on. The money to purchase the firm's capital structure, its fixed costs, can either be borrowed or taken from retained profits. If it is borrowed then the firm needs to pay for the privilege. The price of capital is interest. Students do not, I believe, need to be lectured on borrowing and interest. If you run an overdraft then your bank will charge you interest for the privilege. If capital is funded from retained profits then the firm is sacrificing savings and the associated profits. The rate of interest represents the opportunity cost of these foregone savings.

Land and rent

Land is a fixed factor. The total amount of land in a country is fixed. Land is the ground on which production takes place. Land could be used for growing apples in an orchard, building a leisure centre or playing tennis at Wimbledon. In microeconomics, the reward paid to land is rent. The use of the term 'rent' evolved in the nineteenth century.

As an example, we could think of a plot of land that is fixed in its supply. Due to climatic conditions, the plot of land can only be used for the production of oranges. The supply curve of land is vertical or perfectly inelastic. The price of land is demand determined. Demand can change but supply cannot. The price or rent of the plot is shown in Figure 13.1.

The fixed supply of land for the production of oranges is supply curve S. The present demand curve for the plot of land is D_0 and the price of the plot of land is p_0. This is the rent. The rent or price of the plot is determined by demand. Rent is completely demand determined. The rent is determined by the demand for the land. The demand for the land is determined by the demand for oranges.

If the demand for oranges increases, this leads to the price of oranges increasing. Following this, the demand for land increases, as there are higher profits to be earned from producing the higher priced oranges. The demand curve for land shifts to D_1. The price of land increases to p_1. This price increase does not lead to the price of oranges changing. Rent or the price of land is not a cost entering into the determination of the price of oranges. Rather, it is the price of oranges which determines the price or rent of land. The increase in the price of oranges led to the shift of the demand curve for land, D_1, and the increase in the price or rent of land. The price or rent of the land is determined by the price of oranges. The price of oranges is not determined by the price of land.

FIGURE 13.1 Land and rent

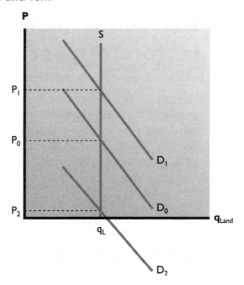

If the demand for land collapsed to D_2 and the price of land fell to p_2, then the owner of the land would still supply the land. The land has no alternative use. The fall in the price of land would not lead to a fall in the price of oranges. The fall in the price of oranges is the fact that has led to the shift of the demand curve for land to D_2.

Changes in the demand for the products or services produced on the land determine the rent. Changes in the rent do not influence the price of the product.

Raw materials, energy and prices

The variable factors of production, such as heating, light and steel, are bought in markets and firms pay either the going rate or a negotiated price depending on their market power. The prices paid enter into the firm's costs.

The entrepreneur and profit

We have covered the entrepreneur and profits on a number of occasions in this book. It is sufficient to say that the entrepreneur would be delighted with supernormal profits, satisfied with normal profits and disappointed with losses. The entrepreneur needs to make a return to make the risk of organising the factors of production and selling the product worthwhile.

Practice 13.1

Lord's Cricket Ground can be used only for cricket matches. The demand for cricket falls. What will happen to the rent paid to Lord's for the use of the ground? What happens first: the change in the attendance price or the change in rent?

Derived demand and factors of production

The demand for this book is not a derived demand. It is a final demand. The demand for the factors of production used in the production of this book is a derived demand. Final-stage demand by consumers for McDonald's Big Macs or computer floppy disks give rise to derived demands for labour, capital, land, raw materials, energy and entrepreneurs. The demand for labour is derived from the need to produce the final product.

Practice 13.2

There are lecturers and graduates. Which is the input and which is the output? Which one is the derived demand?

The labour market and wages

The demand for labour is a derived demand. Labour is hired as a factor of production in the production process. People supply their labour in return for a wage. The labour market can be analysed in at least four ways. The analysis and the outcomes depend on the competitive nature of labour demand and labour supply. The situation in which both labour demand and supply are competitive is analysed first before we move onto more demanding models.

Competition in labour demand and labour supply

This section looks at competitive labour demand and labour supply. The labour market does not have any elements, such as unions, interfering with the competitive process. Labour demand is analysed first.

Labour demand

The demand for labour demand of the firm depends on two factors:

✓ the product being demanded
✓ labour being productive.

The productivity of labour can be measured by its average and marginal returns. The relationship between output (Q) and labour (L) is shown in Table 13.2.

Table 13.2 **The average and marginal products of labour**

Q	L	APL = Q/L	MPL = ΔQ/ΔL
0	0		
			2
2	1	2	
			4
6	2	3	
			6
12	3	4	
			4
16	4	4	
			2
18	5	3.6	
			−3
15	6	2.5	

The first two columns in Table 13.2 are the production function. The third column is the average product of labour (APL). This is calculated by dividing output by the labour used to produce that output (APL = Q/L). The fourth column is the marginal product of labour (MPL) and is calculated by measuring the change in output as more units of labour are employed ($\Delta Q/\Delta L$). The MPL shows the marginal productivity of labour or marginal returns, while the APL shows the average productivity of labour or average returns to labour. The production function, the average product of labour and the marginal product of labour are shown in Figure 13.2.

The production function is S-shaped and shows that the maximum output of 18 occurs when the marginal product of labour is zero. When MPL is positive the production function is rising. If the MPL is negative then production is falling. The

FIGURE 13.2 Total, average and marginal products of labour

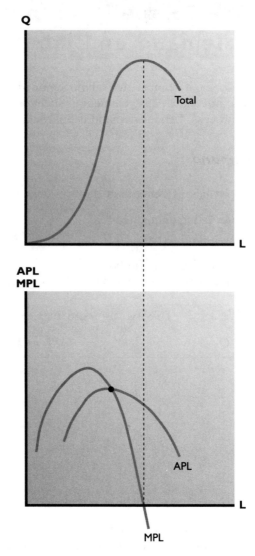

MPL curve is n-shaped and shows rising and falling marginal returns. Marginal product or returns are at their highest when the third worker is employed.

The relationship between the average product of labour (APL) and the marginal product of labour (MPL) is that:

✓ the APL curve is rising as long as MPL is greater than APL
✓ the APL curve is falling when MPL is below APL
✓ the APL curve is at its greatest when MPL equals MPL.

This coverage is very similar to the total, marginal and average variable cost curves coverage. Remember that with a U-shaped average cost curve, marginal cost is below average cost when average cost is falling. If marginal cost is above average cost, then the average cost curve is rising.

Practice 13.3

The average product of labour is rising. What can be said about the marginal product of labour?

The average product of labour is at its highest. What can be said about the marginal product of labour?

Revenue products

If we know the price charged by the firm then we can calculate the firm's total revenue product of labour (TRP$_L$). The production function tells us the relationship between output and labour. For example, three workers produce 12 units. If the price of the product is £2 then the total revenue product of labour (TRP$_L$) is £24. The revenue generated from employing three workers is the output they produce (Q = 12) multiplied by the price of the product (P = £2). Knowledge of the production function and the price of the product also allow us to calculate the marginal revenue product of labour (MRP$_L$) and the average revenue product of labour (ARP$_L$). Using the production function information permits us to calculate the total, average and marginal revenue products. This is shown in Table 13.3.

Table 13.3 Labour and its revenue products

TRP$_L$	L	ARP$_L$ = APL*P	MRP$_L$ = MPL*P
0	0		4
4	1	4	8
12	2	6	12
24	3	8	8
32	4	8	4
36	5	7.2	−6
30	6	5	

The total, average and marginal revenue products of labour are all simply the total, average and marginal products of labour multiplied by the price of the product. So:

✓ $TRP_L = P*Q$ minus the total revenue product of labour simply shows the total revenue produced from selling the output produced by the workers.

✓ $ARP_L = TRP_L/L = (Q/L)*P = APL*P$ minus the average revenue product of labour shows the average efficiency of labour in money terms. The average efficiency of labour (APL) is converted into money.

✓ $MRP_L = \Delta TRP_L/\Delta L = \Delta Q/\Delta L*P = MPL*L$ minus the marginal revenue product of labour depends on two aspects. The first part is the marginal efficiency of the workforce (MPL) and the second is the market price (P) of the product. The workers could be very efficient and have a high MPL. One example is farmers. If the price of their output is low due to the collapse of a foreign market such as Russia or Malaysia, then the MRP_L will be low. It is important to separate the physical and the monetary efficiency. The marginal revenue product of labour can be considered to be the firm's demand curve for labour.

Practice 13.4

There is a favourable shift in the demand for your product. This leads to an increase in price. What will this mean for:

✓ the marginal product of labour
✓ the marginal revenue product of labour?

Practice 13.5

If your firm's management accountant told you that the marginal revenue product of labour was zero, what could you conclude concerning the firm's:

✓ total revenue product of labour
✓ average revenue product of labour?

The cost of labour

If the labour market is competitive then the intersection of labour demand and labour supply will produce the market-clearing wage. The labour market is competitive because neither buyers of labour (firms) nor sellers of labour (workers) can influence the price of labour, the wage rate. This is the world of the firm being a wage taker just as the perfectly competitive firm was a price taker. It is not the world of trade unions or large employers.

If the firm is a wage taker then the total cost of labour (TC_L) is the market wage (w) multiplied by the number of workers employed (L). Thus:

$TC_L = w*L$.

A wage rate of £10 a day produces the total cost schedule for labour of Table 13.4.

Table 13.4 **The supply of labour (MC_L) in a competitive labour market**

w	L	TC_L	MC_L
0	0	0	
			10
10	1	10	
			10
10	2	20	
			10
10	3	30	
			10
10	4	40	

The relationship between the total cost of labour (TC_L) and workers employed (L) is a positive linear relationship and the result is that the marginal cost of labour (MC_L) is constant. Figure 13.3 shows this relationship.

The marginal cost of labour (MC_L) is constant because the wage rate is constant. The firm can now use the information of the constant MC_L and the marginal revenue product of labour (MRP_L) to calculate the number of workers to employ in order to profit maximise.

FIGURE 13.3 The total cost of labour (TC_L) and the marginal cost of labour (MC_L)

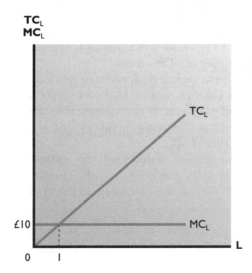

Practice 13.6

Is Tesco, the supermarket chain, a wage taker or a wage maker?

The profit-maximising level of labour

The profit-maximising firm equates marginal revenue to marginal cost to find the profit-maximising quantity. The firm discovers the optimum amount of labour to employ by equating the marginal revenue product of labour (MRP_L) to the marginal cost of labour (MC_L). This is similar to the profit-maximising behaviour of the firm.

| Profit-maximising output | $MR = MC$ |
| Profit-maximising labour | $MRP_L = MC_L$ |

The firm is attempting to maximise the difference between the total revenue product of labour (TRP_L) and the total cost of labour (TC_L) in the same way as the firm tries to maximise the difference between total revenue (TR) and total variable cost (TVC). The TRP_L is the firm's total revenue while the TC_L is the firm's total variable cost. We are simplifying the analysis. It is the main aim of this book. We are treating labour as the catch-all or representative variable factor. Thus the total cost of labour (w*L) is the firm's total variable cost. In the short-run, the firm profit maximises when the difference between TR and TVC is at its greatest. The profit maximising level of labour is shown in Figure 13.4.

The top section of Figure 13.4 shows the TRP_L and the TC_L curves. The firm should hire L* of workers to maximise the difference between its total revenue and its total variable cost.

The bottom section of Figure 13.4 shows three curves. The MC_L curve is shown as a horizontal line. This reflects the fact that the firm is a wage taker. The average cost of labour (AC_L) equals the marginal cost of labour (MC_L). This is the equivalent of marginal cost and average variable cost. We know that when marginal cost is constant it equals average variable cost. The average revenue product of labour (ARP_L) is maximised when it equals the marginal revenue product of labour (MRP_L). The ARP_L curve will allow us to calculate the level of contributions made towards the firm's total fixed cost.

The firm equates marginal revenue product of labour (MRP_L) and the marginal cost of labour (MC_L) to obtain the level of labour to hire. MRP_L and MC_L are equal at points a and e. The profit maximising level of labour is at point a. Look at the top section. At point a, the firm is making a negative contribution to total fixed cost as TC_L is more than TRP_L.

When the firm is employing the optimum level of labour, L*, the unit contribution is ARP_L less AC_L or c−b. The total contribution is the shaded area, the area abcd. We can use this information to produce the firm's demand curve for labour.

Practice 13.7

Your firm can hire any number of workers at a wage of £250 per week. What is the lowest marginal revenue product of labour that would make hiring labour and producing output worthwhile?

The firm's labour demand curve

If the cost of labour (MC_L) falls then the firm will employ more workers. This shown in Figure 13.5.

FIGURE 13.4 **Labour and profit maximisation**

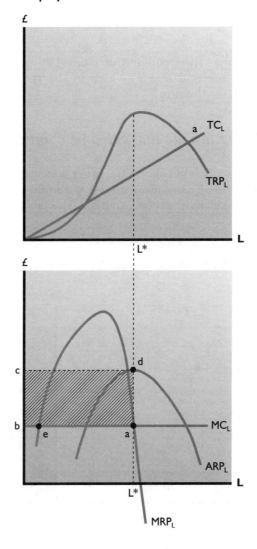

The left-hand figure shows the firm while the right-hand figure shows the market-clearing wage. The firm takes the wage from the market and it becomes their marginal cost of labour. The firm aims to hire the number of workers that will enable it to maximise profits and contributions. This occurs when MRP_L and MC_L are equal. The firm can maximise contributions and profits at points 0, 1 and 2 in the firm figure. The lower marginal cost of labour or wage results in the firm increasing its demand for workers. The firm's demand curve for labour is the marginal revenue product of labour curve below the average revenue product curve. Points 0, 1 and 2 are on the firm's demand curve. Thus wage rates of w_0, w_1 and w_3 are marginal costs of labour which the firm can cope with given their MRP_L curve. The wage rate w_h is too high for the firm. This wage and marginal cost of labour lie above the firm's ARP_L curve. If the firm employed workers when the wage was w_h it would make negative contributions to total fixed cost. Therefore, the firm's demand curve for labour is the MRP_L curve below the ARP_L curve.

Practice 13.8

Figure 13.5 shows three equilibrium points between the MRP_L and the MC_L curves. These are points 0, 1 and 2. Which of the three points produces the greatest contributions for the firm?

Competitive labour market and competitive producer

The previous section has shown the firm's demand curve for labour when the firm is a wage taker. We will continue with this assumption and add another: that the firm is also a price taker in its product market. The labour equilibrium condition is:

FIGURE 13.5 The firm's demand for labour and a competitive labour market

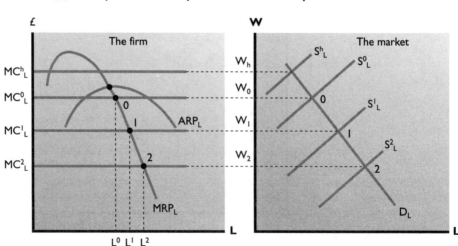

$$MRP_L = MC_L$$

Remember that the marginal revenue product of labour is the marginal product of labour (MP_L) multiplied by the firm's price (P). The firm, remember, is a wage taker. So:

$$MRP_L = MP_L*P = MC_L = w$$

The marginal cost of the firm shows the relationship between changes in output and changes in total cost. If the marginal cost is £4 then this is the outcome of the wage paid to hire the extra worker and the extra output produced by the worker. If the wage were £100 then the worker must have produced 25 units. Thus:

$$MC = w/MP_L = £100/25 = £4$$

We can use previous knowledge to show that marginal cost equals price. The wage rate (w) is the marginal cost of labour (MC_L) and the labour equilibrium for the firm is $MRP_L = MC_L$. The marginal revenue product of labour is MP_L*P. Thus:

$$MC = w/MP_L = MC_L/ MP_L = MRP_L/ MP_L = MP_L*P/MP_L = P$$

This should be familiar to you from the coverage of perfect competition. The perfectly competitive firm prices at marginal cost. The firm hires labour up to the point where MRP_L equals MC_L and produces output up to the point where price equals marginal cost. The two conditions are equivalent.

Competitive in labour market	*Competitive in output market*
$MRP_L = MC_L$	P = MC

Practice 13.9

Draw the labour equilibrium figure for the firm and the output equilibrium figure for the firm.

A non-competitive labour market

Competition and exploitation

The competitive labour market allows the firm to hire any number of workers at the market-clearing wage (w). This is the firm's marginal cost of labour. Workers are paid the market-clearing wage and this equates to the marginal revenue product of the last worker employed. The firm makes profits from the efficiency of its workforce. If the first worker produces five units of output and the firm can sell each of the five at a price of £5, then the marginal revenue product of labour

(MRPL) of the first worker was £25. If the firm hires the worker in a competitive labour market and pays a wage of £20, then the firm makes a contribution towards fixed cost of £5 from the first worker's effort. The firm stops hiring workers when the extra revenue form the worker's effort (MRP_L) equals the extra cost of the hiring the worker (MC_L). **Workers with MRP_L > MC_L are exploited.** There is very little they can do to alter this situation as they have no power in the labour market.

Practice 13.10

Use the firm's labour figure to show the level of exploitation resulting from MRP_L > MC_L. What is this area equal to?

Monopsony

Monopsony is the labour market equivalent of product market monopoly. The monopolist is the sole supplier in the output market. The monopsonist is the sole buyer of labour. It is difficult to think of a national monopsonist but there are examples of local monopsonists. Coal mining is an example of monopsony, as is farm employment dominated by a single landowner. In both examples, the provider of employment is protected from competition by barriers. The most important are geographical barriers and collusion. The employer is the only major employer locally and it is therefore difficult for workers to obtain alternative employment locally. Even if they could secure local employment in the same or alternative work, it would be in the employer's interests to collude against the workers and keep their wages below the competitive wage. Remember that the competitive wage is the marginal cost of labour.

The total wage bill is the wage paid multiplied by the number of workers employed (w*L). If the monopsonist wishes to hire more workers then it will be necessary to offer a higher wage. The higher wage will have to be paid to all the workers. The wage paid is the average cost of labour (AC_L). This is shown in Table 13.5.

Table 13.5 The supply of labour (AC_L) and a non-competitive labour market

L	Wage (AC_L)	Total wage	Marginal cost of labour
0		0	
			3
1	3	3	
			5
2	4	8	
			7
3	5	15	
			9
4	6	24	

The first worker is paid a wage of £3. The average wage is also £3. Thus the wage equals the average cost of labour (AC$_L$). The monopsonist wishes to hire a second worker. The wage needs to rise to £4 to attract the second worker. Both the second and the first worker will be paid £4. The total wage bill is £8, the average wage is £4 and the marginal cost of labour is £5. The marginal cost of labour is the £4 to secure the second worker plus the increase in wage of £1 for the first worker. This results in a marginal cost of labour of £5.

The wage paid is the average cost of labour. This is the monopsonist's labour supply curve. The marginal cost of labour lies above the average cost. The fact that the monopsonist increases the average cost of labour or wage in order to attract more workers causes the marginal cost of labour to rise. The monopsonist hires labour up to the point where the marginal revenue product of labour equals the marginal cost of labour. This is shown in Figure 13.6.

The monopsonist employs a workforce of L$_M$ and pays a wage of w$_M$. The workers are exploited because they produce a marginal revenue product of labour of A but are only paid a wage of M. The worker gets a wage, the average cost of labour, that is less than the worker's marginal revenue product. In a competitive labour market, the workers would be paid a wage of w$_C$ and there would be employment of L$_C$. The competitive market-clearing equilibrium is at point B.

Practice 13.11

Is the monopsonist a wage taker or a wage maker? What do you expect the workers to do?

FIGURE 13.6 Monopsony and the wage

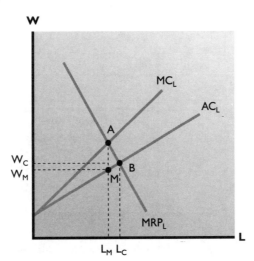

Enter the union

The trade union enters the firm's labour market with the aim of protecting the workforce. The union will control the supply of workers. Again, the labour environment will be uncompetitive. The union will act as a monopoly supplier of labour and use its power to challenge the power of the monopsonist. The union can have numerous objectives. We will look at only one union objective: maximising the wage of the existing workforce. The union will attempt to get the monopsonist to pay the workers a wage where the workers' entire marginal revenue product is paid as a wage. This would be point A in Figure 13.6. All exploitation would be removed. The union will use its power or strength to set a wage at which all exploitation is removed. This is shown in Figure 13.7.

The union sets w_U as the minimum wage. It will not work at a wage below w_U. If the monopsonist tried to pay below w_U then the union would react with industrial action. The monopsonists' labour supply curve and average cost of labour (AC_L) curve becomes w_UuAC_L. The union makes the monopsonist's supply of labour curve horizontal and AC_L equals MC_L when the labour supply curve is horizontal. The firm equates the new MC_L with the MRP_L and pays a wage of w_U. The equilibrium labour situation is still L_M. The union has achieved its objective of securing the maximum wage for the unionised workforce without threatening the employment prospects of the existing workforce.

Practice 13.12

How would the analysis change if the objective of the union were to want to secure the labour market-clearing situation for the unionised workforce? This is the market-clearing position point B in Figure 13.7.

FIGURE 13.7 Monopsony and the union

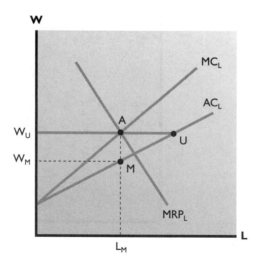

Capital and interest

Capital is the fixed cost structure of the firm. The firm needs to pay for the capital structure. The fixed costs can be financed by bank borrowing or using retained profits. Whichever method is used to finance the purchase of the capital structure the rate of interest will play a part. If the funding is provided by the banking sector then the firm will need to repay the loan over a period of time. In addition, the firm will be required to pay interest on any outstanding debt. If the capital is financed from retained profits then the company must be aware of the opportunity cost of using the retained profits for financing its fixed cost expenditure. The firm could deposit the retained profits in the highest possible savings account. The interest earned from the best alternative use of the retained profits is the opportunity cost of the retained profits.

The relationship between capital and interest is negative. An intuitive explanation is that the government increases the rate of interest to control the demand for credit in the economy. The demand for fixed factors or capital is a demand for credit, finance or funding. Increases in the rate of interest will lead to firms' reducing their demand for capital, as capital has become more expensive.

The marginal efficiency of capital

The marginal efficiency of capital (MEK) is the return earned on capital projects or fixed costs. In a simple example, the firm has total fixed costs of £100. This is its capital structure. The total revenue obtained from using the fixed factors in their most efficient use is £250. The total variable cost of production is £110. The firm makes a profit of £40 (TR – TC) and a return on the initial capital structure of 40 per cent. The firm should be content to pay a rate of interest up to 39 per cent to finance its capital structure.

Firms should rank their capital projects in order of their MEKs. The first capital project undertaken by the firm should be the project with the highest marginal efficiency of capital. The last capital project to be undertaken by the firm should be the one yielding the lowest MEK. This suggests that a firm's potential capital projects can be scheduled against its marginal efficiencies. This is shown in Figure 13.8.

The MEK schedule is downward sloping. The first capital project undertaken is the one yielding the highest return. Firms should be able to form an estimate of their MEK. If they cannot estimate their MEKs then it will be very difficult to gauge the profitability of their capital projects. The Millennium Dome is a capital project and a very expensive capital project at that. The capital cost is estimated to be in

the order of £750 million. Critics are of the opinion that the government does not know the marginal efficiency of the Dome. It is also argued that the MEK is so low that the government should have used the capital for other, more important, uses – such as increasing the pay of university lecturers!

The MEK and interest rates

If a capital project has a marginal efficiency of 9 per cent then it is only profitable if the capital can be financed at a rate of interest of less than 9 per cent. The Bank of England's Monetary Policy Committee determines interest rates in the United Kingdom. Financial institutions take the rate set by the Bank of England as the minimum rate and adjust the rates at which they are prepared to lend based on the Bank of England's rate of interest. Financial institutions such as merchant banks adjust their lending rates to include a premium to cover the risk or creditworthy status of the borrower. Higher interest rates will make some capital projects unprofitable as the MEK is now below the higher rate of interest. The relationship between the marginal efficiency of capital and the rate of interest is shown in Figure 13.9.

The financial community sets a rate of interest of i_0 and is happy to supply capital to anyone who can repay the loan. The supply of capital at interest rate i_0 is S_{K0}. The capital market equilibrium is capital project's K_0 at point 0. The authorities decide to increase the rate of interest to curb the threat of price inflation. The rate of interest rises to i_1. Capital projects between K_0 and K_1 are now unprofitable. The new equilibrium in the capital market is point 1. The higher rate of interest has killed off a number of capital projects.

Practice 13.13

What impact did the rise in UK interest rates from May 1997 to October 1998 have on the number of capital projects over the period?

FIGURE 13.8 The marginal efficiency of capital

MEK

MEK schedule

0   K

FIGURE 13.9 The MEK and the rate of interest

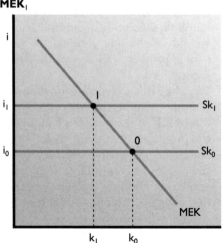

Practice 13.14

The financial crisis in Asia during 1998 increased the risk premium attached to loans. Banks were frightened by the risk of default. What would this do to the MEK schedule?

Summary

This chapter's coverage is not intuitively appealing. The concepts covered do not have readily available real-world examples. Despite these drawbacks, an understanding of the factors of production and their rewards and markets is important.

✓ The demand for the various factors of production is a derived demand. The demand for David Beckham is a derived demand. It is derived from the fact that some people have a demand to watch Manchester United play football. They are willing to pay to watch United games. Manchester United combines the required factors of production, one of which is Beckham. Beckham needs to be rewarded. He is rewarded very well.

✓ All factors of production need to be paid a reward in order to entice them into providing their services. I like my work but I work to live. I, as a labour factor, look at the wage reward I will get. The same is true of all the factors of production.

✓ Rent is the one quirky reward. Land is rewarded by rent and the important thing to recognise is that the demand for the product produced on the land determines the rental reward of the land. The rent does not determine the price of the final product. Rather it is the demand for the final product which determine the rent. When Arsenal decided to play some of its Champions League matches at Wembley during 1998/9, it was the high demand by Arsenal supporters which determined the high rent Wembley plc charged Arsenal for the use of the stadium.

✓ The reward or price paid to a factor of production depends on the nature of the factor market. If the market is competitive then the factor will receive a reward equal to its marginal cost. If the producer of the good has power as a monopsonist then the factors of production will be exploited. When labour is faced by a monopsonist, the usual reaction is to use countervailing power in the form of a trade union. My trade union bargains with a single group to determine my wage and wage increases.

✓ The other big factor, capital, requires a reward. Capital's reward is interest. I do not believe that students require too much coverage on debt and interest payments. Capital projects yield a return to the firm and are profitable if their marginal efficiency exceeds the cost of borrowing.

The microeconomics coverage has ended. The final chapter looks at taking the fear out of assessments in microeconomics. Presumably you read this book because you were frightened by various aspects of microeconomics. The biggest fear factor is, I think, that students realise they will be required to be assessed in a subject they are initially scared of. The final chapter looks at methods of coping with assessment.

Answers for Chapter 13

Answer 13.1

1. A fall in the demand for cricket will lead to a reduction in the rent paid for the use of Lord's.
2. The fall in the price of attendance will precede the fall in the rent.

[*Note*: In the mid-1990s the price of wheat fall significantly. This led to the rent of wheat-growing land falling. Did the fall in the rent lead to the fall in the price of wheat, or was it the other way round?]

Answer 13.2

1. Lecturers are the input. They are a factor of production. I know that at times they do not appear to be a factor of production, but they are.
2. Graduates are the output.
3. The demand for lecturers is the derived demand. If the demand for graduates falls, then the demand for lecturers will decrease.

Answer 13.3

1. If the average product of labour is rising, then the marginal product of labour must be greater than the average product of labour. The MRP_L curve is above the ARP_L curve when the ARP_L is rising.
2. If the ARP_L is at its greatest then MRP_L equals ARP_L. The figure looks like:

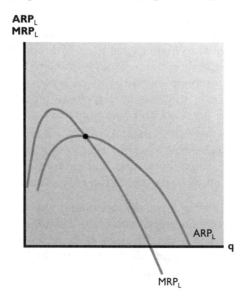

Answer 13.4

1. There will be no change in the MPL as this is not a function of the price.
2. The MRP_L will increase, as MRP_L is MPL*P and the price has increased.

Answer 13.5

1. If MRP_L were zero, then the total revenue product of labour would be maximum.
2. If MRP_L were zero, then the ARP_L would be positive, not at its maximum and to the right of its highest point.

Answer 13.6

In my opinion, Tesco is a wage maker. It negotiates with the workers' union and pays attention to what the other supermarkets are paying but there is no market for checkout workers.

Answer 13.7

The marginal cost of labour is £250. The profit-maximising firm should hire labour up to the point where MRP_L equals MC_L. Thus, the lowest MRP_L is £250.

Answer 13.8

Point 2. This is the lowest marginal cost of labour. The firm obtains the greatest contributions when the marginal cost of labour is at its lowest.

Answer 13.9

The two figures, with the labour equilibrium first, look like:

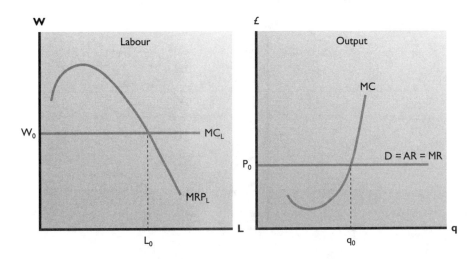

Answer 13.10

The figure looks like:

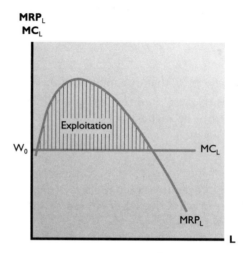

The area of exploitation ($MRP_L > MC_L$) is equal to the shaded area, which bounds the MRP_L curve above the MC_L curve. The firm gets a surplus from its workers as long as MRP_L exceeds MC_L.

Answer 13.11

The monopsonist is a wage maker. I would expect the workers to form or join a union.

Answer 13.12

There would be a fall in the wage but an increase in the number of workers. The wage falls from w_u to w_m. The figure looks like:

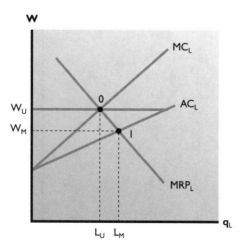

Answer 13.13

The increase in UK interest rates during this period should have reduced the number of capital projects. The evidence showing that it did reduce investment is the increase in unemployment, which started in mid-1998.

Answer 13.14

The MEK schedule will not be affected by the increase in interest rates. The cost or supply curve of capital or loans will shift upward. Fewer capital projects will be undertaken.

TAKING THE FEAR OUT OF ASSESSMENTS IN MICROECONOMICS

When the going gets tough the tough get going.

This will help

Students appear to have a fear of microeconomics. This is understandable given the language used, the diagrams covered and the mathematical nature of the subject. It is also the case that students appear to have a fear of assessments. This does not appear to be confined to economics. It appears to cover both coursework assessment and examination assessment.

Students tend to find examinations more difficult than coursework assignments. The key to conquering any type of assessment is practice, practice and more practice. The more you know, the easier it is to answer questions. I am in favour of students doing revision but only if the revision is topping up previous learning and practice. If the revision is really attempting to learn the subject for the first time then it is too little, too late. It is always better to do a little each week than to try to do a lot in one go. Do you leave the washing up to accumulate in the sink for a week or more? I think not. You do the washing up daily. Do the same with your learning.

The idea is to learn the microeconomics as you go along rather than leaving it for the period immediately before the coursework assessment or examination. Prepare, practice and present should be the student motto. I know that it is not, but it should be. Preparing and practising make life much easier.

Introduction

The purpose of this chapter is to try to present strategies for dealing with coursework and examination assessments. The coverage is based on the experience I have gained during 20 years of teaching economics and marking assessments in microeconomics in higher education. I am not suggesting that I have all the answers. I do not. I simply have 20 years of experience and may be able to help take some of the fear out of assessment.

By the end of this chapter, you will be able to:

✓ plan strategies for answering coursework and examination questions
✓ understand what makes an answer good or bad from the marker's perspective
✓ write better coursework and examinations.

The strategy

To succeed you need a strategy. Only time will tell if it is the correct strategy. We will deal first with a strategy for coping with examinations. Following this we will look at a strategy for conquering the fears of coursework.

Examinations

Before you reach the exam

Start your strategy before you reach the examination. There is, unfortunately, no substitute for work. Students worry when they should be working. I have yet to see worry help a student pass an examination. The key to preparing before the exam is to follow the lecture programme, attend all lectures, seminars/tutorials and practice. Learning microeconomics is a sequential activity. Understanding demand helps you to understand elasticity and indifference analysis. If you are set work for seminars then try to do that work. You will usually find that the answers to the set questions have been covered in the lecture and/or that the lecture programme material covers the questions. The more you work before an exam the easier the exam will be.

The question

You have prepared before the examination. Well done! Now you are in the examination hall with the exam paper on the desk in front of you. First, be confident and see the exam as a challenge. Do not be frightened by the exam. Read all the questions carefully and decide which one(s) you will answer. You look at the questions and decide that your first attempt will be to answer question number three. Do not start writing yet. The question is: 'Perfect competition produces ideal outcomes in the long-run.' Discuss.

The answer

The answer consists of four parts: The plan, the introduction, the discussion and the summary and conclusion. First, we look at the plan.

The plan

You need a plan. The more work you have done before the exam, the easier it will be to prepare your plan. Look at the question and decide what the question is actually asking.

A number of students will launch into an answer without thinking or planning. They will write everything they can remember about perfect competition in an unstructured manner. They may well secure enough marks to pass. It is unlikely, however, that they will get above 50 per cent. They may ever get a fail grade.

The question requires the student to discuss the outcomes of perfect competition in the long-run and also to suggest why the outcomes are thought to be ideal ones. The question does not require a discussion of the assumptions and the movement from the short-run to the long-run.

Before you start your answer:

✓ List all the factors that come into your head concerning the outcomes of perfect competition. You are listing at the moment and not planning. Listing comes first, followed by planning (the numbers in the list are part of the planning process). Your list could look something like:

  – price and marginal cost, 2

  – price and average cost, 3 and 4

  – average cost is minimum, 3

  – profits in the long-run, 4

  – normal profits, 4

  – allocative efficiency, 2

  – productive efficiency, 3

  – the nature of perfect competition, 1

  – the firm and the market, 1

  – contrast with monopoly, 5.

  I would recommend that you try to list at least ten different points. Obviously, the more work and practice you have covered before the exam, the easier it will be to make a list.

✓ Organise the list into your answer plan. I advise students to collect the points into a number of paragraphs. You could place a number at the end of each point indicating the points that will form a paragraph, as in the list already prepared. Thus, paragraph 2 will cover allocative efficiency and price and marginal cost.

✓ Now decide on the opening paragraph of your discussion and the order of the opening paragraph. I would start with the nature of perfect competition and the firm and the market. However, there is something to do before you write the first paragraph of the discussion. You need an introduction.

The introduction

The first thing the marker will read is the introduction. You need to introduce your answer to the marker and outline what you will say in the main body of your answer. First impressions ... I suggest that you use an introduction that includes the question and the structure of your plan. It could take the form:

In this question, I will explain why perfect competition generates outcomes, which are described as being ideal. To do this the answer will cover four themes. The first section will look at the nature of perfect competition, the firm and the market. This will be followed by comments on allocative efficiency. The third section will examine productive efficiency. The fourth part will cover normal profits. Comparisons will be made with monopoly and the answer will finish with a brief summary and some concluding remarks.

You have said in the introduction what it is that you are going to say in your essay. Now make sure that you say it.

The discussion

The discussion is the main body of your answer. Table 14.1 shows the hierarchy of skills usually included. You need to describe certain things such as the nature of perfect competition but remember that the marker knows the subject matter. The marker is looking for knowledge and comprehension. These are the basics and include coverage of the practical aspects and the correct diagrams. In addition, the marker will be looking for higher order skills such as application and analysis of theory and evidence, synthesis and evaluation.

Table 14.1 The hierarchy of skills and the classification achieved

Skills	Classification
Knowledge and comprehension	Third – 40 to 49
Knowledge and comprehension Application and analysis	Lower Second – 50 to 59
Knowledge and comprehension Application and analysis Synthesis	Upper Second – 60 to 69
Knowledge and comprehension Application and analysis Synthesis Evaluation	First – 70+

✓ The knowledge and comprehension coverage is highly descriptive. It is a rote effort. If you want to get a higher grade, you must show higher level skills. The only way to achieve these higher level skills is to read, work and practice.

✓ By planning your discussion coverage in paragraphs, and within paragraphs you will cover the **knowledge** and **comprehension** requirement. The higher skills require a discussion that seeks to make the reader aware of the point of the question. These go beyond a definition of allocative efficiency and attempt to explain the importance of allocative efficiency.

✓ Explaining is significantly different from defining. To explain you need to be able to reason with **analysis** and **application**. **Synthesis** shows your ability to generate solutions from examples. A question asks for coverage of competition and substitutes. You synthesise by including the example of Reebok and Nike.

✓ **Evaluation** is your attempt to say whether the market for running shoes is a competitive one. You can only achieve mastery of these skills with practice. At the end of your discussion, you will need a brief summary and a conclusion.

Summary and conclusion

The summary should be a brief coverage of the salient points. It is not a repetition of your discussion. The summary seeks to highlight the important aspects of the discussion. It should be only five or six sentences. It reinforces your discussion and leads to the conclusion.

The conclusion can be balanced or it can agree or disagree with the question. The conclusion will depend on the tone of your discussion. Whatever your conclusion is, it is vitally important that you have one. Examiners look for conclusions so include one.

Structure of your answer

The previous coverage suggests that you have an introduction followed by your main body, the discussion. The answer should finish with a brief summary and a concluding section. **Say what you intend to say (introduction), make sure you say it (discussion) and finally say what it is you said (summary and conclusion).** Model your answer on the television or radio news coverage. There is an introduction with the highlights. The highlights are then defined, explained and analysed in detail. The reporter attempts to synthesise and evaluate. The news ends with a summary of the important news stories. If they can do it, so can you.

Coursework

The structure of a coursework answer should be the same as the structure of an examination answer. To repeat, there should be an introduction, a discussion and the coursework should end with a brief summary and a conclusion. The marker will be looking for the higher order skills of knowledge and comprehension, application and analysis, synthesis and evaluation here, too. The further up the hierarchy you can travel, the higher the grade you will secure.

Answer the set question

As with an examination question, always read the coursework question. Then read the question again. Now that you understand what the question demands of you, make sure that you supply the right answer. Students tend to engage in the practice of:

✓ answering the question by focusing on a phrase or term
✓ writing everything they know about the selected phrase
✓ producing a knowledge and comprehension coverage.

All this does is to get a mark between 40 and 49.

Suppose the coursework question were: 'Why is the concept of price elasticity of demand important for business decision makers?' This question asks the student to:

✓ define and explain the concept of price elasticity
✓ show an understanding of the relationship between price changes, price elasticity and total revenue
✓ display evidence of how price elasticity is applied in the real world
✓ comment on the problems of trying to use price elasticity.

The first point is your demonstration of knowledge and comprehension. With the second point, you apply your understanding of how the firm could maximise total revenue and use your knowledge to analysis what the firm needs to do. The third point calls for synthesis. You present evidence of how firms use price elasticity. This could be London Transport or package holiday firms. The final point requires an evaluation of the problems of attempting to use price elasticity in the real world.

Keep to the word limit

If the coursework has a word limit, then make sure that your paper's word count is within 10 per cent of the limit. If the coursework asks for 2000 words, then do not write more than 2200 or under 1800 words. The word limit is part of the assessment strategy. You may be penalised for failing to keep to the word limit. Keeping to the word limit is good practice for the world of work. You may be required to write a briefing paper for your line manager. The limit is 500 words. You will lose the confidence of the line manager if you present a 2000-word briefing note. It will be returned to you unread. You may seriously damage your promotion prospects.

If you word process

It is not essential to word process coursework. It may, however, be required. Students believe that word-processed coursework gets a higher mark than hand-written work. This is not my experience. This is because students are not trained secretaries and do not submit word-processed coursework in a professional manner. The spellchecker is not used. The student can spell the words. If the work had been hand written then the spelling would have been correct. However, the student is not a trained typist and so makes typing errors. I have done this through all the typing for this book. Thank goodness for the spellchecker! If you have a spellchecker, use it. Use all the advantages the computer gives you. These include grammar checker, thesaurus and word count. Make sure, also, that the pagination is correct. And remember, it is frustrating to mark word-processed coursework that has spelling mistakes.

Summary

This chapter tries to follow the structure of a good answer. The chapter opened with an introduction:

✓ The introduction tried to set the scene for what was to come. The introduction should be interesting and capture the imagination of the reader. The introduction is important. It is followed by the main body, the discussion.

✓ The discussion section should be organised and used to answer the set question. It should not be a knowledge and comprehension coverage. It should take the reader through Knowledge and Comprehension, Application and Analysis, Synthesis and Evaluation. Remember KCAASE.

✓ The discussion will be followed by a brief summary which leads into the answer's concluding remarks.

It seems a shame that students work hard on the module material but do relatively poorly in their coursework and examinations. The answer is to practice all aspects of the module. Practice writing exam answers.

Practice, practice, practice ...

GLOSSARY

A

Accountant's definition of profits has total cost that does not include entrepreneurial opportunity cost. The accountant's measurement of profit, therefore, exceeds that of the economist. *See* Chapter 7.

Administered price. The firm makes the price. Price is based on average cost. *See* Chapter 10.

Advertising elasticity of demand (AED). Measures the relationship between quantity demanded and advertising. The measure uses percentage changes. If the value is greater than 1 then the good or service is advertising elastic. *See* Chapter 9.

Allocative efficiency. If supply equals demand then the market is allocating resources efficiently. The measure of allocative efficiency is that price equals marginal cost. If price exceeds marginal cost then resources are not being allocated efficiently. *See* Chapter 11.

Average cost (AC). Given by total cost/output. Average cost depends on the type of economies the firm experiences and is calculated using TC/Q. *See* Chapter 6.

Average cost curve. Shows the diagrammatic relationship between output and average cost. If the average cost curve is falling then the firm is experiencing economies. *See* Chapter 6.

Average cost of labour (AC$_L$). The total cost of labour divided by the number of workers employed. In a competitive labour market, the average cost of labour equals the wage rate. *See* Chapter 13.

Average fixed cost (AFC). Given by total fixed cost/output. Average fixed cost falls as output increases, and is calculated using TFC/Q. *See* Chapter 6.

Average fixed cost curve. Shows the diagrammatic relationship between output and average fixed cost. *See* Chapter 6.

Average physical product of labour (APP$_L$). The total output divided by the number of workers employed (Q/L). *See* Chapter 13.

Average product of labour curve. Shows the relationship between the average product of labour and the number of workers employed. *See* Chapter 13.

Average variable cost (AVC). Total variable cost/output. Average variable cost depends on the type of average returns made by the variable factors and is calculated using TVC/Q. *See* Chapter 6.

Average variable cost curve. Shows the diagrammatic relationship between output and average variable cost. If the average variable cost curve is constant, then the firm is experiencing constant average efficiency from its variable factors. *See* Chapter 6.

B

Bliss point. The point at which the consumer maximises total utility. The highest possible indifference curve is achieved given the income or budget constraint. In technical language, the slopes of the indifference curve and the budget constraint are tangential. *See* Chapter 3.

Branding. An attempt by firms to product differentiate their product. It may be achieved through advertising or features identifying the product such as a logo. *See* Chapter 12.

Budget constraint. Sets an upper limit on the amount we can consume. The budget constraint is our income. *See* Chapter 3.

C

Capital market. Where the demand for and supply of capital interact to produce the rate of interest. *See* Chapter 13.

Cartel. A form of collusion. The cartel aims to reduce output below the competitive level. OPEC is the classic example. *See* Chapter 12.

Collusion. Firms collude to decide on an outcome. Against the spirit of competition. *See* Chapter 12.

Complements. Goods or services demanded together. An example is the printer and the paper. *See* Chapter 2.

Constant returns. The variable factor of production is

constantly efficient. *See* Chapter 5.

Contributions to fixed costs. The difference between total revenue and total variable contributions. This is the cashflow of the business. Contributions are achieved when price exceeds average variable cost. *See* Chapter 7.

Cross-price elasticity of demand (XED). Measures the relationship between the quantity demanded of good A and the price of B. The measurement uses percentage changes. If the XED is positive, then A and B are substitutes. If the XED is negative, then A and B are complements. *See* Chapter 9.

D

Decreasing returns. The variable factor of production is becoming less and less efficient. *See* Chapter 5.

Demand curve. A diagrammatic relationship between the price of the good or service and the quantity demanded of the good or service. *See* Chapter 2.

Demand factors. The factors explaining the level of market demand. The main demand factors are price, price of substitutes, price of complements, income, tastes, interest rates and expectations. *See* Chapter 2.

Derived demand. An intermediate demand. Labour is a derived demand. It is demanded so that a good or service can be supplied. The demand for labour is not a final demand. The demand for the good or service that labour helps to produce is a final demand.

The demand for fish and chips is a final demand. *See* Chapter 13.

E

Economies of scale. A long-run concept. If the long-run average cost curve is falling, the firm is experiencing economies of scale. *See* Chapter 6.

Economist's definition of profits. Total cost includes entrepreneurial opportunity cost. The economist's measurement of profits is less than that of the accountant. *See* Chapter 7.

Effective demand. Real, not desired, demand. Wants are insatiable but income is limited. *See* Chapter 2.

Elasticity. Measures the relationship between the change in the independent variable and the change in the dependent variable. *See* Chapter 8.

Elasticity: the average approach. This approach uses the average of the start and finish price and quantity-demanded values. It thus guarantees that the elasticity value is the same whether we measure up or down the demand curve. *See* Chapter 8.

Entrepreneurial opportunity cost. The economist includes this cost in total fixed costs. The reward required to entice the entrepreneur into taking the production risk. *See* Chapter 7.

Equilibrium. No tendency to change. Market equilibrium is when demand equals supply. The equilibrating factor is price. *See* Chapter 10.

Expectations. Our view of the future. What should we do? Buy now or wait? We cannot predict

the future but it is wise to prepare for it. Microeconomics can help us to prepare for the future. *See* Chapter 2.

External economies of scale. Measures shifts of the long-run average cost curve. If the LRAC curve is shifting downward then the firm is achieving external economies of scale. *See* Chapter 6.

F

Factors of production. The factors that combine to produce or supply a good or service. They include labour, management, capital, raw materials and land. *See* Chapters 4, 5, 6 and 13.

Fixed factors. The factors that cannot be altered in the short-run. *See* Chapter 5.

Full-cost pricing. A pricing practice based on average cost. The price fully covers the cost of production. *See* Chapter 10.

G

Giffen good. A good with an upward-sloping demand curve. Named after Sir Robert Giffen. The good has a negative income effect, which is strong enough to overcome the substitution effect. The outcome is that a fall in price produces a fall in quantity demanded, and an upward sloping demand curve results. *See* Chapter 3.

I

Income as demand factor. A demand shift factor. Increases in income normally cause the demand curve to shift to the right. *See* Chapters 2 and 3.

Income as reward. The compensation for working. *See* Chapter 13.

Income consumption curve. Used in indifference curve analysis. The income consumption curve (ycc) shows what happens to the demand for the two goods following a change in income. If the ycc is positively sloped then the two goods are normal. If the ycc is negatively sloped then one of the goods is either inferior or Giffen. *See* Chapter 3.

Income effect. The change in price has a real effect on income. If price falls then, real income increases. The income effect can be positive, zero or negative. The income effect is the key to normal, inferior and Giffen goods. First, calculate the substitution effect. The remaining change in demand is due to the income effect. *See* Chapter 3.

Income elasticity of demand (YED). Measures the relationship between quantity demanded and income. Measured in percentage terms. If YED is less than 1 then the good or service is income inelastic. *See* Chapter 9.

Increasing returns. The variable factor of production is becoming increasingly efficient. *See* Chapter 5.

Indifference curve. A mapping of the total utility derived from two goods. Total utility is unchanged on the same indifference curve. *See* Chapter 3.

Indifferent – different combinations of the two goods produce the same total utility. *See* Chapter 3.

Inferior good. A good with a negative income effect but not strong enough to overcome the substitution effect. The consumer will purchase more following a price reduction. The demand curve is downward sloping. *See* Chapter 3.

Internal economies of scale. Measures movement along the long-run average cost (LRAC) curve. If the LRAC curve is falling then the firm is achieving internal economies of scale. *See* Chapter 6.

K

Kinked demand curve. The demand curve of the price leader in oligopoly. The kink establishes a stable price. *See* Chapter 12.

L

Labour market. Where the demand for and supply of labour determines the wage. It can be competitive or non-competitive. *See* Chapter 13.

Land. The ground used as a factor of production. The reward paid to land is rent. *See* Chapter 13.

Long-run. Production period when all factors of production are variable. *See* Chapter 5.

M

Managerial economies. The ability of the management to move the firm along the long-run average cost of the firm. If there is movement up long-run average cost, this is due to managerial diseconomies. *See* Chapter 6.

Marginal cost (MC). The change in TVC /change in Q. It shows the extra cost of producing one more unit of production and is calculated using $\Delta TVC/\Delta Q$. *See* Chapter 6.

Marginal cost curve. Shows the diagrammatic relationship between output and marginal cost. If the marginal cost curve is falling then the firm is experiencing increasing returns to its variable factors. *See* Chapter 6.

Marginal cost of labour (MC_L). The change in total cost of labour divided by the change in the number of workers employed. In a competitive labour market, the marginal cost of labour equals the wage rate. *See* Chapter 13.

Marginal efficiency of capital (MEK). The marginal efficiency of capital is the return earned on a capital project. *See* Chapter 13.

Marginal physical product of labour (MPP_L). The change in output divided by the change in the number of workers employed ($\Delta Q/\Delta L$). *See* Chapter 13.

Marginal product of labour curve – Shows the relationship between the marginal product of labour and the number of workers employed. *See* Chapter 13.

Marginal profit. The change in total profits. Calculated from the difference between marginal revenue and marginal cost. *See* Chapter 7.

Marginal returns. The change in output resulting from a change in a factor of production. *See* Chapter 13.

Marginal revenue (MR). The change in total revenue as output changes. *See* Chapters 2 and 7.

Marginal revenue product of labour (MRP_L). Shows the relationship between changes in the firm's total revenue product of labour (TRP_L) and changes in the number of workers employed. In a competitive labour market the marginal revenue product of labour equals MPP_L*P, while in a non-competitive labour market it equals MPP_L*MR. *See* Chapter 13.

Marginal utility. The change in total utility. Marginal utility = Δtotal utility/ Δgoods consumed. The change in goods consumed is usually one. *See* Chapter 3.

Market-determined price. Price is determined by the interaction of demand and supply. The firm takes the price from the market. *See* Chapter 10.

Market structure. Models a particular group of firms in terms of their structure, conduct and performance. The four market structures are perfect competition, monopoly, oligopoly and monopolistic competition. *See* Chapters 11 and 12.

Mark-up. The factor by which price is marked up on average cost. *See* Chapter 10.

Maximising total revenue. Marginal revenue is 0 and price elasticity equals -1 (unitary). *See* Chapter 8.

Monopolistically competitive. A market structure, similar to perfect competition, with a downward-sloping demand curve for the firm. This is due to product differentiation and results from either slight differences in the nature of the product or branding. *See* Chapter 12.

Monopoly. A market structure with one producer. This market structure is criticised because

the monopolist uses single producer power to exploit the consumer. *See* Chapter 11.

Monopsony. A single buyer of labour. An example would a sugar plantation in Central American. *See* Chapter 13.

Movement along. Changes in the price of the good or service cause movement along the demand and supply curves. An increase in price causes movement up the demand and supply curves. *See* Chapters 2 and 4.

N

Nationalisation. A firm or market which is controlled by the government and not private interests. *See* Chapter 11.

Normal good. An increase in income leads to an income in quantity demanded. There is a positive income effect. The demand curve is downward sloping. *See* Chapter 3.

Normal profits. Price equals average cost. The firm receives a normal or fair return, which is included in average cost. *See* Chapter 11.

O

Oligopoly. A few firms dominate the market. The defining feature is action and reaction among the firms. This is a market structure with interdependence between the firms. The UK supermarkets are an example of an oligopolistic market structure. *See* Chapter 12.

Opportunity cost. The cost of doing one activity related to its best foregone alternative. I am not running as I type this! *See* Chapter 7.

P

Perfect competition. A market structure in which the outcomes are argued to be perfect. The perfect outcomes are the result of the competitive structure of the market. *See* Chapter 11.

Price. The amount paid for a good or service. *See* Chapters 2, 4 and 10.

Price ceiling. An attempt to place a maximum price below the market determined price. Usually introduced to protect consumers from high prices. Used to limit the rent paid on private rental accommodation. *See* Chapter 10.

Price consumption curve (pcc). Used in indifference curve analysis. This curve shows what happens to the two products following a price change. The curve can be used to see if the good experiencing the price change is price elastic, inelastic or unitary. *See* Chapter 3.

Price elastic. Demand is responsive to a price change. The percentage change in quantity demanded dominates the percentage change in price. A decrease in price will increase total revenue. *See* Chapter 8.

Price elasticity of demand (PED). The relationship between price changes and quantity-demanded changes. Measured in percentage terms. Usually negative as an increase in price leads to a decrease in quantity demanded. *See* Chapter 8.

Price floor. An attempt to guarantee a minimum price above the market-determined price. Usually introduced to increase the income of poor groups such as farmers. *See* Chapter 10.

Price inelastic. Demand is not responsive to a price change. The percentage change in quantity demanded is dominated by the percentage change in price. A decrease in price will decrease total revenue. *See* Chapter 8.

Price leadership. The dominant firm in oligopoly decides on the market price and the other firms follow the leader. *See* Chapter 12.

Price of factors of production. The price paid to entice a factor into the production or supply process. They include wages, salaries and interest. *See* Chapters 4, 5, 6 and 13.

Privatisation. A firm or market which is denationalised and thus subjected to market discipline. *See* Chapter 11.

Product differentiation. Products in the same market (e.g. sports shoes) are separated from one another by branding features such as Air, Gel and Pump. *See* Chapter 12.

Production efficiency. The firm produces at the minimum point of the average cost curve. Production is at the lowest possible average cost. *See* Chapter 11.

Production function. A two-dimensional graph showing the relationship between output and the factors of production. There are short-run and long-run production functions. *See* Chapter 5.

Production possibility curve. Shows the upper limit placed on production. The concave slope can be used to calculate opportunity cost. *See* Chapter 5.

Profit maximisation. Occurs when marginal revenue equals marginal cost and all extra or marginal profitable

opportunities have been exhausted. *See* Chapter 7.

Profit profile. Shows the relationship between total profits and output. *See* Chapter 7.

Profits (Π). The difference between total revenue and total costs. Profit maximisation is argued to be a business objective. The reward paid to the entrepreneur. The level of profit can be normal or supernormal. *See* Chapter 7.

R

Rate of interest as demand shift factor. The price of credit or loans. Interest rates influence the demand for durables such as double glazing and fitted kitchens. An increase in interest rates causes the demand curve to shift to the left. *See* Chapter 2.

Rate of interest as the price of capital. Interest is the reward received by savers. They supply the capital and receive interest as a reward for sacrificing present consumption. *See* Chapter 13.

Raw materials. Part of the firm's factors of production. Raw materials are a variable factor of production. *See* Chapter 13.

Rent. The reward paid to land. *See* Chapter 13.

S

Scarcity. The microeconomic problem. Our wants are insatiable. The supply of goods and services is limited. How the wants are supplied is the microeconomic problem. *See* Chapter 1.

Shift of. Changes in the explanatory factors, except price, cause the demand and supply curves to shift. *See* Chapters 2 and 4.

Short-run. A production period in which at least one factor of production is fixed. The fixed factor is usually a dominant part of the firm's capital structure. *See* Chapter 5.

Slope. The rate of change between two variables. The demand curve is a slope. A downward-sloping demand curve shows that the slope of the relationship between price and quantity demanded is negative. The two variables have a negatively sloped relationship. The upward-sloping supply curve shows a positive relationship between price and quantity demanded. *See* Chapter 3.

Substitutes. Goods or services that compete for consumer demand. An example is apples and oranges. *See* Chapter 2.

Substitution effect. A price decrease always leads to an increase in quantity demanded. The substitution effect is always negative. Use the old indifference curve and the new budget constraint. *See* Chapter 3.

Supernormal profits. Price exceeds average cost. The firm obtains a reward in excess of the required entrepreneurial opportunity cost. *See* Chapter 11.

Supply curve. A diagrammatic relationship between the price of the good or service and the quantity supplied of the good or service. *See* Chapter 4.

Supply factors. The factors explaining the level of market supply. The main supply factors are price, price of factors of production, technology, business aims and expectations. *See* Chapter 4.

T

Tastes. A demand shift factor. Strongly influenced by advertising and peer group pressure. *See* Chapter 2.

Technology. A factor of production. The spellchecker facility is an improvement in computer technology and improves the productivity of the user. *See* Chapter 4.

Tied goods or services. Goods or services that are consumed together. An example is the Duracell torch and the Duracell torch battery. *See* Chapter 9.

Total cost (TC). The total cost of producing the level of production. Total cost is the sum of total variable cost and total fixed cost. TC = TVC + TFC. *See* Chapter 6.

Total cost of labour (TC_L). The average cost of labour multiplied by the number of workers employed. In a competitive labour market, the total cost of labour equals the wage rate multiplied by the number of workers employed. *See* Chapter 13.

Total fixed cost (TFC). The cost of employing the fixed factors. A short-run concept. Total fixed cost does not vary with output. *See* Chapter 6.

Total revenue. The result of multiplying price and quantity demanded. Total revenue is the same as sales revenue. TR = p*q. *See* Chapters 2, 3, 7 and 8.

Total revenue product of labour (TRP_L). The total revenue of the firm is the firm's total revenue product of labour. APL*P is the total revenue product of labour if the labour market is competitive. If the labour market if non-competitive then the total revenue product of labour equals APL*MR. *See* Chapter 13.

Total revenue profile. Shows the relationship between total revenue and quantity demanded. If the demand curve is downward sloping then the profile is dome-shaped. *See* Chapters 2 and 8.

Total utility. The consumer gets marginal utility from each unit of the good or service consumed. Total utility is the sum of all the marginal utilities. *See* Chapter 3.

Total variable cost (TVC). The cost of employing the variable factors. Total variable cost varies positively with output. *See* Chapter 6.

U

Union. Workers grouping together to engage in collective action. The union seeks to challenge the power of the employer. *See* Chapter 13.

Unit profit. The difference between price and average cost. *See* Chapter 7.

Unitary elastic. The percentage change in price is equal but opposite to the percentage change in quantity demanded. The value is −1. A change in price has no impact on total revenue. *See* Chapter 8.

Util. A util is a measurement of utility. *See* Chapter 3.

Utility maximisation. The consumer gets the maximum satisfaction from the combination of goods and services purchased. No other combination of goods and services produces utility maximisation. *See* Chapter 3.

V

Variable factors. The factors that are changed to vary short-run supply or production. *See* Chapter 5.

W

Wage. The reward paid to labour. *See* Chapter 13.

Wants. The goods and services that we want. Wants are effective if we are willing and able to purchase the wants. *See* Chapter 2.

INDEX